# MENACE IN EUROPE

# MENACE IN EUROPE

## WHY THE CONTINENT'S CRISIS

## IS AMERICA'S, TOO

# CLAIRE BERLINSKI

THREE RIVERS PRESS

NEW YORK

Published in the United States by Three Rivers Press, an imprint of the Crown Publishing
Group, a division of Random House, Inc., New York.
www.crownpublishing.com

Three Rivers Press and the Tugboat design are registered trademarks of Random House, Inc.

Originally published in slightly different form in hardcover in the United States by Crown
Forum, an imprint of the Crown Publishing Group, a division of Random House, Inc.,
New York, in 2006.

Library of Congress Cataloging-in-Publication Data
Berlinski, Claire.
Menace in Europe : why the continent's crisis is America's, too / Claire Berlinski.—1st ed.
Includes bibliographical references and index.
1. Europe—History—21st century.   2. Europe—Civilization—21st century.   3. Europe—
Relations—United States   4. United States—Relations—Europe.   I. Title.
D2020.B47 2006
940.56'1—dc22                                                          2006000484

ISBN 978-1-4000-9770-8

Printed in the United States of America

Design by Leonard Henderson

10 9 8 7 6 5 4 3 2 1

First Paperback Edition

*For my grandmother . . . who has seen it all*

I know that Europe's wonderful, yet something seems to lack;
The Past is too much with her, and the people looking back.

—Henry Van Dyke

# CONTENTS

# MENACE IN EUROPE

# CHAPTER 1

# EUROPE ON FIVE DOLLARS A DAY AND A FLAMETHROWER

I KEEP A SPIRAL-BOUND notebook on my desk filled with miscellaneous notes—the usual collection of ideas that seem insightful at three in the morning but substantially less so at daybreak, ideas that may well have been insightful but have been lost to posterity because my handwriting is indecipherable, scraps of overheard dialogue, observations made from the windows of trains.

One scrawled passage in particular stands out now. The date was July 3, 2005. "Within six months," I wrote, "there will be another major terrorist attack or political assassination in Europe." I am embarrassed to admit that my next thought, apparently, was that this would be inconvenient for me, since it would necessitate making major revisions to this book.

Three days later, Trafalgar Square erupted in celebration at the announcement that London would host the 2012 Olympics. The next morning, as the rush hour drew to a close, four suicide bombers detonated themselves in central London, killing 52 people and injuring 700 more. Papers with headlines from the previous evening had not yet been pushed off the newsstands: "Blimey! It's London's turn!" said one, and I can only imagine how those jolly words must have appeared to commuters staggering off the smoke-blackened London Tube.

Four more bombings were attempted on the London transport

system two weeks later. This time, the bombs failed to detonate and the bombers survived, leaving behind forensic evidence that permitted police to ascertain their identities. Both the living and the dead bombers were *British,* born and raised—homegrown monsters who had not yet been apprised of the news that democracies don't breed terrorists. Some were from comfortably affluent families. Some had been living handsomely for years on state benefits. It now appears that al Qaeda, which took credit for the attacks, recruited some of the bombers at a Muslim community center in Leeds—one funded by the British government and the European Union.[1]

It was revealed in the weeks following the attacks that quite a number of British Muslims do not much care for their fellow Britons. According to a poll conducted shortly after the bombing, a full 32 percent of British Muslims agreed that "Western society is decadent and immoral and Muslims should seek to bring it to an end." Toward that goal, 1 percent—a seemingly small proportion until one considers that this comprises some 16,000 British Muslims—described themselves as willing, even eager, to embrace violence to destroy that society. According to the same poll, 6 percent of British Muslims saw the bombings as justified, 56 percent "understood why some people behave in that way," and 16 percent felt "not loyal towards Britain."[2] This is not, of course, a problem limited to Britain: every European country is now home to large populations of alienated, unassimilated Muslims who despise the West.

As the portrait of the bombers became clearer, sharply illustrating these fissures in Europe's social fabric, a large cohort of the professional commentariat proclaimed themselves shocked. I believe I heard the same people, several months later, proclaiming themselves shocked by the news that Kate Moss uses cocaine. Those of us who had been paying attention were not shocked at all.

This protest, for example, outside the U.S. embassy in London on May 20, 2005, was the kind of clue some of us had been noticing:

> Shouting, "Down, down USA; down, down USA," the protesters
> called for the killing of Americans, the death of the U.S. president,

the death of British Prime Minister Tony Blair, the bombing of Britain, and the annihilation of the U.S. capital: "Nuke, nuke Washington; Nuke, nuke Washington! Bomb, bomb the Pentagon." . . . "Death, death Tony Blair; death, death Tony Blair. Death, death George Bush," the protesters chanted. . . . Holding their Qurans high, they called for death and mayhem, praising the destruction of New York's twin towers on September 11, 2001, and saying the White House is next.[3]

I did not think these demonstrators were just joking then, and I certainly do not now.

The trend has been in evidence for years. British-based terrorists were involved in the planning and execution of the suicide bombing of American embassies in Kenya and Tanzania in 1998. They were involved in the planned attack on the American embassy in Albania. They were associated with the attempted attack on Los Angeles International Airport in 2000 and, most important, with the September 11 attacks on New York and Washington.

One week after the London bombings, it was reported that Mohammed Sidique Khan, believed to have been the operation's field commander, had been in contact with a suspected recruiter for an extremist group in New York. Two other men linked to the plot had direct ties to the United States: one had traveled recently to Ohio; another had been a student at an American university.[4]

I have those same handwritten notes beside me now. On the evening of July 7, 2005, having spent the day following the news on the Internet and exchanging e-mails with my friends in London, I wrote these words: "The same thing will happen soon in the United States, and the bombers will come from Europe." They will come from Europe because it is comparatively easy to enter the United States if you carry a European passport, and because Europe is—as it always has been—the breeding ground of the world's most dangerous ideologues.

Although I take as much satisfaction as the next woman in being right, I'd much prefer to be wrong about this. Unfortunately, I don't think I am.

## THE RETURN OF THE REPRESSED

To judge from the number of books published in recent years about the challenges of renovating a farmhouse in Tuscany or Provence, large swaths of Europe are now populated by middle-aged American divorcées, living large on alimony and greatly occupied by the tending of their new olive terraces. As far as they are concerned, the chief problem with life in Europe is the difficulty of coaxing the medieval plumbing in their newly acquired Renaissance villas into action. (These women are survivors. They *grow* from this tough experience.)

Many Americans know this version of Europe—Alimony Europe, *Fodor's* Europe, *Europe on Five Dollars a Day*—quite well. They know it from books and movies, they know it from their summer vacations. They remember backpacking through Europe after graduating from college. *Amsterdam was great, until Flounder fell in the canal.* They think wistfully of that ad in the back of the *New York Review of Books:* "Dordogne—18th-century stone manor. Antiques, all original beams, 18' cathedral ceiling, fireplace, pool. 28 bucolic acres of woods, meadow, fruit and walnut trees, stream. Must be willing to feed goats." When they visit Europe, they travel from one historic and lovely city center to another, making use of Europe's convenient railroads. They do not visit the places most Europeans actually live, and know little about them.

Indeed, most Americans born after the Second World War have grown up thinking of Europe, Western Europe in particular, as not much more than a congeries of windmills, gondolas, dissipated monarchs, and peculiar toilets. They have considered the political and moral essence of Europe, when they have considered it at all, to be much like our own. They have, of course, heard the stories about the cancerous, deranged *thing* of the past, but that Europe, they believe, is long dead, vanquished by the United States in the First and Second World Wars, resurrected in our image through the Marshall Plan. Europe? It's free, prosperous, peaceful, and democratic now, right? We don't need to worry about it anymore.

Yes, Europe *is* peaceful, prosperous, free, and democratic, relatively speaking. It is not Sierra Leone, and I'm not saying it is. I do not propose we worry overmuch that German nationalists will hijack commercial jets and pilot them into our skyscrapers. American troops stationed in Italy may leave their bases without benefit of armored convoys, unworried about the threat of capture and beheading by enraged fundamentalist papists. All of that is true; it would be absurd to deny it. Europe's achievements since the Second World War have been real and significant. There is unprecedented prosperity on the Continent, with standards of health care and education that in many places exceed those in the United States. The Great Powers of Europe are no longer cannibalizing one another. The Furor Teutonicus has for the moment subsided. No doubt, much of the darkness has been repressed.

But the repressed is known for returning.

Since the collapse of the Soviet empire, and particularly since September 11, some Americans have begun to sense, uneasily, a certain lack of love from our transatlantic brethren. Many Europeans did not seem to grasp the enormity of September 11, and never denounced the event as forthrightly as we had expected. The rift over the Iraq War exposed an extremity of anti-American passion that simply made no sense, particularly given that European intelligence agencies were, like ours, persuaded that Saddam Hussein was developing weapons of mass destruction, still more so because European cities would have been the obvious targets of those weapons. Iraq was, after all, believed to be building not long-range but *medium*-range ballistic missiles. To any European capable of reading a map, the implications of this should have been obvious. The spectacle of European leaders and citizens declaring themselves, in all seriousness, to be more alarmed by American imperialism than by Saddam's quite rightly made many Americans wander to their bookshelves and begin thumbing through their copies of *Let's Go: Mexico.*

The American political analyst Robert Kagan has suggested, reassuringly, that the divide is not as serious as it looks: it is just that Americans are from Mars, and Europeans are from Venus. Now, I am all for interplanetary diplomacy—who isn't?—but having lived in Europe for most of my adult life, I see things just a little differently.

## BLACKMAILED BY HISTORY

I use the word *Europe* here as a shorthand. I mean by this the former members of the European Community, a distinct historic entity comprising most of Western Europe and Great Britain. These nation-states are united now by their entangled pasts and their common dilemmas. I am writing about *this* Europe because it is the Europe I come from and the Europe I know; having never lived in Eastern Europe, I will leave that subject to someone who has.

I come from this Europe in the sense that my grandparents, musicians born in Leipzig, were refugees from the Nazis; they crossed every border in Europe from Danzig to Bilbao in their flight from Hitler's armies. Their lives—and thus mine—were shaped by Europe's history. I know this Europe because I have lived in it for many years, studied its languages and history in its universities, and worked in its economies; I have closely examined its legal and medical systems, its bureaucracies, its rental markets, and its tax codes—not so much out of academic curiosity but because for anyone living here, a close examination is inescapable. These are, therefore, personal stories.

They are unified, however, by two larger themes—and a set of questions.

The first theme is that Europeans are behaving now as Europeans have always behaved. Many seemingly novel developments in European politics and culture are in fact nothing new at all—they have *ancient* roots in Europe's past. And what is that past? From the sack of Rome to the Yalta Conference, that past has been one of nearly uninterrupted war and savagery. Ethnic wars, class wars, revolutionary wars, religious wars, wars of ideology, and genocide are not aberrations in Europe's history; they *are* its history. An interregnum from these ancient conflicts endured from 1945 to the end of the Cold War, when Europe's destiny was in the hands of the two superpowers. With the collapse of the Soviet empire, however, history has reasserted itself. Those disturbing sounds you hear from Europe are its old, familiar ghosts. They are rattling their chains.

The second theme is that this history has culminated in a peculiar, palpable European mood. Europeans, especially young Europeans, sense in their lives a cultural, spiritual, and ideological void, one that is evident in the art, the language, the literature of contemporary Europe; in the way they talk about their existence in cafés, in discotheques, and on the Internet; in their music, in their heroes, in their family lives; and above all in the way they face threats to their own civilization—and ours.

At the same time, Europe now confronts an entirely new set of questions, ones to which no European leaders or thinkers have offered a coherent answer, about the ultimate effects of European integration, changing demography, massive immigration from former European colonies, and the expectations to which the postwar welfare states have given rise. Without understanding this history, this mood, and these questions, there is no understanding Europe. Without understanding Europe, we cannot construct an intelligent relationship to it.

## HOPELESSNESS AND THE VOID

Two historic events in particular are reverberating throughout Europe today. The first is the death of Christianity. From the time of Constantine's conversion, Europe was above all a Christian continent, with every aspect of its political, social, and family life refracted through the prism of Christian faith. But Europe has in the past several centuries seen a complete—*really* complete—loss of belief in any form of religious faith, personal immortality, or salvation. In 2005, the death of Pope John Paul II occasioned profound, spontaneous grief, to be sure, but the emotion was an atavism: church attendance in most Western European countries is less than 5 percent, a statistic ultimately much more telling than the weeping crowds in St. Peter's Square. For all the pope's charisma, he was completely unable to persuade Europeans to return to the traditional beliefs and rituals that once defined them. The first draft of the new European Union constitution did not include a single mention of Christianity. Almost a third of the Dutch no longer know why Christmas is celebrated. When asked by pollsters to name an inspirational figure, British respondents placed Christ well below Britney Spears.

The past two centuries of European history can be viewed as a series of struggles to find a replacement for what Europe has lost. Until recently, nationalism in Europe has been a substitute for religious belief. In France, for example, the idea of France itself and its civilizing mission has lent meaning to the lives of Frenchmen, just as some mystical Aryan ideal has served as a substitute for religious belief in Germany.

The second event, the complete catastrophe of the two World Wars, put an end to that, and to every other form of idealism in Europe besides. Europe is still experiencing postwar aftershocks that are at once deadening and deadly. All secular substitutes for faith, and particularly those based in a notion of the supremacy of European culture, have lost their hold. What Frenchman can stand before the graveyards of Ypres or Verdun and without choking on the words profess his allegiance to the *mission civilatrice?* The nation-state, the arts, music, science, fascism, communism, and even rationality—all of these were *substitutes* for Christianity, and all failed.

My point in making these observations could easily be misunderstood: I am not an apologist for the Church, an enemy of secularism, or an advocate of religious revivalism; I am in fact a secular Jew who is delighted never to have faced the Inquisition. I am simply reporting what I see. Not much seems to be left here now beyond pleasure and personal relations, and these do not seem to be enough to keep hopelessness at bay. A poll conducted in 2002 found that while 61 percent of Americans had hope for the future, only 42 percent of the residents of the United Kingdom shared it. Only 29 percent of the French reported feeling hope, and only 15 percent of the Germans.[5] These statistics suggest—to me, anyway—that without some transcendental common belief, hopelessness is a universal condition. I do not believe it an accident that Americans are both more religious and more hopeful than Europeans, and more apt, as well, to believe that their country stands for something greater and more noble than themselves.

The father of modern sociology, Emile Durkheim, famously observed the prophylactic effects of religion on suicide, arguing that suicide rates may usefully be considered a measure of a society's state of disillusionment. In many European countries, suicide is now the second most prevalent cause of death among the young and middle-aged, exceeded only by transport accidents. Despite the prevalence of firearms, suicide in the United States is only the eighth leading cause of death. The American suicide rate is about half that of France. Suicide rates in the Islamic world are dramatically lower.

If the death of Christianity has left a void, what now is filling it? Bizarre pseudoreligious substitutes, of which anti-Americanism and antiglobalism are only the most obvious. The roots of European anti-Americanism are complex—they are in Europe's failed domestic politics, in the universal human propensity to turn complaints outward in preference to subjecting oneself to scrutiny, in humiliation over the loss of the leadership role Europe played from the Age of Exploration to the Great War. But most interesting is the quasi-religious and messianic, even orgiastic, aspect of this anti-American ideology, especially in its coupling with undifferentiated antimodernism and anti-Semitism. Particularly revealing are the words and slogans of activists who conceive of their program as essentially spiritual or transcendental—French farmers, for example, who practice what is in effect a form of crop worship, or the extremely influential German neo-Protestant fruitcake Eugen Drewermann, who writes,

> . . . whether in the battle against racism amongst influential circles in the US south . . . whether against the absolutely unfair trade conditions on the world market in exchange relations of raw materials and manufactured goods to the permanently aggravating disadvantage of Third and Fourth World countries . . . every little

"success" in the fight against injustice, inhumanity and violence, is undoubtedly a little more "nearness" to the kingdom of heaven which Jesus wanted to bring us.*

George Orwell, observing the rise of fascism in Europe, described the worship of power as "the new religion of Europe." Anti-Americanism, predicated in part on fascism's mirror image, the revilement of power—especially when that power is somebody else's—answers many of the fundamental needs once filled by the Church. There is a transcendent and common goal. There are crusades. There is a pleasing sense of moral superiority. There is community. There is zeal, a sense of belonging, even ecstasy in anti-American protest movements—yet there is rarely an explicit belief in God, for that is now widely viewed in Europe as the mark of primitivism.

Europe's anti-Americanism significantly antedates the presidency of George W. Bush. It has been a theme of European politics for some two hundred years, suppressed only during the Cold War, and then just barely. It is through ignorance of this tradition that American observers attribute Europe's recent satisfied spasm of anti-Americanism to our presumptively incompetent diplomacy or our military presence in Iraq. It is more helpful to place this emotion in the context of Eric Hoffer's still-relevant observations about mass movements. These, he asserted, have distinct characteristics in common, no matter how disparate the subjects. They are convenient ways of avoiding personal responsibility. They can exist without a God, but will fail without something to hate. They are attractive to people whose lives are meaningless. They give hope to existence. And they are interchangeable: No matter the goals of the movement, the people involved are the same.

---

*These remarks are particularly rich inasmuch as Drewermann is best known for complaining bitterly in an interview with *Der Spiegel* that Americans "live in the delusion that they, as a magnificent nation, were specially appointed by God to direct the course of world events." Interview with Eugen Drewermann, "Psychoanalysis: Why Bush Must Conduct This War," *Der Spiegel*, February 11, 2003.

## IT'S OUR PROBLEM

*It's their problem, not ours.* That's what many Americans believe.
For the most part, Europe is regarded by American policymakers as
an irrelevant museum at best, a squawking nuisance at worst. The
silent premise animating American policy is that we have more important things to worry about—terrorism, Iraq, nuclear proliferation,
hurricanes. These *are* problems that should cause us all to lose sleep.
But recall where the lives of American soldiers have *in fact* been
squandered in the past century: in Europe, 344,955. In all other conflicts combined—including Vietnam, Korea, and the Persian Gulf—
less than half this number of Americans have perished.

Why should this concern us now? We are, after all, in the process
of removing troops from Europe. Can't we just leave them to their
own devices and forget about them at last? No, we can't. Would that
we could. A united Europe, even to the limited extent that it is united,
is a major power—one bigger than the United States in territory and
population. A morally unmoored Europe, imploding under the weight
of social and economic pressures few politicians in Europe will even
forthrightly describe, no less address, poses a threat to American interests and objectives everywhere on the planet. It threatens our trade
policy and our economy. It threatens our policies in Iraq. It threatens
our attempts to mediate the Arab-Israeli conflict, particularly given
the alarming recrudescence of anti-Semitism on European soil. It
threatens our posture toward North Korea. Toward China. Toward
Iran. Toward Afghanistan. Toward Sudan. It impedes our efforts to
prevent terrorism and halt the advance of Islamic radicalism.

This is not a hypothetical: There are radical Islamic terrorist cells
in every major European city. The September 11 attacks were plotted
in Hamburg. The assassins of Afghanistan's Northern Alliance leader,
Ahmad Shah Masood, carried Belgian passports. Zacarias Moussaoui,
who trained to be the twentieth hijacker on September 11, was born in
France and educated in Britain. I could extend this list for pages. If Europe is unable to assimilate its immigrants, if Europe is a breeding

ground for anti-Americanism and Islamic radicalism—and it is—this *is* our problem, and we need to understand why this is so.

Islamic radicals are far from the only problem in Europe. We have already been drawn back into armed conflict on European soil, where "Never again" has proved an empty slogan. Confronted with genocide—yet again—in the former Yugoslavia, European diplomats bickered helplessly until the United States intervened. Jacques Poos, the foreign representative of the European Community, surveyed the scene in 1991 and declared, "The hour of Europe has come!" Distinctly under-awed Bosnian Serb forces responded by capturing European peacekeepers and tying them to trees. The hostages offered no resistance, and their governments did nothing to retaliate. When Bosnian Serbs entered Srebrenica, the Dutch forces charged with the protection of the refugees failed to fire a single shot. The Serbs separated some 7,000 men and boys from the women, hauled them away, and slaughtered them. This kind of Europe—passive, paralyzed, and fundamentally in disaccord with American idealism—is very much our problem. Our history is too deeply intertwined with Europe's to imagine it could be otherwise.

Throughout Europe, crude anti-Americanism now substitutes for serious attempts to construct farsighted foreign policy. European bookstores are full of titles such as *American Totalitarianism; No Thanks, Uncle Sam; A Strange Dictatorship;* and *Who Is Killing France?* (The answer to the last question is, of course, the United States. Given the hectic imperial schedule we have apparently adopted, it is odd that the author believes killing the French would be high on our priority list.) The French journalist Thierry Meyssan has argued that no airplane crashed into the Pentagon on September 11; instead, he proposes, the American secret services and America's military-industrial complex invented the story to prime their sheeplike countrymen for a war of imperial conquest against Afghanistan and Iraq. The level of anti-American hysteria in France is such that his book, *The Horrifying Fraud,* was a galloping best-seller. Shortly before the beginning of the Iraq War, a poll showed that 30 percent of Frenchmen hoped the United States would be defeated by Saddam Hussein. It is one thing to oppose the war in Iraq on strategic grounds or out of heartfelt dopey pacifism; it is another to hope for the *triumph* of a genocidal maniac who transformed his own country—and its neighbors—into an abattoir. Who in his right mind hopes for the victory of a dictator who fed his opponents into industrial shredders and shoveled uncountable numbers of his compatriots into mass graves?

The popular Belgian musician Raymond van het Groenewoud recently wrote a hit song titled "Down with America." The lyrics are easily remembered: "Down with America! Down with the jerks from America. Down with America!" In Britain, newspaper headlines have proclaimed the United States to be the "world's leading rogue state" and "an unrepentant outlaw." In a comparison widely echoed by German entertainers, writers, playwrights, and talk show hosts, Germany's former justice minister, Herta Däubler-Gmelin, suggested an equivalence between President Bush and Hitler—this from a cabinet-level official, not some adolescent protester, an educated woman who *should* be fully conversant with the history of Nazism, the rape of Czechoslovakia, Poland, Belgium, Holland, France, Luxembourg, Denmark, Norway, Romania, Yugoslavia, and Greece. She has heard of the Holocaust, I'm sure. She must be aware that some 52 million people perished in the Second World War. But these same critics, whose well-developed organs of indignation are so exceptionally sensitive to the infamies visited upon the globe by the United States, have had little to say about the outrageous human rights records of Libya, Sudan, Saudi Arabia, Iran, or China. When *these* countries are mentioned, the critics may be found coughing discreetly into their napkins and decorously picking lint from their neckties.

France and Germany, having long luxuriated under the American defense umbrella, appear now at long last to have converged upon a foreign policy principle: systematically undermining diplomatic and military initiatives emerging from the United States. European leaders who reviled the United States for deposing Saddam Hussein by force were consistently unable to propose, or even formulate in outline, any thoughtful or viable policy alternative beyond the one that had already been tried without success for twelve years. France and Germany were not content merely to voice their own objection to our diplomatic and military policies in Iraq; they obstructed both, aggressively lobbying African nations to vote against us in the United Nations and, it is credibly rumored, blackmailing Turkey with the threat of exclusion from the European Union should it permit the United States to stage operations from its bases.[6] France was the principal investor in Saddam Hussein's regime and remains the chief lender to Iran, Cuba, Somalia, Sudan, and nearly every other kleptocratic state the United States seeks economically to isolate. Wherever French lending institutions hesitate, German ones pick up the slack; their banks are the biggest lenders to North Korea, Syria, and Libya.[7]

In October 2005, a commission led by former U.S. central bank chief Paul Volcker concluded its lengthy investigation of the United Nations' oil-for-food program. The commission reported that in exchange for French diplomatic support, Iraq adopted an "explicit policy of favoring companies and individuals based in France." Beneficiaries of Iraqi kickbacks received oil barrel allocations based on their level of opposition to the sanctions regime. (Now mind you, countless European politicians piously insisted that this very same sanctions regime had not been given enough time to work.) The Volcker Report alleges that Jean-Bernard Mérimée, France's former special adviser to the secretary-general of the UN, received oil allocations for 6 million barrels from Iraq; French businessman Claude Kaspereit received allocations for more than 9.5 million barrels; former French diplomat Serge Boidevoix received 32 million barrels; Gilles Munier, the secretary-general of the French-Iraqi Friendship Association, received 11.8 million barrels. Munier, by the way, has been a particularly loud critic of American policy in Iraq. Former French interior minister Charles Pasqua was given allocations for 11 million barrels. Upon receiving this news, he is said gleefully to have exclaimed, "I will be the king of petrol!"[8] (The line is almost too camp to be believed. It's something Dr. Evil would say while dangling Austin Powers above a tank of hungry sharks.)

This is our problem, not that we ever asked for it. It is infuriating, of course. I am hardly the first person to observe that were it not for

American soldiers and taxpayers, Russian tanks would long ago have rolled straight to the Atlantic, the troops pausing only to perform a traditional Cossack dance on the rubble of the Elysée Palace and then urinate on the remains of the flower beds. Indeed, one rarely hears discussed in Europe the threat now posed by Russia's descent into neo-imperial authoritarianism, but this is not because no such threat exists: it is because we may be counted on to nullify it. The United States still stations 26,000 combat personnel and 34,000 military support and administrative personnel on 294 military installations in Europe. It has cost us many billions of dollars to maintain these bases since the end of the Second World War. This is money that we have not spent on social welfare programs in America—nor has it been returned to those who earned it—and it is money that Europe *has* spent on its own social welfare programs.

But Europe should interest us for another reason: We share its problems. America is Europe's cultural, political, intellectual, and social progeny. Many of the problems now confronting Europe are also present, in lesser but growing form, in America. Hysterical anti-Americanism, for example, is widespread in America itself. It is not only Europeans who have compared the American president to Hitler. Europe is a test case, a laboratory, that shows us *exactly* where some of these ideas lead. It is significant that the French sheep farmer and antiglobalization activist José Bové has such a large American following. Before joining his herd, Americans might wish to know exactly who he is, where he comes from, and what people like him have already wrought in Europe.

Many Americans are besotted with Europe. They look to contemporary European political culture and its social institutions for inspiration; they admire Europe's welfare states and believe American social welfare programs should be modeled on them. Paul Krugman, for example, has urged us in the pages of the *New York Times* to "learn from" the French and their admirable family values, which he believes to be nurtured by the shorter French workweek.[9] France's government regulations, he writes, "actually allow people to make a desirable trade-off—to modestly lower income in return for more time with friends and family—the kind of deal an individual would find hard to negotiate."

Has Paul Krugman ever set foot on French soil? One wonders. The argument is, first of all, laughable on the face of it. For one thing, the most important family value is to have a family in the first place, and it is a notorious source of concern to French economists that French rates of marriage and reproduction have for years been drastically lower than those in America. Second, there's no evidence at all that the French are spending that leisure time with their families, even when they have them: During the great European heat wave of 2003, the corpses of the elderly were stacked up by the thousands in makeshift warehouses outside Paris because the French took their abundant vacation time and went to the Riviera, leaving their parents behind to perish. Their *families?* Where does he get these crazy ideas? Krugman may vaguely recall the French expression *cinq à sept,* which means "five to seven" and refers to the hours of the afternoon during which the French commit adultery, the traditional French pastime. *That's* what they do with that leisure time. There is, of course, no comparable expression in America—from five to seven in the evening, Americans are too busy *working.*

More seriously, Krugman does not for a moment consider the other consequences of those regulations—consequences that one encounters every day living in Paris. Among them is France's intractable structural unemployment, which bears a direct relationship to its inability to assimilate its Islamic immigrants, and thus the growing, murderous radicalism of its slums.

The riots that erupted in the suburban ghettos of Paris in November 2005—where unemployment among the young on average exceeds 30 percent and is, in some areas, as high as 50 percent—are in large part attributable to the very policies Krugman would have us emulate. The worst violence France has seen since 1968 quickly spread to more than 200 cities and towns, as well as neighboring countries. Curfews were imposed throughout France. The president declared a state of emergency. In some parts of France, commerce and transportation were brought to a halt. Lyon shut down its entire public transportation system following the bombing of a train station. In Bordeaux, a bus exploded when hit with a Molotov cocktail. Thousands of vehicles and several public buildings were completely destroyed. There were many serious injuries and one death. By the time this book is in print there may be more. It would seem that a great many French families—or their children, at least—enjoy spending their leisure time torching cars, throwing firebombs, and choking on tear gas. Surely it would be no very cynical asperity to suggest that these kids would be better off working.

There are many Americans who, like Krugman, suspect that Europeans and their leaders are, as they style themselves, more sophisticated, worldly, and politically mature than Americans and their leaders. They believe that Europe's antipathy toward America is a proportionate and rational response to American failings.

I encourage them to feel uneasy in these sentiments.

# CHAPTER 2

# SELF-EXTINGUISHING TOLERANCE

On January 30, 2005, in Rotterdam, the Netherlands'
largest film festival canceled a showing of *Submission,* a short
film about the suffering of women in Islamic cultures. Theo van Gogh,
the director, had several months before been slain on the streets of
Amsterdam by a Dutch-Moroccan Muslim who found the film offensive. The festival had planned to show *Submission* as part of a program titled "Filmmaking in an Age of Turbulence." Also on the
agenda were films that had been censored in Russia, Indonesia, and
Serbia: presumably the program's intended moral message was one of
pious opposition to censorship. But when the documentary's producer,
Gijs van de Westelaken, of Column Films, received death threats, he
chose with hideous unintentional irony to embody the title of the film
in question. *Submission* was promptly removed from the program.
Added, however, were two Islamist propaganda films, one about the
racism of British authorities, which, the movie offered, was understandably causing young British Muslims to join al Qaeda; the other a
sympathetic interpretation of Palestinian suicide bombings as a natural response to the repressive practices of the occupying Israeli army.[1]
Explaining his decision, van de Westelaken remarked that he did not
want "to take the slightest risk for anyone of our team."[2]

Coincidentally, the showing of the film was canceled on the day of

Iraq's first multiparty elections in half a century. The comparison is instructive. Describing the mood in Baghdad on that day, an Iraqi named Sam posted this entry to his weblog:

> We decided to challenge the terrorists who threatened to wash the streets of Iraq with our blood. We said . . . let them send their dogs to suck our bones we care not! We challenged them and we knew we may die and some of us wear their shrouds and voted in a civilized way with out problems. In one incident in Baghdad an Iraqi Hero suspected a terrorist. He chased him! The terrorist run and the Iraqi hero run after him and captured him. The terrorist blows himself with our hero who died to save many lives.[3]

Another Iraqi in Baghdad, Ali, wrote this after casting his vote:

> This was my way to stand against those who humiliated me, my family and my friends. It was my way of saying, "You're history and you don't scare me anymore." It was my way to scream in the face of all tyrants, not just Saddam and his Ba'athists and tell them, "I don't want to be your, or anyone's slave. You have kept me in your jail all my life but you never owned my soul." It was my way of finally facing my fears and finding my courage and my humanity again. . . . As I was walking with many people towards the center explosion hit and gun fire were heard but most were not that close. People didn't seem to pay attention to that.[4]

Hundreds of Iraqis posted to weblogs like these in the days after the election, expressing similar sentiments. You don't need to take my word for it: Do a quick Google search under the terms "Blog+Iraq" and you'll find them. Granted, there is no way to verify that these sites are authentic. Perhaps they were all created, as some charge, by the CIA.[5] If that's true, well then, *chapeau!*—and I apologize for all the times I made fun of you, old buddies. It's good to know our men in black have their act together at last.

But frankly, that seems unlikely. I watched CNN that day like everyone else. You saw what I saw, I'm sure: illiterate desert tribesmen, in dusty robes, walking for miles to reach the polls; young Iraqis carrying the elderly and the infirm in their arms to the voting booths; wizened women, dressed from head to toe in black, defiantly holding up their purple fingers to the cameras. I'm quite satisfied that the CIA didn't stage all of that and convince all the news stations, al-Jazeera included, to broadcast the phony footage.

Story after story reported on that day suggested that the sentiments expressed on these websites were typical. An Iraqi man who had lost his leg in a car bombing the year before announced to the press that he would have crawled to the polls if he had to. Voters stepped around the body of an exploded suicide bomber outside a polling station and in a particularly superb gesture spat on his corpse. Voters turned out in numbers that surpassed predictions, in percentages that exceeded any recent American election. They did so in the face of terrible danger: Thirty-five Iraqis were murdered on election day. In one instance the terrorists, apparently striving to set some kind of world record in depravity, used a kidnapped child with Down syndrome as an improvised explosive device.

The comparison to the mood of capitulation in the Netherlands is so striking that it cannot but arouse our curiosity. Of course it is understandable that the festival's administrators were spooked by the death threats. Surely the Iraqi voters were spooked, too. Why such a stunning discrepancy in bravery and defiance? Why did we see the Dutch capitulating to terrorists on the very day that Iraqis were—literally—spitting on them? Why, in fact, have we recently seen this kind of capitulation to Islamic radicalism over and over again throughout Europe?

## BARGAINING WITH DEPRAVITY

This is not the first time we have seen something like this in the Netherlands. The French have been widely and deservedly condemned—

and are to this day remorselessly ridiculed—for collaborating with the Nazis. They have never lived that down, despite the extraordinary French record of bravery in the First World War, which left almost every French village bled white and depopulated of young men.* Everyone familiar with the history of the Second World War knows that the French offered little resistance to the Nazi program for the destruction of French Jewry. It is not widely appreciated that the Dutch record is even worse. Perhaps it is because Anne Frank's diary is so well known that people now imagine Holland to have been overbrimming with sturdy towheaded heroes who at terrible risk to themselves stashed Jews in their attics. Careful readers will note, however, that the Frank family was betrayed to the Nazis by their neighbors.[6]

There is an important tradition in the Netherlands—as there is throughout Europe—of bargaining with depravity. The Dutch response to Islamic terror has much in common with the Dutch posture toward Nazi terror. Both represent perversions of the noble Dutch tradition of accommodation and tolerance, one that dates from the Dutch Golden Age of the seventeenth century—the age of Erasmus and the birth of humanism—when Dutch art, trade, and science were among the world's most acclaimed. The Jews of Portugal and Belgium fled to the tolerant Netherlands to escape the Inquisition. Scientists and philosophers from all of Europe, including Spinoza and Descartes, took refuge in the Netherlands. But in the past century, Dutch tolerance has had a notable tendency to shade into its ugly cousin—an inability to discern what *cannot* be tolerated.

The Dutch attempted to appease the Nazis. This is not a taunt, it is simply a fact. The Netherlands' elites found much to admire in Nazi Germany during the interwar period, and were particularly sympathetic to Hitler's anti-Communist and anti-Semitic agenda, as this typical comment from Willem Jacob Oudendijk, Holland's acting envoy to Petrograd, suggests:

---

*Courage in conjunction with lamentable military strategy is, of course, not much to celebrate.

Unless . . . Bolshevism is nipped in the bud immediately it is bound to spread in one form or another over Europe and the whole world as it is organized and worked by Jews who have no nationality, and whose one object is to destroy for their own ends the existing order of things. The only manner in which this danger could be averted would be collective action on the part of all powers.[7]

By 1935, the Dutch were cooperating closely with the Germans in arresting their "Marxist and Jewish elements." Many of the German Jews who had taken refuge in the Netherlands following Hitler's seizure of power were forced to flee. In March 1935, Fort Honswijk, south of Utrecht, was redesigned as a concentration camp to contain "undesirable elements." In 1936, the influential newspaper *Nieuwe Rotterdamse Courant* fired its Jewish foreign editor for criticizing the Nazis.[8]

The Dutch royal family was surrounded by National Socialists. When the future queen, Princess Juliana, married a member of the Reiter-SS, Prince Bernhard zur Lippe-Biesterfeld, guests at the wedding party hailed the couple with Nazi salutes.[9] The Nazi diplomat Wolfgang zu Putlitz, assigned to The Hague after a tour of duty in London, fondly recalled the Dutch and their cooperative posture in his memoirs:

In England I had never come across officials in leading agencies who expressed their sympathy for the new Germanism as enthusiastically as in the Netherlands. . . . The National Socialists of Mr. Mussert [the leader of the Dutch Nazis] had supporters in almost all ministries and even among the royal household. . . . There were Chiefs of Police who, summarily, at one signal from Butting [an attaché at the German embassy], deported German emigrants at any time of day or night, and handed them over to the Gestapo. . . . I have never heard that the Dutch government asked for a single document concerning such arbitrary acts, which were known to us by the dozen.[10]

Following Kristallnacht, the Dutch government renounced the Netherlands' centuries-old tradition of sheltering fugitives, declaring that it would no longer accept Jewish refugees. The border was policed with especial care against desperate Jews attempting to escape from Germany. One week after Kristallnacht, the government issued a statement condemning Dutch citizens who privately attempted to rescue Jewish children: "The behavior of Dutch who transfer Jewish children by car or by train to the Netherlands has to be disapproved of."[11]

The Dutch appeasement policy ended as appeasement policies generally do when the German army invaded the Netherlands in May 1940 and overran the country within five days. Jews were swiftly dismissed from government positions and required to register themselves as non-Aryans, a demand to which the Dutch civil service acquiesced without complaint. On February 22, 1941, the first 430 Jews were picked at random, arrested, and deported to the Mauthausen concentration camp in Austria. Within three months all were dead. Soon afterward, the identity cards of Dutch Jews were stamped with the letter *J*, and Jews were forced to wear the yellow star. They were forbidden to travel and barred from public transportation, theaters, libraries, parks, and the homes of Gentiles. As the Nazis demanded, the Dutch implemented the Nuremburg laws on racial purity. Jews were fired from their jobs. The Nazis seized the valuables of Jews and transported them to German banks. During the entire Occupation, with the exception of a single day-and-a-half protest strike in February 1941, organized by the Communists, the Dutch took no public action to protest *any* of these policies.[12]

Indeed, the Dutch cooperated fully in their own moral destruction. The Dutch continued to trade energetically with the Germans, filling 84.4 percent of their orders. (The French filled only 70 percent of German orders.)[13] Dutch policemen arrested the Jews. Dutch officers guarded them in the transit camps. Dutch railway workers deported them for liquidation. Dutch security forces were praised by Himmler for their loyalty and industry. "Very good," the SS leader wrote at the top of a memo documenting their efficient contribution to the Nazi death machine.[14]

Ordinary people were well aware of the fate that awaited those deported. Anyone who says otherwise is speaking nonsense. The Nazis, with the help of the Dutch police, were seizing Jews from orphanages, hospitals, and homes for the aged. Their claim that these Jews were to be conscripted into labor service was patently ludicrous. No one ever received mail from the deported. Even a child like Anne Frank had a perfect grasp of the situation. "The English radio speaks of gassing," she wrote. "Maybe that is after all the quickest method of dying."[15]

When the mass deportations began, in July 1942, the Jewish population of the Netherlands stood at 140,000. Approximately 110,000 Jews were sent in sealed railway cars to the death camps. All but a handful were exterminated. The percentage of Jews who perished in the Netherlands exceeded that of any other country in Western Europe. *This* is why it is particularly disturbing now to see Dutch filmmakers taking orders from totalitarian fanatics who explicitly propose to destroy Dutch democracy and make no secret of their odium toward the world's remaining Jews.

It is not only the filmmakers who have exhibited a disturbing willingness to compromise with fanaticism. The Dutch state funds, with taxpayer money, hundreds of mosques and Islamic clubs headed by radical clerics who are committed to destroying Dutch civic order. In 2003, the Dutch government granted the Arab European League permission to open its first branch in the Netherlands. The league was founded in Belgium by Dyab Abou Jahjah, a former member of Hezbollah and self-described "armed resistor" in Lebanon.[16] It had already incited vicious riots and anti-Semitic violence in Antwerp, and had issued public approvals of September 11. "Sweet revenge," said Jahjah. Jahjah seeks the implementation of sharia—Islamic law—throughout Europe. In the "sharocracy" he envisions, all women will be covered.[17] The organization has pledged solidarity with the Iraqi insurgency: With Dutch troops serving in Iraq, this would seem to be a posture that crosses the line between moral ignominy and treason.

The interim leader of the Netherlands branch of the Arab European League, Jamil Jawad, opened the league's inaugural meeting by calling for the destruction of Israel. He then demanded the abolition of the Netherlands' drug-selling coffee shops and legal brothels. His successor, Mohammed Cheppiah, urged that homosexuals be stoned to death. The league's press officer, Naïma Elmaslouhi, announced that she found unproblematic the sight of Moroccan youths chanting "Hamas, Hamas, gas all the Jews" on the streets of Amsterdam, as they did during protest marches in 2002.[18] (This was reported in the *NRC Handelsblad,* commonly regarded as the Netherlands' highest-quality newspaper. Elmaslouhi subsequently denied making the remark. I know who I believe.) When, in November 2003, terrorists believed to be linked to al Qaeda detonated bombs throughout Turkey, killing more than 50 people, Elmaslouhi expressed her "support and understanding" of the murderers. They had, after all, blown up two synagogues. "I am against the killing of innocents," she said, "but how do you know who is innocent?"[19] As far as I know, she has not denied making this remark. Following the Madrid train bombings that left nearly 200 dead and hundreds more injured, Jahjah, the league's founder, remarked in a televised debate that a similar attack was likely in the Netherlands. "It's logical," he said. "You make war with us, we make war with you."[20]

Why on earth should the Dutch tolerate this, an official, legal terrorist organization dedicated to erasing Dutch tolerance?

## OH, UNBELIEVING FUNDAMENTALISTS: THE MURDER OF THEO VAN GOGH

Dutch courage does exist, however, and has recently been personified by the politician and author of *Submission,* Ayaan Hirsi Ali, who happens to have been born in Mogadishu, not Holland. The daughter of a politician forced into exile by the Somali civil war, Hirsi Ali was raised throughout Islamic Africa and the Middle East, and thus observed the lives of Muslim women from a number of bleak perspectives. When Hirsi Ali turned twenty-three, her father announced her engagement to a kinsman in Canada, a man twice her age who grandly proposed to sire six children in a row. Hirsi Ali was en route to Canada, transiting Germany, when she slipped off the plane and fled, seeking and receiving asylum in the Netherlands. She spoke not one word of Dutch.

She was an uneducated woman with no financial resources. In one gesture, she exiled herself from everything familiar to her, from her family and her culture, even from her language. Supporting herself with cleaning jobs, she studied Dutch, acquiring a now-legendary fluency. She put herself through college, where she studied political thought from the Greco-Roman era to the present. She was particularly fascinated by the writings of John Stuart Mill. She joined the Dutch Labor Party and won a seat in the Dutch parliament, becoming prominent as an advocate for abused Islamic women. She denounced the forcible imposition of the veil, incest, spousal battery, and the monstrous practice of female genital mutilation. She carefully documented thousands of these crimes among Muslim immigrants in the Netherlands.

Astonishingly, her stance on these issues was both controversial and rare. Antipathy came not only from Muslims, from whom she received a steady influx of death threats, but from her own political party, which demanded she abandon her campaign. "They don't want to believe Muslim women in the Netherlands are beaten and locked up in their homes," she said, "or that girls are murdered for holding hands with a non-Muslim boy. When I took it up with the Labor Party they sided with the Islamic conservatives, and told me to stop, so that's when I became really inflamed."[21]

Hirsi Ali left the Labor Party and joined the Liberal Party, where she has led a campaign against the Dutch government's expensive support for the multiculturalism programs that, she argues, have succeeded only in isolating Muslim women still further from Dutch society. She particularly opposes the funding of education for immigrants in their own languages, rather than Dutch, and the government's underwriting of more than 700 Islamic clubs, many headed by radical imams who do not speak Dutch and know nothing about Dutch culture.

*Submission*—the film Hirsi Ali wrote and for which her friend and collaborator Theo van Gogh was murdered—is only eleven minutes long. It depicts women in transparent veils and low-cut wedding gowns, with red lash marks on their flesh and blackened eyes. Texts from the Koran have been inscribed directly on their skin. Among these texts are the passages sanctioning the physical punishment of disobedient women. The women pray out loud, asking Allah for strength to bear their suffering.

I wish I could report that *Submission* is a triumphant artistic achievement. It's awful, actually. It's set to music that sounds like a porn flick sound track overdubbed with the muezzin's call to prayer—*bow-chicka-mow-mow-allahu-akbar!* Even worse than the sound track is the acting, which manages, curiously, to be both leaden and overwrought at once. After eleven minutes of watching these prissy martyred creatures roll their eyes heavenward as they supplicate and whinge to Allah, one finds sympathy for the urge to slap them around. But the film's artistic merits are not the point. No one should die for making a crummy movie. The film's *moral* message is one to which no civilized person—and particularly no feminist—should object.

*Submission* aired in the Netherlands on August 29, 2004. On November 2, 2004, a man dressed in a traditional Moroccan djellaba shot Van Gogh as he cycled to work in central Amsterdam. The filmmaker pleaded for mercy while the assailant stabbed him repeatedly in the chest. When Van Gogh tried to stumble away, his attacker shot him again, stabbed him again, slit his throat with a butcher knife, then used the knife to skewer a five-page letter to his chest, lodging the blade all the way to his spinal column. The letter called for the murder of Hirsi Ali, who was aligned, it said, with "Jewish masters," and threatened several other Dutch politicians, including the Jewish mayor of Amsterdam (who, curiously, responded to the murder by calling for greater trust between native Dutch and Moroccans).[22] It described the sounds the author expected presently to hear throughout the streets of Europe: "Screams, Miss Hirsi Ali, that will cause shivers to roll down one's spine; that will make hair stand up from heads. People will be seen drunk with fear while they are not drunk. FEAR shall fill the atmosphere on that great day."* It concluded:

> I know for sure that you, Oh America, will go under;
> I know for sure that you, Oh Europe, will go under;
> I know for sure that you, Oh Holland, will go under;
> I know for sure that you, Oh Hirsi Ali, will go under;
> I know for sure that you, Oh unbelieving fundamentalist,
>     will go under.

In the ensuing shootout with police, the assailant also wounded a police officer and an eyewitness. The murderer was subsequently identified as twenty-six-year-old Mohammed Bouyeri, an Islamic extremist with dual Dutch and Moroccan nationality. He was believed to belong to a terrorist network affiliated with al Qaeda and linked to the May 16, 2003, terrorist attack in Casablanca that killed forty people. Bouyeri had been born and raised in Amsterdam. Like the London Tube bombers, he was a homegrown European monster. At his trial, he made a point of taunting Van Gogh's mother: "I don't feel your pain. I don't have any sympathy for you. I can't feel for you because I think you're a nonbeliever." He stressed to the court that he would kill Van Gogh again if given a chance: He had, he said, acted out of conviction.

On July 26, 2005—a few days after the second set of attacks on London—Bouyeri was sentenced to life imprisonment. It was the maximum sentence possible under Dutch law, but it must be allowed that many fates are worse than spending one's life in a Dutch prison. *De Telegraaf,* a leading Dutch newspaper, recently published an article about life in the Esserheem Prison, which houses murderers and other violent criminals: "Life is nowhere so relaxed as in Esserheem," said Martin K., who was serving a sentence for two murders. "In our own

---

*The message is obviously of Koranic inspiration. "22/1 Mankind, have fear of your Lord! The quaking of the Hour is a terrible thing. 22/2 On the day they see it, every nursing woman will be oblivious of the baby at her breast, and every pregnant woman will abort the contents of her womb, and you will think people drunk when they are not drunk; it is just that the punishment of Allah is so severe." (Sura al-Haj, 'The Pilgrimage')

café 'Club 91' we have a party every weekend. . . . While enjoying a delicious snack, an ice cream or a malt beer, we play pool or listen to music. If the weather allows, we play tennis, since we have a tennis court outside."[23] Bouyeri retains his right to vote—and to stand for parliament. Prosecutors had asked the court to strip him of both; the judges declined.

Soon after the murder, the Dutch government took some obvious, if long-overdue, measures. It began deporting terrorist suspects, closing extremist mosques, and shutting down Islamist websites. Police stepped up surveillance of radical groups and made quite a few arrests. Yet at the same time, many prominent Dutch politicians and civic officials displayed a public and almost parodic inability to recognize the significance of the murder or respond to it appropriately. Van Gogh was, as his name suggests, a descendant of the artist whose achievements rank among the great triumphs of Western culture. His assassin was a welfare recipient: he had been not only tolerated but nourished by the Dutch state, just as the London bombers had been nourished by the British state. The symbolism of this murder could scarcely be more obvious, and if anyone missed it, the note stabbed to his body should surely have filled in the blanks. After the murder, Deputy Prime Minister Gerrit Zalm made the perfectly self-evident observation that the Netherlands was at war with Islamic extremism. Note his careful phrasing: Islamic *extremism*, not Islam. He was sharply chastised by his colleagues. "We fall," said Green Left leader Femke Halsema, "too easily into an 'us and them' antithesis with the word 'war.'" Many other prominent politicians, including the mayor of Amsterdam (who had been specifically marked for death in the murderer's letter), echoed or applauded her high-minded rebuke. That sort of language, said the mayor, was not helpful and might lead to an "us-and-them" divide.

An us-and-them divide? It *is* you versus them, you phlegmatic Dutch dolts. *Just read the note.* Jan Marijnissen, the leader in the Dutch parliament of the Socialist Party, was not on the note's copy list, apparently: "If rationality is pushed aside," he said primly of the deputy prime minister's comments, "hate could lodge itself in the heads of extremists." I personally suspect that a bit of hate just *may* be lodged in their heads already. Now, this Dutch tolerance business is all very inspiring, but the "them" in question happen to be, as Van Gogh himself put it, "a fifth column of goatfuckers." If these politicians really can't tell the difference between themselves and Islamic extremists, I propose they spend a year living under Islamic law, preferably in one of the countries where Ayaan Hirsi Ali was raised.

In the aftermath of the murder, the stories of perverted tolerance multiplied. In a now infamous incident, a Rotterdam artist created a street mural—on the exterior of his own wall—with the words "Thou shalt not kill." Moroccan youths gathered around the mural and spat on it. The head of a local mosque complained to police that he found the mural offensive and racist. The mayor of Rotterdam ordered the mural, not the Moroccan youths, removed by police. When a video crew attempted to film the destruction of the mural, Dutch police seized the videotape. The Netherlands was once the only country in Europe where figures such as Spinoza could be guaranteed freedom of expression. Now it is the only country in Europe where the Sixth Commandment is subject to immediate censorship.

Immediately following the murder, Hirsi Ali was sped out of the country on government orders. Members of the Dutch parliament were forced into hiding. These developments met with surprisingly little outrage. The parliamentarian Geert Wilders, who has called for closing Holland's radical mosques, now spends every single night in a high-security prison cell; his security guards say they cannot protect him otherwise. He is permitted a weekly meeting with his wife. Can anyone imagine an American senator—John McCain, say—spending his nights in a high-security prison cell because the U.S. government was unable or unwilling to take appropriate measures to protect him?

This particular story is a Dutch one. But the tolerance of Islamic radicals who are dedicated to Europe's destruction is not limited to the Netherlands. Throughout Europe, funded by foreign money, thousands of mosques import a belligerent strain of Islam that rejects assimilation and embraces jihad, the complete subjugation of women, and vitriolic anti-Semitism. France's 1,200 mosques are nearly all funded by foreign money, and most of the imams who preach in them are foreigners. An Algerian-born imam in Strasbourg, Mohamed Latreche, has established the PMF—the French Muslim Party—on a platform that consists largely of demonizing Jews and denying the Holocaust. Representatives of Hamas and Hezbollah participate in his rallies. The imam of Hamburg's al-Quds Mosque, where 9/11 hijacker Mohamed Atta regularly worshipped, announced in a videotaped sermon prior to September 11 that "the Jews and crusaders must have their throats slit." Many prominent Islamic spokesmen in Europe dream openly of the day when the Continent will be governed by sharia. Europe tolerates all of this.

## THE NEW ORDERING PRINCIPLE OF EUROPEAN SOCIETY

Why do we find Europe in the grip of this strange passivity? The diffidence finds its source in the new ordering principle of European society—a form of weak rationality, a kind of utilitarianism. Europeans now obey their authorities not because they rule by divine right, nor because those authorities promise a utopian future, but because law and order are preferable to chaos and anarchy. This is reasonable enough, but hardly a principle to set men alight with passion.

Social and moral structures in Europe are now, essentially, bureaucratic structures: These structures, like Turing machines, serve ends that aren't specified and may not even exist. Throughout Europe, the replacement of supernaturalism with rationalism has led to an open question: *Why must we do things the way we always have?* The response—*No reason, I suppose*—has vitiated innumerable seemingly pointless demands of manners, propriety, culture, and behavior. With the exception of a few core demands, ancient social structures have been in large part demolished. But the loss of many small principles can add up to a catastrophic failure of the system as a whole.

Consider, for example, soaring rates of drunken vandalism in Britain. The culture of loutishness has become so pervasive there that voters now consider antisocial behavior—drunkenness, vagrancy, vandalism, street brawling, public urination—to be their greatest concern. Why is this behavior rising so alarmingly? One explanation: No one now believes, in principle, in any argument stronger than the assertion that there really *shouldn't* be so much drunken vandalism. To this, it is only too easy to reply, "Why the hell not?" Why the hell should people not urinate in public? And why the hell should they fight to protect European civilization?

"The fall of ideologies now casts a deadly shadow over every ideal," writes the French philosopher Chantal Delsol, a professor at the University of Marne-la-Vallée and a shrewd observer of modern Europe. Utopian ideologies, she remarks, were in their capacity to awe and inspire like cathedrals, and Europe has watched the collapse of one cathedral after another.[24] Delsol likens experiments in utopianism, particularly in its communist and fascist expressions, to Icarus's attempts to soar to the sun, and remarks that the failure of these experiments has left modern man as she imagines the fallen Icarus, humbled and paralyzed by self-doubt. (Modern *European* man, I should interject: Americans neither conducted these experiments nor do they live with their consequences.) Modern Europeans have come, as a consequence, to condemn zeal and faith in all their forms, theist or atheist, in preference for bureaucracy, weak solutions of moral relativism, and quiet despair. Delsol is not unsympathetic to this ideological uncertainty and lack of moral self-confidence: Rigid orthodoxy, after all, *did* give rise to both the Inquisition and the Holocaust, she reflects, or at least were associated with both. Europe, in other words, has lost its mojo for good reason.

Lacking any sense of purpose, Delsol observes, and fearful of taking a stand—about anything, even the essentials of self-preservation—Europeans instead enshroud themselves in technological and physical comfort, leading mediocre lives, avoiding risk at all cost, and mouthing vapid, unexamined clichés. She calls these clichés "the clandestine ideology of our time"—clandestine because no overt, passionate adherence to ideology is now socially permissible. Delsol correctly observes, however, that the banishment of the economy of ideology has encouraged a black market to flourish in its place, an underground moral code steeped in sentimentality but untempered by reason and serving no larger, coherent principles.

The code she describes is a close cousin to what is termed, in America, political correctness, but whereas political correctness in the United States is confined for the most part to the universities and the coastal cities, it is the unspoken foundation of the modern European welfare state—a society predicated on an ever-expanding sense of entitlement. Increasingly, Delsol observes, that to which men feel entitled is described as a *right* or, for special emphasis, a *human right*:

> Anything contemporary man needs or envies, anything that seems desirable to him without reflection, becomes the object of a demanded right. Human rights are invoked as a reason for refusing to show identification, for becoming indignant against the deportation of delinquent foreigners, for forcing the state to take illegal aliens under its wing, for justifying squatting by homeless people, for questioning the active hunt for terrorists.[25]

A leading principle of this code is the estimation of "tolerance" above all other virtues. The idea of tolerance, originally defined as the absence of state prohibition against certain ideas and behaviors, has come, she notes, to be conflated with legitimization—the general social acceptance of those ideas and behaviors, to the point of encouraging them with legal and material aid from the state, ultimately to the detriment of the entire commonwealth.* This in turn gives rise to an ambient culture of moral quasi-relativism—"quasi" because, as Delsol rightly

---

*The fruits of this peculiar conception of tolerance may also be seen in the Netherlands' policy on euthanasia, one that may briefly be summarized as *Don't get sick in a Dutch hospital*. A policy widely applauded for its tolerance in fact permits Dutch doctors to kill deformed newborns, the retarded, and a great many elderly people who have specifically indicated that they have no desire to die. According to the Dutch government's own investigation, an average of sixteen people in the Netherlands are killed each day by their doctors without their consent. See the Remmelink Report by the Committee to Investigate the Medical Practice Concerning Euthanasia, *Medische Beslissingen Rond Het Levenseinde, Sdu Uitgeverij Plantijnstraat* (The Hague: 1991). On the so-called Groningen Protocols concerning the killing of infants by doctors, see, e.g., Toby Sterling, "Netherlands Hospital Euthanizes Babies," Associated Press, November 30, 2004. See also Richard Miniter, who reports that more than 10 percent of Dutch senior citizens surveyed feared being killed, against their will, by their doctors: "The Dutch Way of Death: Socialized Medicine Helped Turn Doctors into Killers," *Wall Street Journal*, April 28, 2001.

observes, its adherents unquestionably accept moral absolutes ("one must be tolerant"), yet tend simply to *affirm* that they indignantly reject moral absolutism. Delsol finds this pernicious, of course, and rightly so: One need only to look at the Netherlands to see exactly where it leads.

## THE NIHILIST ASSASSIN RETURNS

At the time of his death, Theo van Gogh was preparing a documentary about the murdered Dutch politician Pim Fortuyn, whose assassination prefigured Van Gogh's by exactly 911 days. The story of Fortuyn's death and its aftermath is particularly illustrative of this European tendency to conflate tolerance and somnolence.

On May 6, 2002, nine days before the general election in which he was expected to win the balance of power in the Dutch parliament, Fortuyn gave a radio interview in the dozy city of Hilversum, a residential suburb of Amsterdam. As he exited the radio station and entered the parking lot, he was shot five times from behind, at close range, in the head, chest, and neck. Attempts to revive him were unsuccessful. A thirty-two-year-old Dutchman, Volkert van der Graaf, was arrested minutes later at a nearby gas station, covered in Fortuyn's blood, the pistol still on his person.

Upon hearing the news, Belgian prime minister Guy Verhofstadt declared that he had believed something like this was "impossible in this day in age, in the European Union, in the 21st Century."* Two years later, no one would express surprise—dismay, yes, but not

---

*He wasn't paying attention, then. Only seven weeks before, Marco Biagi, a senior adviser to Italian prime minister Silvio Berlusconi, had been gunned down by the Red Brigades. The fact that Verhofstadt was either unaware of this or indifferent to it suggests something about the degree to which Europe has truly been integrated: not so much as some claim, evidently. It *is* true that Fortuyn's murder was the first political assassination in the Netherlands since 1584, when William the Silent was shot to death in the city of Delft. Perhaps the Belgian prime minister was inadvertently expressing a common, if rarely articulated, European sentiment: Italians can be expected to shoot their politicians (that's Sopranoland down there, after all), but when the placid Dutch begin shooting one another, it is time to worry.

surprise—that an event like this could occur in the European Union. We are all aware now that the place has a few problems.

Although Fortuyn was widely described after his death as a neo-fascist, this is ridiculous. Ideologically, he was closer to traditional figures on the European left than on the right. This was a man with portraits of Marx and Lenin hanging on the walls of his home, for God's sake. The former Marxist sociology professor—that's right, *Marxist* sociology professor—embraced the Netherlands' permissive laws on drugs and prostitution. He supported the Netherlands' policy on euthanasia.* He was an open homosexual who applauded Holland's full legalization of same-sex marriages, although he himself had no taste for monogamy or domesticity and frequently called attention to the racial diversity of his bedmates as proof of his liberal bona fides. Given his views, it scarcely even makes sense to call Fortuyn a man of the Right, no less a fascist.

How, then, did Fortuyn acquire his reputation? His alleged fascism amounted to two positions: He had come to view the Netherlands' highly collectivized economy as overweening; he favored economic decentralization and privatization. Given that most Dutch citizens pay more than half their incomes in taxes, his ideas were hardly far from the mainstream, although they obviously represented an evolution from his early Marxism. But no one could truly be shocked that a modern European politician might adopt these views after the fall of the Berlin Wall, particularly given the visible stagnation of Europe's more regulated economies.

More notoriously, he ran his campaign on an anti-immigration platform. Specifically, he opposed Islamic immigration, because wide-scale Islamic immigration, he held, threatened the Dutch tradition of *left*-wing permissiveness. Islamic immigrants, he pointed out, tended

---

*In this regard, it is true, Fortuyn's support for Holland's euthanasia policy did have something in common with fascism—Nazism, in particular—but in the modern European political tradition, it has been the Left, not the Right, that has favored permissive laws on euthanasia. It is one of those many issues where the line between the modern Left and the historic Right begins to blur.

to take a dim view of homosexuals such as himself. His homosexual friends had been attacked in the streets by Muslim youths; imams in Holland's mosques openly called for homosexuals to be stoned to death. Traditional Islamic values, he observed, were incompatible with the sexual openness and equality practiced in the Netherlands. He deplored forced marriages, honor killings, and female genital mutilation, all of which had been brought to the Netherlands by Muslim immigrants and by no other kind of immigrant. He was deeply disturbed by Islamic anti-Semitism. He observed, correctly, that young men from Islamic countries committed a disproportionate share of street crime in the Netherlands, and that levels of that crime had been rising sharply. Fortuyn was widely pilloried in the press for referring to Islam as "backwards." Less often was it noted that he made this comment in response to a Rotterdam imam's remark, on prime-time television, that homosexuals were worse than pigs. That *Fortuyn* came to be portrayed as the intolerant one in this exchange is a wonderment.

The Netherlands—the most densely populated country in Europe— did not need more immigrants for any social or economic reason, Fortuyn argued. But unlike Jean-Marie Le Pen, the leader of France's National Front to whom he was unfairly compared, Fortuyn did not call for the expulsion of immigrants already in the Netherlands.* In fact, he called for *more* government spending on health care, housing, and education, most of it to be directed toward the country's immigrant population to better facilitate their integration. To call this a fascist political program is to denude the term *fascist* of all meaning. If Fortuyn was a fascist, then Dick Cheney is an anarchosyndicalist and I am a Whig.

The press made another serious category error in describing Fortuyn's assassin. Van der Graaf, who at the time he murdered Fortuyn was thirty-three years old, was white and Dutch-born. The media made much of the fact that he was a vegan. If you mention his name to the average European, that's the word they will search for—"Oh yes, that vegan." It's true that he was an animal-rights activist who as a

---

*Le Pen is, indeed, a Holocaust denier and a crypto-fascist.

teenager had laundered oil-soaked birds. But it is absurd to imagine that this had anything to do with Fortuyn's death. Fortuyn was not known for having any opinion at all about animal rights: his party had scarcely formulated an opinion on the issue. When Van der Graaf subsequently confessed the crime, he stated that he had killed Fortuyn to protect "vulnerable members of society." By this he clearly did not mean the short-toed treecreeper or the black-tailed godwit.

But it would be an equal mistake to see Van der Graaf as an Islamist sympathizer or even a deranged but sincere defender of minority rights. Psychiatrists inspected him closely and found him perfectly sane. His alleged sympathy with the Netherlands' most vulnerable members was transparent window dressing, an excuse calculated to appeal to a Dutch public and judiciary that reflexively find that vocabulary heartwarming. In truth, Van der Graaf had never before in his life lifted a finger to assist Dutch immigrants. He had never attempted, through any legal means, to help any human member of society.

This is a particularly interesting point: *He had no real reason for murdering Fortuyn.* He could not explain his action in terms of any coherent ideology. The murder was a piece of sanguinary performance art detached from any set of principles—violence for the sport of it. Police found in his garage condoms filled with a chemical explosive made of calcium chlorate and sugar. Nearby were flasks of sulfuric acid. They found a timer device and anarchist publications in his attic, along with floor plans for the homes of other Dutch politicians. Van der Graaf later told the courts that he found these things "exciting and interesting."

Van der Graaf is an old figure in Europe—a vague, disaffected sociopath who is for some reason attracted to the word *anarchist* and who feels most fully alive when people die and things explode. He might have stepped right off the pages of *Demons,* Dostoevsky's portrait of the murderous young nihilists of czarist Russia. Indeed, Van der Graaf's spiritual ancestors were the *narodniki,* the group whose terrorist wing, the People's Will, undertook a campaign of political assassinations throughout Russia that culminated in 1881 in the murder of Czar Alexander II. The *narodniki* inspired anarchists and political assassins throughout Europe, who spent the next thirty-odd years picking off heads of state before achieving their ultimate triumph, setting all of Europe ablaze, in 1914, with the assassination of the Archduke Franz Ferdinand. It is important to remember how it all ended: These kinds of assassinations are contagious, and their consequences have been known vastly to exceed the imaginative capacities of their authors.

King Umberto I was stabbed in Naples, in 1878, by the anarchist Giovanni Passanante. The king survived, only to be assassinated in 1900 by the anarchist Gaetano Bresci—another vague, disaffected sociopath who had, he said, taken the action for the sake of the common man. "Strange that he should have committed such an act, I thought," wrote his insane contemporary Emma Goldman, a Lithuanian-born American anarchist. "He had impressed me so differently from most of the other Italians I knew. He was not at all of an excitable temperament and not easily aroused."[26] Sociopaths rarely are, actually. The personality type is quite fixed. If you consult the *Diagnostic and Statistical Manual of Mental Disorders* under "antisocial personality," you will see these characters described: few emotions, little remorse, a taste for mayhem.

In France, the great Anarchist Terror lasted from 1892 to 1894. The French terrorist Ravachol, the living symbol of violence for its own sake, committed his first murders in 1886 when he broke into the home of an elderly recluse and split his skull with a hatchet, then chased down and killed the man's elderly servant. Realizing that he had found his calling, he subsequently took to bombing judges, prosecutors, and army barracks, dabbling on the side in robbing graves. At his trial, when convicted at last of murdering his landlady, he professed his commitment to anarchist principles and, much like Van der Graaf, declared himself to have been acting on behalf of the weaker members of society. He remains a cult hero among French anarchists: If you search under his name on the Internet, you will find websites devoted to his memory—and to urgent action on behalf of Mumia Abu-Jamal, *bien sûr.*

Ravachol served as the inspiration for a host of sociopathic French terrorists, including Auguste Vaillant, who in 1893 threw a nail bomb from the public gallery in the Palais Bourbon into the chamber, injuring twenty deputies; and Emile Henry, who in 1894 tossed a home-made bomb into a crowd because he found its members "pretentious and stupid." The terror culminated on June 24, 1894, when an Italian anarchist, Sante Jeronimo Caserio, assassinated the French president, Marie-François-Sadi Carnot.

The Empress Elisabeth of Austria—widely regarded as one of the most beautiful women in Europe—was killed in 1898 by the Italian anarchist Luigi Luccheni. Mark Twain, living in Austria at the time, was particularly anguished by her death. He described Luccheni thus in a rather maudlin letter to his friend, the Reverend Joseph H. Twichell:

> And who is the miracle-worker who has furnished to the world this spectacle? All the ironies are compacted in the answer. He is at the bottom of the human ladder, as the accepted estimates of degree and value go: a soiled and patched young loafer, without gifts, without talents, without education, without morals, without character, without any born charm or any acquired one that wins or beguiles or attracts; without a single grace of mind or heart or hand that any tramp or prostitute could envy him; an unfaithful private in the ranks, an incompetent stone-cutter, an inefficient lackey; in a word, a mangy, offensive, empty, unwashed, vulgar, gross, mephitic, timid, sneaking, human polecat.[27]

He was, in other words, a classic specimen of the type.

The European influence spread to America, as it so often does. Leon Czolgosz, a figure very much like Van der Graaf, assassinated President William McKinley in 1901. Czolgosz was a recluse, as most of them were. This trait, too, is often characteristic of sociopaths. He spent much of his time reading socialist and anarchist newspapers. When he was arrested, police found a folded newspaper clipping about Gaetano Bresci in Czolgosz's pocket. Evidently, he had spent many hours studying Bresci's life and career. Sentenced to electrocution, his last words were: "I killed the president because he was the enemy of the good people—the good working people. I am not sorry for my crime." None of these killers had an intelligible plan for the future. All claimed to be acting on behalf of some oppressed or marginalized section of society. All were in fact acting on behalf of no one.

In light of this, Europe's response to Fortuyn's assassination—a recrudescence of a deadly European disease—was bafflingly tepid and equivocal. *El Mundo,* a leading Spanish newspaper, appeared to blame Fortuyn for his own death, seeing his execution as the natural consequence of his "incendiary racist calls," labeling him an "heir of Nazism," and sympathetically portraying his assassin as "fearful and harassed by demagoguery."[28] The editorial stopped just short of applauding the murder. "The brown parties of Europe have a new martyr," sneered *Aftonbladet,* Sweden's leading newspaper.*[29] (Not long afterward, the Swedish foreign minister, Anna Lindh, was stabbed to death in a department store by a deranged Serb sympathizer, although her assassin was so clearly off his trolley—when asked to choose a lawyer, he requested Tom Cruise—that it would be a stretch to relate this murder to much of anything.)

Astonishingly, the Dutch courts declined to give Fortuyn's murderer the maximum life sentence. Although he showed few signs of remorse, he was sentenced to only eighteen years' imprisonment. He was fined 34,000 euros. He is widely expected to be free by 2014—well before I'm eligible to collect Social Security. The Dutch judiciary certainly sent a terrifying message with that verdict: Assassinate a politician on Dutch soil and you can expect a *very* stiff fine.

Any terrorist considering this case would be hard-pressed not to come to the conclusion that assassinating public figures in the Netherlands is an eminently cost-effective proposition. At the risk of appearing intolerant, I must observe that when a country's politicians face the prospect of life in a high-security prison cell but their murderers don't, one worries about that society's incentive structure.

---

* "Brown" is shorthand for Brownshirt, or Nazi.

CHAPTER 3

# WHITE TEETH

WHO ARE THESE YOUNG ISLAMIC RADICALS, and why is Europe breeding so many of them? Let us look at this question in Britain, where they have most recently made their presence so obvious.

First of all, they are not, as is often asserted, an infinitesimal fraction of the population. According to a December 2002 poll conducted by Britain's ICM Research for the BBC, 44 percent of British Muslims agreed with the statement that al Qaeda's attacks were a justified response to American aggression. Another 9 percent declared themselves unsure. Nearly 60 percent did not believe al Qaeda had been responsible for the September 11 attacks anyway. Seventy percent believed that Britain and the United States had declared war on Islam. Another 10 percent were unsure.[1] Similar results have since been replicated in many other well-constructed opinion polls.

Islamic radicalism now flourishes among alienated young first- and second-generation immigrants in London. In the north, in cities such as Bradford, Birmingham, Leicester, and Oldham, it is epidemic. The London transport bombers were part of a large cohort of such men in Leeds. Shortly after the bombings, a Whitehall minister warned the prime minister that al Qaeda was recruiting affluent, middle-class Muslims in British universities to carry out terrorist attacks in Britain. Lord Stevens, the former Metropolitan police chief, noted separately that as many as 3,000 British-born or British-based Muslims had passed through Osama bin Laden's training camps.

Nor are these men silent and hidden. Immediately after the attacks, Muslim radicals living in Britain publicly and vocally defended the terrorists' actions. On July 8, Hani al-Siba'i, head of the al-Maqreze Centre for Historical Studies in London, described the attacks as "a great victory."[2] Anjem Choudary, the U.K. leader of the Islamist group al-Muhajiroun, remarked that "in reality the real terrorists are the British regime, and even the British police, who have tried to divide the Muslim community into moderates and extremists, whereas this classification doesn't exist in Islam."[3] Less than a week later, London's *Guardian* offered one of their trainees, Dilpazier Aslam, a forum to relieve himself of his opinions about the bombing. Like the terrorists, he wrote, he was "a Yorkshire lad, born and bred," and although he did not mention this in his editorial, he was also an Islamic extremist—a member of Hizb ut-Tahrir, an organization dedicated to restoring a global caliphate under Islamic law. Hizb ut-Tahrir has been banned throughout the Middle East and most of Europe. It is an organization every bit as radical as al Qaeda. "Second- and third- generation Muslims," Aslam explained to readers, "are without the don't-rock-the-boat attitude that restricted our forefathers. We're much sassier with our opinions, not caring if the boat rocks or not."[4] It is a revealing measure of contemporary Britain's climate that less than a week after the slaughter of 52 London commuters by second- and third-generation Muslims, one of its leading news organizations could be so egregiously tone-deaf as to offer a forum to a young, male Islamist who suggests, by association, that suicide bombing is a form of sassy boat-rocking.

Britain has, clearly, been infected by a malefic and virulent ideology. As elsewhere in Europe, the vector of transmission has been foreign-born radical clerics. Britain has welcomed foreign dissidents since the time of Garibaldi. Following the Soviet withdrawal from Afghanistan, this tradition permitted some of the world's most radical jihadis, Arab clerics who had fought in Afghanistan and faced criminal sentences for terrorism in their native countries, to seek and receive asylum in Britain. Statutes designed to promote racial tolerance permitted these clerics, mostly trained in Saudi-sponsored madrassas, to promulgate delirious hatred of the West from the pulpits of British mosques. London became the international headquarters for radical groups such as Takfir-wal-Hijra, Hizb ut-Tahrir, the Movement for Islamic Reform in Arabia, the Bahrain Freedom Movement, and the Algerian Armed Islamic Group. British authorities studiously ignored this development. Since the 1990s, frustrated French counterterror officials have for this reason referred to the British capital as Londonistan.

The Salman Rushdie affair, in 1989, galvanized Muslim youths throughout Britain; clerics seized upon this opportunity to organize these newly radicalized young Muslim men into a national political force. Islamist sects in Britain openly recruited for the Taliban. While the clerics were Arabs, their followers were, like most Muslim immigrants in Britain, chiefly men of Bangladeshi and Pakistani origin. Pamphlets so inflammatory they would have been banned in most Middle Eastern countries became widely available in the bookstores of Central London. These tracts, like the note stabbed to Theo van Gogh's chest, assumed as a given that a great jihad had begun and would end only with the West's utter destruction.*

The jihad accelerated after September 11. Well before the July 7 bombings, the town of Luton was covered with "Magnificent 19" posters glorifying the hijackers who flew jets into the Pentagon and the World Trade Center. Islamic terrorists made multiple failed attempts to attack London with conventional and biological weapons before they succeeded: On March 31, 2004, eight Pakistani-born Britons were arrested near Heathrow Airport with half a ton of ammonium nitrate fertilizer, the ingredient used in the massive bombs that exploded in Bali in October 2002, and in Istanbul the following year. One week after the arrest, British police aborted an Islamist plot to detonate a massive bomb full of the nerve agent osmium tetroxide at Gatwick

---

*Because they were written in Arabic, they were unread and ignored by the CIA. Had they been read, September 11 would not have come as such a surprise. For an important account of this intelligence failure, see Robert Baer, *See No Evil: The True Story of a Ground Soldier in the CIA's War on Terrorism* (New York: Crown, 2002).

Airport. In September 2004, four men linked to al Qaeda were arrested in Britain while attempting to purchase radioactive material for a dirty bomb. The intended targets, police believed, were civilians in a crowded area of London. British authorities at the time described an Islamist strike against Britain as "inevitable." They were right.

Until recently, the claw-handed Cyclops, Abu Hamza al-Masri, preached to vast crowds of Pakistanis, Bengalis, Algerians, and Egyptians outside London's Finsbury Park Mosque. Al-Masri tutored Zacarias Moussaoui, who was to have been the twentieth hijacker on September 11, and Richard Reid, who tried to blow up a Paris-to-Miami jetliner with explosives hidden in his shoes. Al-Masri has been captured on film urging his followers to kill non-Muslims:

> If a *kafir* goes in a Muslim country, he is like a cow. Anybody can take him. That is the Islamic law. If a *kafir* is walking by and you catch him, he's booty. You can sell him in the market. Most of them are spies. And even if they don't do anything, if Muslims cannot take them and sell them in the market, you just kill them. It's OK.[5]

Special points, he stressed, will naturally be awarded in paradise for killing Jews and Americans.

In January 2003, police discovered chemical warfare protection suits at the Finsbury Park Mosque, as well as a range of conventional weapons, fake passports, and suggestively annotated maps of the London Underground. British government officials warned, though, that to suggest the mosque might be harboring or supporting terrorists "would have worrying racist overtones."[6]

More than a year later, al-Masri was at last arrested and the mosque officially shut down. But when I visited in the autumn of 2004, I was assured by the young Muslim men in the cafés and Islamic bookstores nearby that it was still functioning—"just knock on the door"—and that sermons were held outside the mosque as usual on Fridays. They made no effort to conceal this.

## THE SOCIOECONOMIC GROWTH MEDIUM

When *The Muslim News,* a prominent British journal, asked its readers, "Who do you think you are? British-Muslim? British Muslim? Muslim in Britain?" responses such as this one, from "Saghir, United Kingdom," were typical:

> I am most definetly [*sic*] not a British muslim but a muslim living in Britain. I don't ascribe to the corrupt values thoughts [*sic*] of this society. Some people ascribe to the view that if we don't like it here then why don't we leave. Simply because i [*sic*] was born here.[7]

This is *not* inevitable or self-explanatory. It is enormously important to observe that American immigrants rarely feel this intensely estranged from America. There are isolated and much-publicized examples to the contrary, but for the most part, Muslims, like most immigrants, come to America and become loyal Americans. Why should British Muslims feel otherwise? Why, in fact, does the British press generally speak of British Muslims, rather than Muslim Britons?

Not all British Muslims are disloyal to Britain—most aren't—and not all are hostile to America. Terrorist apologetics are *certainly* not limited to its Muslim population. (Note to the *Guardian*: Please be sporting and report that I stress this when writing your otherwise hostile review of this book.) But these views are particularly widespread among Muslims, and there are reasons for this.

The anti-Americanism of British Muslims is often ascribed to their sympathy with their coreligionists on the Arab street, particularly the Palestinians. But it is not at all obvious why British Muslims should be swayed by this. They are, after all, *British*. They have voluntarily made the choice to be in Britain; they live, work, and die in Britain; they—or their children—are educated in British schools; they trade and profit in the British economy; they enjoy a full range of civil liberties in Britain unavailable on *any* Arab street. Why should their loyalties lie with foreign peoples or regimes?

Indeed, in recent history, few Muslims have been particularly concerned with the fate of fellow Muslims in foreign countries, so long as that fate is not in some way bound to the United States or to Israel. With the exception of the al Qaeda fringe and a handful of Indonesian nationalists, no Muslim gives a damn that East Timor is now independent. We certainly do not see the Turks, for example, burning down the Australian embassy in Ankara.

At its fundament, the radicalism of British Muslims has a different source. Like Islamic radicalism throughout Europe, it is a distilled form of anti-Occidentalism. It derives from this group's profound alienation from *Europe*, and from Britain in particular.

A large part of this alienation is socioeconomic. The social and economic composition of the Muslim community in Britain is substantially different from that of the United States. In the United States, Muslims are geographically dispersed; in Britain, they are concentrated and ghettoized. In America, Muslims are largely middle-class professionals: doctors, engineers, academics. In Britain, most Muslims remain stubbornly stuck in the working class or the unemployed underclass.

In the past decade, the unemployment rate for white Britons has been about 8 percent. It has been closer to 30 percent for Pakistanis and 38 percent for Bangladeshis (who are almost all Muslims). The incomes of almost 85 percent of Pakistani and Bangladeshi households are less than half the national average. Muslims do worse than other pupils at all stages of compulsory education. Fewer Muslim sixteen-year-olds are in education, training, or employment than any other ethnic group of the same age. Muslim students take an extra two years to obtain the same qualifications as their non-Muslim counterparts. They are less likely to obtain first- or upper-second-class degrees.*

---

*British universities subdivide university graduates on the basis of their final examination results into Firsts (superclever), Upper Seconds (diligent), Lower Seconds (lazy or athletic), and Thirds (abject dullards). Examination results are published annually, resulting in an unseemly spectacle of lordly gloating—cloaked in false modesty—among those who have received Firsts.

The failure of Muslims to penetrate the centers of political power has been spectacular. There are only two Muslims in the House of Commons; representation in proportion to population would demand at least twenty. Muslims are similarly underrepresented in the senior ranks of the civil service, prison service, police force, criminal justice system, and armed forces.[8] In the summer of 2001, Britain experienced its worst riots in twenty years, resulting in $15 million of damage and 300 injured police officers. The media termed these race riots, but could just as correctly have called them religious riots, since all the rioters were Muslims.

This is not, of course, a problem limited to Britain, as the French, in particular, are now learning to their dismay. The number of Muslims in Europe has doubled in the past decade, and throughout Europe, Muslims remain for the most part uneducated and poor. Crime rates in Muslim neighborhoods are high. Unemployment in those neighborhoods generally vastly exceeds national averages—Muslims constitute half of France's unemployed. The percentage of Muslims in France is roughly equivalent to that of African-Americans in the United States, but not one single Muslim sits in France's 577-seat Chamber of Deputies.

I do not conclude from this that poverty and low achievement are the *causes* of the terrorist impulse. The striking prosperity of the world's most prominent terrorists suggests otherwise. Terrorism is caused by an ideological virus to which neither the poor nor the rich are immune. But this virus is best propagated under certain breeding conditions, and societies with large cohorts of frustrated, unemployed young men find their immune systems markedly compromised when diseases of the soul are at large.

## CHEERFUL MULTICULTURALISM: THE FICTION

Much can be sensed about a society from the books it lionizes. Zadie Smith was all of twenty-four and still living with her mother when the publication of her first novel, *White Teeth*, catapulted her to vertiginous celebrity in Britain. Her panoptic portrait of post-Imperial London traces the lives of Archie Jones and Samad Iqbal, whose friendship was forged in a British tank at the close of the Second World War. They meet again in the early 1970s, when Samad emigrates from Bangladesh to London, destined for frustrated underemployment as a waiter in an Indian restaurant. He brings his shrewd, suspicious bride, Alsana, with whom his marriage has been arranged.

Archie, meanwhile, poleaxed by love at first sight, has wed a Jamaican immigrant, Clara, the teenage daughter of an avid Jehovah's Witness—a marriage no one would think to arrange. A racially heterogeneous generation of Britons issues: from Clara, Irie, who spends much of the book longing for straight hair; from Alsana, twin sons, Magid and Millat. Theirs is a generation of children, as Zadie describes them, "with first and last names on a direct collision course. Names that secrete within them mass exodus, cramped boats and planes, cold arrivals, medical checks."

Jump-cut to the near-present. Watching their sons grow up as Londoners, not Bengalis, Samad and Alsana see in their inexorable assimilation the disappearance of their own culture. "They have both lost their way," Samad mourns. "Strayed so far from what I had intended for them. No doubt they will both marry white women called Sheila and put me in an early grave." To Archie he confides his fear that his children will follow the path of Alsana's Westernized niece: "They won't go to mosque, they don't pray, they speak strangely, they eat all kinds of rubbish, they have intercourse with God knows who. No respect for tradition. People call it assimilation when it is nothing but corruption. Corruption!"[9]

Listening to this lament, Archie—an archetypal Briton, as his name suggests—is at a loss: "He kind of felt people should just live together, you know, in peace or harmony or something." These sentiments do not amount to a stirring defense of European values, but it's worth observing that when confronted with this species of condemnation, few contemporary European intellectuals have anything more vigorous or coherent to say.

When one of the twins, the more intellectual Magid, takes to calling himself Mark, so dismayed is Samad that he kidnaps his son and ships him back to Bangladesh. This, he hopes, will protect Magid from the West and its seductive corruption. He cannot afford to send both sons, so Millat remains in England. But it is Samad who is seduced and corrupted by his shameful and sacrilegious erotic obsession with his sons' music teacher, Poppy Burt-Jones, the perfect, preposterous, patronizing icon of British white womanhood. "'Sometimes we find other people's music strange because their culture is different from *ours*,' said Miss Burt-Jones solemnly, 'but that doesn't mean it isn't equally good, now does it?'"

Irie is achingly infatuated with Millat, the twin who remains in Britain—as is Zadie, to judge from the excruciating longing with which she describes him: "Millat was like youth remembered in the nostalgic eyeglasses of old age, beauty parodying itself: broken Roman nose, tall, thin, lightly veined, smoothly muscled; chocolate eyes with a reflective green sheen like moonlight bouncing off a dark sea; irresistible smile, big white teeth." But he is possessed of "an ever present anger and hurt, the feeling of belonging nowhere that comes to people who belong everywhere." These, we are to believe, are the emotions that drive him to delinquency, and then to religious radicalism. Recruited by the Keepers of the Eternal and Victorious Islamic Nation (the group's acronym is our reassuring clue that it is to be mocked, not feared), Millat travels to Bradford to participate in a ritual burning of *The Satanic Verses*.

Magid, to his father's even greater mortification, returns from Bangladesh a passionate Anglophile. He is unofficially adopted as something like a pet by the neighboring Chalfen family, a smug clan of fully assimilated, unbearably condescending, right-thinking liberal London Jews. Irie and the Iqbals are fascinated by the Chalfens' comfortable integration into bourgeois British life; the Chalfens are equally fascinated by themselves, finding much to admire in their own high-minded commitment to multiculturalism. The analogy between the Chalfens and Britain is clear.

*White Teeth* won the WH Smith book award for new talent, the Commonwealth Writers' first book award, the overall Commonwealth

Writers' prize, the Betty Trask prize, the British book award for new-comer of the year, the Ethnic and Multicultural Media award; the BT Emma best book and best female newcomer awards, the Whitbread first novel award, the James Tait Black memorial prize for fiction, the John Llewellyn Rhys prize, the Orange prize, and the Author's Club first novel award. It was adapted for television. The miniseries based on the novel was as much a sensation as the novel itself. The rapture over this book was enough to make other young novelists take to their beds with envy (I say this from firsthand experience). Britain adored this book, and adored it, I have to admit, for good reason: Zadie is an im-mensely talented writer with an uncanny ear for dialogue. *White Teeth* is a clever book, it is thoughtful, and like only the best of novels, it brings a whole world into being.

But Britain loved this book most of all because of Zadie's vision of modern Britain—a Britain where, as many critics observed, diversity and multiculturalism are lightly and whimsically drawn. *White Teeth* mirrored back to Britain an essentially cheerful and charming reflec-tion of itself—credibly flawed, of course, but basically optimistic. Above all, it is a Britain where the conflicts experienced by immigrants are *funny*—or at least, more comic than tragic.

"Imaginative," writes one reviewer. "This book is imaginative. How on earth did she come up with this storyline?" Actually, I know exactly how she came up with the storyline. I recognized it immedi-ately. Like most first novels, *White Teeth* is essentially autobiographi-cal. Although she denies it, insisting that the book is not based on her own life, Zadie is Irie; like Irie she grew up in North London (blocks from Richard Reid, the shoe bomber); like Irie she is the daughter of an English father and a Jamaican mother; and like Irie she was in love with Millat. His real name is Jimmi Rahman. The book is dedicated to him.

This is not speculation. I know this. I know this because I too was once in love with a Rahman—Jimmi's brother, Zia. Zia is Magid. I knew all the characters in the book, except Zadie herself; for two years they were the center of my life. Zadie's description of the Iqbal family is unerringly apt. But that is not nearly as funny as *White Teeth* suggests.

## THE CHEERLESS REALITY

I met Zia Haider Rahman early one morning in the Junior Common Room of Balliol College at Oxford University. The year was 1991. I was a graduate student, writing a Master's thesis about an aspect of American foreign policy so arcane that my dissertation passed into obscurity even before I finished it. It had been raining for weeks, a low, slanting English rain. Everyone's shoes squeaked. The pantry was serving fried eggs, bangers, toast soldiers with Marmite. No one looked well.

Someone surged to my table uninvited and swept out his arm as though he were flouncing a cape. "I'm *so* glad you invited me to sit with you," he said cheerfully. "I've been waiting for you to do that for ages, you know." He had an aristocratic accent. I was later to learn that he had acquired it from the radio; no one spoke like that where he grew up. He had beautiful white teeth, an erect spine, black hair, black eyes. And presence, he certainly had that.

Within a half hour of urgent, flirtatious conversation we repaired to his tiny smoke-filled room over Staircase XIV, the blackboard against the wall crabbed with tiny mathematical symbols. Within another half hour, we had our first hysterical fight and were both in tears. "Don't you understand," he said, "the upheaval this would cause my family? How *could* you understand?" He was right: I had no idea what he was talking about.

Zia was an exceptionally gifted mathematician, involved in the study of some fiendishly complicated conjecture related to the solution of Fermat's last theorem. He was born in Bangladesh's impoverished, flood-wracked Sylhet Province, and had grown up in a conservative Islamic home in North London. He was the first member of his family to be educated. His unusual mathematical talent conferred great, unexpected prestige upon his mother, a seamstress. It was particularly lucky, from his mother's perspective, because of his corresponding misfortune: He had quite dark skin, which in Bangladesh made him an undesirable commodity in marriage. (Attention multiculturalists: I regret to report that the strange values of other cultures are *not* always "equally good.") His mother was the bane of his existence—and mine. She was determined to leverage the prestige of his education by arranging an excellent marriage for him to another Bengali. I was, as you can imagine, unenthusiastic about this plan.

Zia and Jimmi are not twins. Zia is the eldest of the family. Rendering the brothers as twins was a nice touch, though. By making the characters genetically identical but diametrically unalike, Zadie effectively makes the point that being British is not simply a matter of racial ancestry. As Samad puts it, "The one I send home comes out a pukka Englishman, white suited, silly wig lawyer. The one I keep here is fully paid-up green bow-tie wearing fundamentalist terrorist." The brothers do have one thing in common, however, in both the novel and real life: their violent, bewildering experience of assimilation. The real story upon which Zadie based her novel was hardly "relentlessly funny," as the *Guardian* called *White Teeth,* and it certainly gave no one "hope for a multicultural society," as the *Financial Times* proclaimed.

Zadie has taken fictional license in a number of ways; she has assigned Millat all the charm, and Magid is drawn as a cold and sexless intellectual, which is certainly not how I remember him. Jimmi never became an Islamic radical; he dabbled with Islam, ran a chain of bars, and then trained as an actor. But in emotional essence the story is true. Zia did indeed grow up with his parents' demand that he remain Bengali in a culture where *being* Bengali brings patronizing indulgence— the kind displayed, for example, by the Chalfens, modeled on a very real family in North London who are exactly as Zadie describes them—or outright antagonism. (The critics made much of the fact that the Chalfen family is Jewish. What, they asked meaningfully, does *this* signify? It doesn't signify anything, I suspect: It just so happens that the Chalfens were modeled on a Jewish family. As any novelist will tell you, sometimes you borrow from real life because it's there.)

Growing up, Zia, like so many immigrants from the Subcontinent, was bullied and beaten; he was insulted in the street. Once, when we were dating, he came home covered in coffee. It had been thrown on him from the window of a speeding car. Even upon coming up to Oxford, he was harassed; racist graffiti was scrawled on his door, forcing him to switch colleges. That was how he had come to be at Balliol, a college better known for its tradition of tolerance.* "When I went into the bar of an Oxford College in my first term, I was chased out," he recalled when I last spoke to him. I had heard the story before. "I'd made some friends, I was loud. I had a swastika daubed on my door. When I told the dean of the college, he looked very skeptical. Weeks passed, matters grew worse, and then I received a note from the dean saying that he had made enquiries and apparently my claims were 'not without foundation.'

"I walked to Balliol. Within an hour I met two fellows, my grades were checked, and Balliol accepted me. The following year, at my old college, one of the people who had attacked me was sent down. He had poked someone's eye out for bringing a black person to a party. One would have thought this would be unheard of at Oxford in the late twentieth century. So that was Oxford."

He recounted this to me recently in his apartment near the City of London, blocks from Brick Lane, London's largest Bengali neighborhood. Brick Lane bustles with cheap curry restaurants, sari shops, greengrocers selling sacks of rice, vats of ghee, exotic tubers and fruits. Zia is now a corporate lawyer for an American law firm where, he said, "the color that matters most is the color of money. Clients don't give a damn who wrote the memo. Where there's a great deal of money at stake, people tend to focus on content." Recently, he said, a newcomer to the firm noted the domination of exotic names on Zia's department's letterhead. "Do you have to be Asian to work in this department?" he asked. Zia's coworker looked up from a stack of briefs. "No, you just have to be fucking smart," he replied.

---

*Oxford University comprises thirty-nine self-governing colleges, each with its own character and traditions. Generally, it is nearly impossible to transfer from one college to another. The circumstances must be quite unusual, as in this case they were.

Zia's loft apartment, on the top floor of a converted brick-wall warehouse, is furnished in the modern, masculine style that became popular in New York during the 1980s stock-market boom, with oak floors, recessed spot lighting, chrome and glass, Italian leather. Apart from the antique maps of Bengal on the wall, there is no clue that Zia has any connection to the Indian Subcontinent. His handmade book-shelves, however, are full of volumes on Islam, Christianity, the clash of civilizations; there are rows upon rows of novels by authors from all over the world—though notably few from the U.K.; books are over-flowing onto his windowsills and kitchen table, dog-eared and haphaz-ard. Zia has spent his life trying to figure out where he belongs and what it means to belong. "I've often been asked, 'Do you consider yourself British?'" he said in response to precisely that question. "I think the fact that people ask is infinitely more interesting than any an-swer I could give."

During the two years we spent together, my inability to under-stand Zia's difficult relationship with Britain was a constant source of friction. From my perspective, Zia's sensitivity to racial slight bor-dered on paranoia. He could discern subtle racism in the most trivial of gestures, a single raised eyebrow. He was capable of brooding for hours about a shopkeeper who spoke to me before speaking to him—evidence, in his view, of the way the British thought it impossible for him to be romantically attached to a young white woman, the way they saw him as nothing more than a "dirty little Paki." Those words were the identifying epithet of his youth. His desperation to succeed and to prove himself, his ambivalence about dating Western women, his willingness to take seriously his family's insane demands—none of this made sense to me. He was British, I thought, and since there could be no going back, he might as well get on with things.

But he was right, and I was wrong. I was callow and insensitive. I do see that now. My mistake was to assume that his experience and mine were essentially analogous. After all, like most Americans, I too am a recent descendant of immigrants. My grandparents, German and Polish Jews, refugees from the Nazis, arrived in New York in the early

1940s. But being Jewish has always been, to me, completely compatible with being fully American. In the few instances where I have encountered anti-Semitism in America, there has been no sense of inevitability about it: it has been a queer aberration, so out of place as to be ludicrous. I grew up with a deep, intuitive sense of full entitlement to everything America has to offer. Not only do I not view America as essentially anti-Semitic, I perceive my country as a haven from the world's anti-Semites. Certainly, in being Jewish I am in an important way different from the majority of Americans, but I have never experienced this as a *wound*. For Zia—and for many other immigrants in Britain—it is just that: a wound that cannot be healed.

"A sense of belonging," he subsequently wrote to me, trying to explain this better, "is crucial on a fundamental human level, because it is linked to the most basic question of how we give meaning to our lives. A sense of belonging, of rootedness, turns us into a link between history and posterity, and in doing so it hands us a purpose. We become part of a greater story. . . . I think that when we start to think about identity or a sense of *belonging,* as a premise, a condition, for creating meaning out of life, rather than merely in terms of political or racial fault lines, we could open up new ways of thinking about ideas that have ossified under the weight of platitudes. A feeling of belonging to Britain means feeling you're part of the British story."[10]

At dinner with Zia one evening in London, I mentioned in passing that more than once, when I've returned to the United States, the immigration officer has inspected my American passport and said, "Welcome home."

"If any official here," Zia replied, "had ever, ever, even *once* said that to me, I would have died for England on the spot."

## "AN HONORARY WHITE MAN"

Zia took an expected First at Oxford, then spent two years at Cambridge. We broke up. He abandoned mathematics. He received a scholarship to Yale, then worked for a few years for a prestigious investment banking firm in New York. The time he spent in America was a revelation: In America, he said, he was "a regular Joe," not only to his professors and colleagues but to women as well. "Maybe they regarded me as an honorary white man—who knows and I don't care. It didn't matter to me because I was always treated well." In Britain, he told me, he had been either fetishized by rebellious English women or simply unsexed; in America, he felt himself fully a normal man.

"I still feel an enormous amount of affection for America and Americans," he told me. "I felt much more sexual in America. How the outsider is sexualized is as much a political matter as the legal rights conferred on him or denied to him. I felt that I was being acknowledged as a sexual being, in a way that I wasn't so much in Britain. London is very cosmopolitan, and Oxford and Cambridge are very cosmopolitan, but it's most curious that in my three years at Oxford and two years at Cambridge, and all my time in London before I went to the States, I didn't have a single English girlfriend. . . . And the background, to put it in context, is that I did have many girlfriends, but none of them were English. The women I had been seeing and dating, who were interested in me, and in whom I was interested too, were all foreigners in Britain—Italians, French, Indians, Americans, bright foreigners in Oxford and Cambridge. Not English. In America it was no problem at all. Sure, it might have been different if I'd been African-American or even African, but I'm not. I was in an unusual environment, of course, New Haven and then New York City, but American women in these cities—well, I was made to feel welcome."

A suggestive set of statistics might indicate that Zia's experience was not unique. Intermarriage rates among Muslim immigrants in Britain are dramatically lower than in the United States. Fewer than 10 percent of Muslim immigrants marry native Britons. In the United States, the figure is probably closer to two-thirds.[11] It is impossible to know whether this distinction tells us more about prevailing attitudes toward religion in the two countries or prevailing attitudes toward race; the two cannot be disaggregated, since the majority of Muslim immigrants in both countries are also nonwhite. It is also impossible to say whether these statistics reflect differences in the attitudes of the immigrants, the attitudes of their hosts, or both. But it *is* possible to say that hybrid relationships, and particularly intermarriage, may reasonably be considered the ultimate indicator of the true state of a society's ethnic integration, for intermarriage demands a willingness to see one's culture of origin genetically diluted and ultimately annihilated. Only those fully committed to their adoptive country propose marriage to its natives, and only those who view immigrants as full equals accept. Clearly, in this regard, the United States and Britain are different.

Zia returned to England, where he became a lawyer. Later, he returned to Bangladesh, where he campaigned as a human rights lawyer and anticorruption activist. But there he discovered to his dismay that he was even more an outsider and a curiosity than he was in England. "I was returning to an imaginary homeland." In *White Teeth,* Samad's confidant Shiva, another waiter, asks rhetorically, "Who can pull the West out of 'em once it's in?" Zia couldn't, evidently, any more than anyone else can.

## THE BITTER EXPERIENCE OF IMMIGRATION

Hanif Kureishi published his semiautobiographical novel, *The Buddha of Suburbia,* in 1990. In a memorable scene, Karim, the half-Pakistani protagonist, is told by his friend Helen's father not to see her anymore. "'We don't like it,' Hairy Back said. 'However many niggers there are, we don't like it. We're with Enoch. If you put one of your black 'ands near my daughter I'll smash it with a 'ammer! With a 'ammer!'"[12] The reference is to Enoch Powell's 1968 "Rivers of Blood" speech, in which the Conservative shadow cabinet minister spoke with ill-tempered passion against immigration, inciting a wave of racial violence throughout Britain. *White Teeth* also alludes to this event, though in this reference the speech is portrayed as ancient and irrelevant.

"Conspicuously absent from *White Teeth,*" Zia said to me, "is the anger. Where have all the angry books gone? These new books don't feel like Hanif Kureishi." British novels, Zia reflected, no longer "talk about bitter experiences, about experiences of racism, domestic violence, chauvinism, and if they do, it's made saccharine, sanitized. We don't see the very dark aspects of racism. That's something that divides the book from reality—the real experience." And strangely, he noted, these new British novels are written by women, not men.

So what, I asked him, *was* the real experience? "The real story," he said, setting his tea on the floor and fidgeting abstractly with his hands, "is very complicated, and becoming more and more complicated. Whereas before it might have been generally accepted that Asian men and women were the victims of racism, there's a growing body of opinion that this is not the case—they're now enfranchised, co-opted, we hear. This really isn't so." As we spoke, his voice repeatedly trailed off as he attempted to marshal his thoughts; sometimes he paused for as much as half a minute. It made him sound fragmented and disorganized, but I realized later when I transcribed the tape that in fact he was speaking in lucid, complete sentences.

"The truth is: It *wasn't* so cheerful. Immigration is a very bitter experience for many people, and it was for us. It was difficult, it was a struggle. My father worked heroic hours, he was very rarely at home. My mother worked very long hours. We were all quite hot-tempered, quite fiery people, and there were fireworks. They were rather more alarming than the book portrayed. The police were called out. And there was a constant feeling of alienation. The book does bring that out, in my character: the alienation from family, the alienation of many, though not all, young Asians from their parents. Zadie does deal with that. The man who became the Chalfen character in the novel, whom you've met. . . . I remember when I was eighteen, sitting in his kitchen, we had a discussion, and in the course of the conversation, he came to a sudden stop and said, 'Where on earth did *you* come from?' and I was struck by that, struck by it because I felt hurt, not by him but by the comment—there wasn't any malevolence in the comment—but it made me keenly aware that I wasn't regarded as forming a continuum with my family.

"My family was in many respects very typical . . . or if not typical, we had characteristics typical of Bangladeshi families but in accentuated form. We were atypical in that we were all very bright, all regarded by our peers and teachers as being very talented, which meant that we confronted problems other Asians might not have. Some of our experiences of racism were in contexts where people would say they didn't like our 'brashness.' That was racism—it was pretty obvious. If you're loud—well, people don't like an uppity nigger. Before Oxford, I remember one Christmas when there was a Christmas tree in the foyer of my school. These three boys didn't like me. I was loud, but in a socially unattractive way. I was a debating champion, editor of the school magazine, and pupil governor—I was never behind the bike sheds. The three boys set on me. I remember it very well, because one of them was Jewish. I remember marveling at the irony of this Jewish boy pushing a Muslim into a Christmas tree. I wanted to say to him, 'What are you doing? Your people have been herded into ovens and you're calling *me* a Paki?'"*

Zia's brother Jimmi evidently made a much greater impression on Zadie than he did on me. I remember him as a vague, angry teenager but don't recall much more about him. *White Teeth* was written and published shortly before September 11, and the character based on Jimmi, Millat, seems by contemporary standards a benign Islamic radical. Millat does nothing more sinister than burn a book he has never read. But Zadie's plot device was suggestive. Was she correct to draw a connection between incomplete assimilation and Islamic radicalism?

Zia thought so. "The grievance of terrorists *must* operate on a very personal level," he reasoned. "When you read about terrorists, you'll read about arguments rooted in history, and in some slight committed by some Christian king against an Islamic ruler in the distant past. . . . And the explanations *are* rooted in history, they're fantastic, those explanations, but what seems to be missing is an account of the knot of emotions inside a terrorist, that knot of fire, that personal dimension,

*Zia later asked me to stress that this boy is now a friend of his. Consider it stressed.

that anger, that fear, that personal grievance. I live in the East End of London and I see a lot of angry Asian males. I see them walking in groups of twelve, I've seen them smashing things, I've watched as they set a car on fire. I see a lot of anger, and the statistics bear it out—the crime rate, I have friends who work in the emergency department of the local hospital. . . . I've wondered whether the anger that I have felt is qualitatively in the same category. Whereas my anger found expression and voice—not outlet—in articulate, nondestructive ways, theirs is turned outward, into other-destructive ways. So I might even sometimes fault myself for something that's really someone else's problem, but they rightly identify it as someone else's problem. The mistake they make is in what they choose to do about it."

If Muslim men turn their anger outward, Muslim women, it might be surmised, turn it inward: young Pakistani and Bangladeshi women, while rarely seen smashing cars, have the highest rates of suicide and attempted suicide in Britain.

But what, I asked him, is that anger about, exactly? "The anger is about being alienated from British society, and the great danger now is that as more and more Asians become visibly co-opted, the exclusionary forces have the protection of that fact, they can hide behind it. But things remain difficult—very difficult. There are still gaps in salary, in achievement rates, gaps that econometricians tell us—after factoring out unemployment, educational underperformance, social exclusion, and dozens of other candidate causes—are not attributable to anything but racism and discrimination, not even to the class structure. But my anger is not just directed at the establishment, or society, but also at the Asian community, with which I'm in profound disagreement. They have as much, maybe more, to answer for."

"What kind of disagreement?" His voice had become so quiet that I was worried it wouldn't register on the tape recorder. He reached over to switch it off. He told me that he was worried about maligning the Bengalis, that nothing disgusted him more than a man who would denigrate his own people. After thinking quietly a bit more, moving about uncomfortably in his chair, he permitted me to switch it on again, but he remained uneasy. "They aren't equipped to deal with modernity. They come from villages—I come from a village, I'm a villager, I was born in a village, I lived in a village, I spent several formative years in a village—and there's very little in a village that will equip you with the necessary skills. . . . A villager from rural Sylhet is going to have a hard time dealing with taxes, elections, is not going to have a sense of civic duty, he's never had recourse to institutions. If you want a dispute resolved you go to the local holy man, or the village elder—there are village elders on council estates* here in London, but that just demonstrates that they're trying to re-create their village structures here; they're not really integrating. Look, I sit on the board of governors of a school in Brick Lane. More than 80 percent of the children are Sylhetis from Bangladesh, yet there is not one Sylheti parent on that board. Many of these children are taken off to Bangladesh by their parents for months, even years at a time, interrupting their education. I help out in a reading program run by my firm at another school. The kids are wonderful, they still have brightness in their eyes, but they read the storybooks like drones. They can read the symbols, but ask them to explain what they've read and you see that they've barely taken in a word, and this at an age when their comprehension should be much better. How can that be? Well, after school, these kids are taken off to local madrassas by their parents, where they recite pages and pages from the Koran without understanding a single word—Arabic is a foreign language. For these kids, recitation *is* reading. This is how their parents are educating them. There is so little active engagement on the part of Sylheti parents in the education of their own that school governing bodies in Tower Hamlets struggle to reach a quorum, and people like me, who don't even have children, let alone children at the school, are welcomed onto the boards.

"The kids are growing up with a sense that there's something to be taken from Britain, in between extended visits to the home country, but they don't participate in this society. They look to the state to provide things for them; they're not rooted in the community; they lead lives with one foot in the airport. . . . They don't want to belong, they

---

*Council estates are the equivalent of housing projects.

don't want to become part of the British story. Someone needs to tell them—because their parents aren't—that our lives are short and the only story we can join is the one going on around us. There's no time to lose. If you don't like it, change it, or get out and join another story—either way, you've got to be part of some story to hold off the meaninglessness."

What *is* Britishness? And why don't Muslim immigrants want to become part of the British story?

## ASSIMILATION IS DEATH

No one really knows what Britishness is. If you ask people in Britain what gives their lives meaning, the answer will often be football. Waiters, bus drivers, kids hanging out on street corners, they will all say the same thing: "Football's our religion." That turn of phrase strikes me as significant, although what it means, I have no idea.

One reason Muslim immigrants don't want to become British is that becoming British means losing their faith, their sense of purpose and identity. Being British offers none of those things; if it did once, it certainly does not now. No other ideology now broadly on offer in Britain—certainly not football—can account for human existence or place that existence in a wider, meaningful pattern. British academic life is now dominated by the condescending strain of atheism promulgated by Richard Dawkins, who holds the Chair for the Public Understanding of Science at Oxford University. His remarkably unattractive worldview manages to be not only spiritually empty but also intellectually embarrassing—as evidenced, for example, in his campaign to relabel atheists "brights."

British Christianity has become a vaporous shadow of its former self. Senior figures in the Anglican Church have described the story of the Crucifixion and Resurrection as no more than a metaphor; some have confessed that they do not believe in God. Cathedrals have been converted into nightclubs, the crucifix is a fashion accessory, and the word *religion* is a brand name for young women's dancewear. The religious beliefs of politicians are hardly ever mentioned in the course of political debate. Tony Blair's press attaché is reported to have told reporters, "We don't do God."

In the United States, by contrast, levels of churchgoing are high. Christianity, in its literal and evangelical form, is a vital presence in both political rhetoric and popular culture. But even American Christianity is nowhere near as muscular as Islam. Islam's vitality is such that it is now the fastest-growing religion among native Britons. (The runner-up is a form of evangelical Christianity much like that of the American Southern Baptists.) Converts include some of the country's most prominent aristocrats and celebrities. The great-granddaughter of the Liberal prime minister Herbert Asquith has converted to Islam; Prince Charles's interest in Islam, it has been bruited, is more than ambassadorial.* The Muslim Charles Le Gai Eaton, a former diplomat and author of *Islam and the Destiny of Man,* reports regularly receiving letters from "people who are put off by the wishy-washy standards of contemporary Christianity. . . . They are looking for a religion which does not compromise too much with the modern world."

Is it possible to become British without abandoning Islam? Of course. But it is not possible to become fully British without abandoning Islam in its more radical forms—in other words, embracing a dilute Islam that is no more compelling than Britain's dilute Christianity. Perhaps this is why so many immigrants view assimilation as something literally worse than death.

## A DIET FOR THE SPIRITUALLY FLABBY

I was struck, when I returned to Britain recently after an absence of almost ten years, to find that middle-class Britain had become obsessed with health food and dietary purity. It was once rare to see

---

*Delicious though this rumor may be, it is almost certainly untrue.

fresh vegetables served in Britain, but now the nation is raising organic produce, shunning red meat, flushing toxins from its collective system, and taking colonic purges. This last, evidently, is Diana's legacy.

Dr. Gillian McKeith—her doctorate in Holistic Nutrition comes from a mail-order diploma mill in Alabama—painstakingly inspects her clients' excrement on her national television program, *You Are What You Eat*. This astonishing display of prime-time copromancy is wildly popular. Her book of the same name was a national number one best-seller. "If dieting has become a sort of religion," writes the editor of a popular British lifestyle magazine, "then Gillian McKeith must be this year's top guru."[13] British psychiatric professionals have reported a notable rise in orthorexia, a previously unknown mental disorder in which sufferers, fixated upon righteous eating, starve to death.

Phiroze Nemuchwala is a British psychotherapist; his specialty is the treatment of psychosomatic illness. We have been friends since we met by chance in a bookstore nearly twenty years ago. Of late, he has noticed that many of his patients on restrictive vegetarian diets—women especially—are suffering from depression, anxiety, and susceptibility to coughs and colds. He is beginning to suspect that they are malnourished. I asked him what, in his view, was at the psychosocial heart of Britain's strange food fixation. "Religion," he said immediately. His patients, having like most Europeans rejected theism, are embarking upon a desperate quest to conquer the unacceptable prospect of disease, aging, and personal extinction. (He offered the suggestion, too, that women who declared themselves repulsed by the very thought of eating red meat frequently presented with intense sexual conflicts and a great deal of unconscious rage.)

Phiroze's practice consists mostly of upper-middle-class white Britons, the majority of them women. In recent years, his professional approach has changed. "For the first ten years of my practice I worked very much as a Freudian," he said. He did not, in his practice, discuss "deep, fundamental, powerful values like truth, integrity, action, will, clarity, awareness—indisputable values" for him. These concepts are not generally considered by psychotherapists in Britain to be relevant to mental health. "I was not talking about those concepts, and I was quite determined not to. One can do a pretty good four-year, twice-a-week analysis with someone and the word *love* never comes up. Because if the patient doesn't mention it, it's not really the therapist's place to. And eventually, after some ten years of this, I found this way of working a little bit sterile, and I found that it was missing the deep point. And I suppose my own explorations into psychology, philosophy, and literature were inclining me toward an idea that love, integrity, compassion, courage—values that are common to all religions, values that date from Socrates, eternal human values—were more important than I'd realized."

The focus of his practice now is on imparting those common religious values that, he believes, give life meaning. These are ideas, Phiroze notes, for which his clients, when they come to see him, don't even have a vocabulary. "Until recently in Europe it was about serving Christ. They didn't really think about that, they were just offered it at the age of three, as soon as they could speak. But the people who come here don't have a whole set of ideas like that. What I try to get across to them is that there has been this current of thought in world thinking for three or four thousand years, and that certain things are agreed to be deeply meaningful and certain things are generally agreed to be not so. I call them true deliverers of the Good Life. I contrast this with false deliverers, things that promise to deliver but don't really—the obvious ones being money, sex, fame. Media and advertising will tell us that if you buy these sunglasses, this handbag, then you will have the good life, and you will be blessed, and you will be in the elect, you will be special. But the truth of it is that the much more religious and philosophical ideas of love, courage, integrity, dignity, respect, compassion, authenticity, genuineness—*these* are the things that will deliver the Good Life."

Phiroze does not, however, tell his clients that they should embrace these values because they are, simply speaking, good values. "I never suggest they should do this because it's the right thing to do. I say, 'In my observation and study, and personal experience, these work better, and what I advise you to do, in the empirical, scientific tradition of the West, is experiment.' So I say to them, 'Well, try it out. Try it for this week until next Friday, doing this, and come back and tell me if it yielded a better harvest of good feeling than buying that pair of Ray-Bans did last month.' And without fail, they come back and tell me that yes, being much more honest with their sister, boyfriend, child, parent did yield meaningful, worthwhile results. They feel more deeply anchored in themselves, their self-respect has gone up, and they see very readily that what I call the True Deliverers are better deliverers than earning a bit more money, getting promoted, buying a new car, losing a bit of weight. I don't have a religious type of belief, a faith belief, that these are the things that work. I have *found* them to be things that work." These are, as he puts it, "a mishmash of religious ideas," though he never mentions God to his patients, and calls himself an atheist.

"My patients don't think much about the search for meaning. I encourage it. They don't come here saying, 'What's it all about?' Perhaps they come here because of depression or anxiety. Usually when we've cleared all that up, in the third year, I raise the question, 'What do you want your life to stand for, what do you think you're here for?' And almost without exception they get fascinated by that and do another year with me.

"I love that stage of work."

His patients are hungry for *something,* obviously, as are the patients of Dr. McKeith. Is it really so surprising that presented with a choice between Islam, which offers a coherent and absolute set of answers to these questions, or its alternative, which seems in modern Britain all too often to be a bracing colonic purge, many recent immigrants have found the former more compelling?

## CORRUPTION, GHETTOIZATION, AND A PERVASIVE SENSE OF UNFAIRNESS

There is more to this complicated story, though, than the empty flabbiness of Britain's secularism and the horror it inspires among Muslim immigrants, or at least Zia thinks so. "What we're seeing in the East End of London is a ghettoization," Zia told me, "and nobody's doing anything about it—certainly not at the level at which something would have to be done. The local government of Tower Hamlets is riddled with waste, if not outright corruption, and it's very difficult for people to criticize the local government, because the counselors are Bangladeshi, so accusing them of corruption might look like racism."

Tower Hamlets, the area around Brick Lane, is a small, densely populated London borough adjacent to the eastern boundary of the City. It has the largest Bangladeshi population in the country. There is severe economic deprivation throughout the borough, and if Zia is right, the local government isn't helping. "In order to help the economically and socially excluded who don't speak English as a first language, well-meaning liberals insist that every pamphlet produced by the borough advising its citizens of their rights to health care, education, social services, and so on, every form and leaflet, has to be translated into a dozen languages. This introduces an enormous cost, especially when you think that new local and central government programs are being rolled out at a rate of knots with every passing fad of public policy. But aside from the cost, it's either useless or dangerous. When you go to the doctor's surgery,* the leaflets in Bengali remain piled high—nobody takes them. My friends in local government confirm that reams of these translations get pulped. Here's the terrible irony: They don't get used because the literacy rate among Sylhetis is very low—the literacy rate in Bengali, that is. Sylhetis don't even speak Bengali, they speak a dialect or another language, call it what you like. But this business of translation is useless and worse still it is very likely dangerous. The provision of services in Bengali means Bangladeshis are drawn to Tower Hamlets and remain there. The reception at my doctor's surgery here counts a number of Sylhetis among its staff. As a Sylheti in Tower Hamlets, you can conduct all your exchanges with official Britain, in the doctor's surgery, at the unemployment benefit office, at the social services office, in your mother tongue.

---

*In Britain, a doctor's office is called a surgery.

Why on earth would you not come here and why on earth would you ever leave? This is a ghetto. We have got to get every generation speaking English as well; we've got to abandon the dogma of multiculturalism."

Tower Hamlets is the setting of Monica Ali's book *Brick Lane,* another extremely successful recent novel about Bengalis in Britain written by another attractive young woman of exotic ethnic extraction. Despite Zia's complaint that the modern British novel is not angry enough for verisimilitude, *Brick Lane* portrays the bewilderment and alienation of Bengali immigrants in Britain quite successfully—and proposes, as well, that these emotions morph readily into Islamic radicalism and hatred of America.

Ali recounts the story of Nazneen, an obedient Bengali villager sent to London as a teenager to marry a stranger twice her age. When Phiroze spoke of his wasting vegetarians, I thought of Nazneen, who is astonished to discover that in Britain it is the poor who are fat. Nazneen's daughters, like the children in *White Teeth,* dismay their father, Chanu, with their enthusiasm for assimilation. "And what is their culture?" Chanu asks contemptuously of the British. "Television, pub, throwing darts, kicking a ball." Like Zadie Smith's character Samad, Chanu schemes to take his children back to Bangladesh against their will.

Nazneen's rebellion, late in life, comes in the form of an extramarital affair with a virile young Muslim radical, Karim. His anti-Americanism—and the anti-Americanism of Muslim immigrants generally—is assumed by the author as a given: At the community meetings Karim convenes, the debate is not about *whether* British Muslims should oppose the United States, it is about *how* to oppose the United States. The outcast of the group, who objects to violence on the grounds that it is not sanctioned by Islam, is a black convert— the only one who is not of Bengali origin.

"So there's a lot of anger," Zia concluded. "There's the anger and the fear of the terrorist, the vandal on the street, but there's anger too in the lawyer, the physician, the banker. I've wondered if when you see someone passionate *against* something, against unfairness, whether behind that passion there is anger. I know angry Asian men who will only discuss their anger behind closed doors in the company of friends." He had, he told me, thought of writing a novel about these angry men.

A woman he had met the weekend before was sleeping in his bedroom. She was already besotted with him and he was already bored with her. Several more women called him on his cell phone as we spoke. His life did not seem a vale of tears. I interrupted him. "Look, Zia," I said, gesturing around me at his apartment, the leather sofa, the panoramic view of London's skyline, "you're one of the most successful people I know, by any measure. It would seem that Britain has been good to you. Why are *you* angry?"

He didn't seem surprised by the question. Perhaps he'd heard it before. "It's a curious need," he answered, pausing at length between clauses as if retrieving them from deep storage, "that we all have, which is to be treated fairly. We all must feel that we are being treated fairly. We hear people saying all the time, 'Since when was life supposed to be fair?' And yet we all absolutely *rage* against injustice. Injustice perpetrated against an individual coupled with injustice perpetrated against the individual because he's part of a wider group, not only is that an unfairness, it's obliterating of his uniqueness. It's *so* disregarding. Not even a moment's thought about his uniqueness. The desexualizing—it's bound to make you angry."

Zia began to speak now as if facing a jury, no longer using the first person. "Everyone faces adversity. And everyone must position himself in such a way not only to overcome adversity but to find challenges equal to his talents. Now, we all do things, we all find creative ways of negotiating through difficulties. That doesn't mean we don't have them. If you see someone who's done moderately well, what you see is someone who's done moderately well. What you won't see is what obstacles he had to overcome. It almost smacks of greed for that person to argue that he's been treated unfairly—it *is* unseemly—but I think it's unfair to deny him that argument, because whether that argument is a valid one is entirely to do with matters of fact, which we may or may not be able to ascertain, but it is a factual question, not a moral one. How do I account for my success? I'm an outlier. I'm random. There are many, many more who have much more talent than me, many more, I am sure, who never broke through. And in the whole of life, you will get a few like me, who have had the happy confluence of circumstances. I've been lucky."

As he finished his sentence, the woman who had been sleeping as we spoke walked into the living room in her pajamas. She stared at Zia with infatuated eyes. He sighed.

## THE GREAT SATAN'S SECRET WEAPON

Zadie's book suggests a particularly important truth: In the war against Islamic radicalism, Europe's chief weapon will be its enormous seductiveness. While Europe has been home to history's most extraordinary forms of religious fanaticism, European civilization has also had a corrosive effect on the religious life, whether Catholic, Protestant, or Jewish. There is no reason to expect the Muslim experience to be different. The temptations of Western civilization, as the characters in British novels repeatedly discover, are corrosive; and even sending one's children back to Bangladesh is no proof against them. That which disgusts the Islamists—alcohol, promiscuity, faithlessness, decadence—will for many be their undoing. These are what Europe has to sell, and they are commodities that have repeatedly proved more appealing than abstract salvific ideologies—at least, in the long run.

The Berlin Wall did not fall simply because the Soviet Union was militarily and economically bankrupt, nor even because the citizens of the East longed to be free. It fell because those citizens said "Screw this" to communism's utopian message. They wanted video recorders, not the dictatorship of the proletariat. They wanted Michael Jackson albums. They wanted motorcycles. They wanted *Penthouse* magazine, combination washer-dryers, twenty-four-hour convenience stores, rave music, and a lot of Ecstasy to go with it. Communism provided none of that.[14] The West, by comparison, demands no adherence to grim, self-sacrificing ideologies, even as it offers infinite possibilities for pleasure in the temporal realm. Of course it is that very same seductiveness—accompanied by the complete absence of a redemptive message, the *disdain* for redemptive messages—that introduces into the West its anomie and hopelessness, but surely it is far better to have newly faithless immigrants moping around the cafés, fretting about the toxins in their diet and complaining that none of it makes any sense, than to have them planning to blow up buildings. Unfortunately, it is that very anomie and hopelessness that prevents the West from defending itself aggressively even when the buildings actually are blown up.

The eminent Middle East historian Bernard Lewis has remarked that when the mullahs call America the Great Satan, the Satan in question is not *our* incarnation of evil, but theirs—"the adversary, the deceiver, above all the inciter and tempter who seeks to entice mankind away from the true faith."[15] In the Orientalist mythology described by Edward Said, the East is a seductive female and the West is a conquering male. But it can equally well be viewed as precisely the inverse.[16] The West tempts the faithful and the West devours religion, not so much by subduing it militarily as by offering something so much more immediately attractive: personal autonomy, sexual freedom, nice things to buy. Europe has snuffed out Christianity, and sooner or later it will probably do the same to Islam. With luck, it will do so before Islam manages to wreak too much more damage. But given how much easier it is to destroy than to build, there is no guarantee that it will do so in time.

## TOO MUCH BLOODY HISTORY

Let me make one thing clear: No one but a fool would argue that the United States is free of racial and religious tension, that immigration is an uncontroversial issue in America, or that there are no Islamic radicals in the United States. It is a difference of degree—but differences of degree can be so great as to amount to a difference of kind. The fundamental ethnic divide in the United States is not between established

Americans and recent immigrants but between whites and blacks. The historic origins of this divide are obvious: Black Americans came to the United States not as willing immigrants but as slaves. Relations between blacks and whites in the United States remain less than perfectly harmonious, but it is laughable to imagine that a significant number of black Americans would consider martyring themselves to destroy Western civilization.

The historic origins of the divide between native Britons and Muslim immigrants are often held to be equally significant: the immigrants were once the colonized, and the native Britons, the colonizers. In *White Teeth*, describing his obsession with Poppy Burt-Jones, Samad reveals the greatest source of his shame: Poppy Burt-Jones is English.

"That is the worst of it," said Samad, his voice breaking. "English. White. English."

Shiva shook his head. "I been out with a lot of white birds, Samad. A lot. Sometimes it's worked, sometimes it ain't. Two lovely American girls. Fell head-over-heels for a Parisian stunner. Even spent a year with a Romanian. But never an English girl. Never works. Never."

"Why?" asked Samad, attacking his thumbnail with his teeth and awaiting some fearful answer, an edict from on high. "Why not, Shiva Bhagwati?"

"Too much history," was Shiva's enigmatic answer, as he dished up the Chicken Bhuna. "Too much bloody history."

That bloody history, it is often said, is why Britain is unable to integrate its immigrants as the United States does. But it is *not* the fact of colonization per se. Non-Muslim immigrants from the Indian Subcontinent in Britain—Hindus, Parsis, Sikhs, Jains—are wealthier and better educated than other ethnic groups in Britain, including whites and Jews.[17] Nor is this a function of national origin. Although most Hindus in Britain come from India, Hindus from Bangladesh—a minority so small that they scarcely register on the census—are by every socioeconomic measure as successful as those from India. The 1.2 million

Hindus in Britain are never found rioting in the streets of industrial towns as their Muslim counterparts do. Nor do they bomb London's subways. Yet the obstacles to political and economic success in Britain that apply to Muslims should in principle apply to Hindus, should they not? All have dark skin, and thus presumably encounter the same degree of institutional racism. All come from countries that were colonized. All come from vastly different, non-Western economic traditions. When I pointed this out to Zia, he replied that I was asking the wrong question. "The proper question is whether, all other things being equal, outcomes for this cohort of Hindus are as good as those of their white counterparts. The fact that they have done well tends to mask what studies show, which is that as a group they would have done even better but for discrimination. (Also, it's important to bear in mind that discrimination has mutated in Britain; if people can discern the difference between a Vindaloo and a Madras curry, it should come as no surprise if most people can tell a Muslim name from a Hindu one.)"

Perhaps. But the crucial difference is not discrimination, nor even any beliefs or habits of mind particular to Islam. It is that, as Zia remarked, the Muslims come from villages. Through a series of historical contingencies, Muslim immigrants for the most part *arrived* in Britain poor and uneducated, whereas other immigrants from the Indian Subcontinent did not.

Consider this: For nearly 800 years India was ruled by Muslims, and it is for precisely this reason that British colonizers smashed their privileged political, social, and cultural position. This policy was above all driven by a practical power logic—and justified as a liberation of Hindus from the rule of an oppressive minority—but ancient religious antipathy clearly made the task a pleasure. While Islam and Hinduism were of inherently equal theological anathema to British Protestantism, Islam was viewed by colonists and colonized alike as the old, familiar enemy of Christendom—the Crusades here shaping the recent past, and by this means the present. Hinduism, by contrast, was viewed as a quaint, faintly contemptible, and unthreatening paganism.

Having crushed the Sepoy Mutiny in 1857, Britain abolished the

East India Company, placing India under the direct control of the Crown. British administrators, incorrectly attributing the mutiny to the Muslims alone, confiscated Muslim properties and restricted Muslim employment in the army, revenue department, and judiciary. Advertisements inviting applications for government jobs noted specifically that Muslims would not be appointed. The Inam Commission, appointed to study Mogul legal structures for landholding and revenue farming, concluded by seizing some 20,000 Muslim estates, ruining countless ancient Muslim families. The British built schools in India designed specifically to cultivate Western habits of thought, making no provisions for religious education. A new Hindu elite, the Bhadralok, emerged from these schools, swiftly filling the vacancies in government offices formerly held by Muslims. Muslims, having been given excellent reason to fear the destruction of their culture, refused to be educated in these institutions, further withering their political role in the colonial system. It is not really a surprise that Hindus were more willing than Muslims to accept the adulteration and Anglicization of their religion as the price of power. Historically, Hinduism has always profited from its polytheistic syncretism and ability to assimilate foreign influences; it is common, for example, to find Christ images or the Virgin Mary among the pantheon of deities in a Hindu household.

Following decolonization, and in many cases much before decolonization, Hindus—as well as Jains, Sikhs, and Parsis who profited similarly under the British Empire—came to Britain as highly qualified teachers, doctors, businessmen, and army officers, often with several degrees apiece. They spoke excellent English and had generations of experience with administrative and commercial institutions modeled on British ones. They were in consequence at a tremendous assimilative advantage.

Indian Hindus were, moreover, active traders in East Africa, where they dominated the banking and financial services. Muslims, owing to Islamic prohibitions on usury, have never evidenced much of a flair for these industries. Upon achieving independence, African states nationalized banks and private businesses, strictly regulating their economies, and in the early 1970s, Idi Amin confiscated the property of Indian businessmen and expelled them from Uganda. The urbane, commercially experienced Hindu immigrants who came to Britain as a consequence have become, unsurprisingly, remarkably prosperous.

Muslims, however, for the most part arrived in Britain as unskilled rural laborers. The partition of India in 1947 caused the displacement of large rural populations from Pakistan, including Bangladesh, particularly in the Punjab and Mirpur. The simultaneous construction of the Mangla Dam in Pakistan displaced another 100,000 people. While some relocated to other parts of Pakistan, many immigrated to Britain. In this, they were encouraged by the British government, which hoped to preserve British textile mills in the north and midlands through the import of low-cost Commonwealth labor. Britain *deliberately* encouraged unskilled, uneducated, politically unsophisticated Muslim immigrants to fill its factory jobs. So did most other European countries: Germany, for example, imported a massive labor force of unskilled Turks to do the jobs Germans no longer cared to do. They came from the least-developed areas of rural Turkey. Moving to *Istanbul* would have been a great shock; Germany might as well have been the moon. This was true as well of the North Africans who immigrated to France, Spain, Italy, and the Netherlands. Throughout Europe, the vast majority of Muslim immigrants were already the poorest citizens of their native societies—this, precisely, is why they migrated. As Zia remarked, traditional village life is poor preparation for economic advancement and civic integration in a modern, secular city.

In Britain, the focus of the modernizing economy soon shifted from labor-intensive industries to those requiring specialized skills and education. Unskilled immigrants consequently found themselves not only unemployed but in natural competition with Britain's white underclass, who predictably failed to embrace them. It is obvious why this group of immigrants has fared poorly in Britain, as have their offspring.

Here is a critical point: Education and social class upon arrival in Britain, above all, appear to account for the radically different markers of assimilative success evidenced in these communities, far more so

than religious belief. The evidence? Muslims whose parents were educated, English-speaking professionals upon arriving in Britain seem to
fare quite well—just as well as Hindus, in fact. There just don't happen to be very many of them.

Hassan Alam, who also studied with me at Oxford, is the son
of Muslim physicians from a comparatively prosperous northern
province of Bangladesh.* He finds Zia's descriptions of immigrant life
unrecognizably angst-ridden. He wondered in a letter to me,

> Why do you think he paid so much heed to the prejudices and
> idiosyncrasies of his parents? Not going out with your girlfriend
> in public is a Bangladeshi rite of passage. It's like puberty (except
> it's still happening in your 30s). No reason for him to get so hung
> up on it. We all go through it. He should have just lied to his par-
> ents and listened to Morrissey in his bedroom like the rest of us.

Hassan is quick to emphasize his admiration for Britain, for its tolerance and pluralism. His Bengali relatives can visit Britain, wear
clothes that distinguish them as Muslims in a predominantly Christian
country, find and eat halal food, and worship at a mosque without
harassment. In Saudi Arabia, he notes, no Christian would enjoy a
similar freedom. Britain's ethnic diversity, he says, is "fantastic."

Hassan didn't much care for *White Teeth;* he found it unconvincing
and overwritten. He wondered why all these comely first-generation
immigrant novelists felt compelled to write about Islamic radicalism,
forced marriages, and social alienation. Why, he asked, did these novels insist on depicting abusive, hypocritical male characters, men who
were inevitably secret fornicators despite their ostensible piety? Why so
many long-suffering, oppressed women who by the end of the novel
enjoy a feminist awakening? "Why can't they do us the courtesy,"
he asked, "of portraying us as unique, complex people?" These, I
thought, were an interesting echo of Zia's words, but their premises
and implications were remarkably different.

---

*He has asked me to use a pseudonym; this is not his real name.

Most immigrants, he insisted, were not destined for unwanted arranged marriages or wracked with anger about their alienation or plotting to blow up buildings. Immigrants were capable of thinking about other things, normal things, the things Bridget Jones thinks about. He was toying with the idea of quitting his job as a management consultant and writing a book about the *real* Bengali immigrant experience.

This alone seems to be the universal constant of the Bengali immigrant experience: the desire to write a novel about it.

## HOW TO RAISE A GOOD LITTLE EUROPEAN

On my last visit to London, I found myself chatting with Phiroze in his consulting room, an opulent study with drawn brocade curtains and a coal fire. Sculptures on the mantel of his fireplace represent different aspects of the emotional world. There is one for depression, one for the gentle mother, one for the hurt child. Socrates depicts wisdom. Until recently, I had thought it striking that none of the sculptures had Asian faces. On this visit, though, I noticed the addition of a placid Buddha's head.

Psychotherapists of Asian descent are extremely rare in Britain, as are Asian patients. Almost none of Phiroze's patients have been other Asians. Even middle-class Asians are unlikely to consider practicing or entering psychotherapy, a discipline intimately linked to the core of Western intellectual culture, to its art and literature and high drama, to representation and abstraction, to the enlightenment ideals of self-fulfillment and the pursuit of personal happiness. Immigrants of his background, Phiroze surmised, had little patience for these concepts and were uncomfortable discussing feelings and the self, particularly sexual feelings. The admission of rage and resentment toward one's parents would be unthinkable in many Asian families, and spending money to talk about oneself would be an unacceptable self-indulgence.

Phiroze lives and practices in a massive, somber stone manor on London's Blackheath, an upper-middle-class neighborhood of carefully tended rosebushes, manicured lawns, and white professionals. He has lectured, conducted seminars, and performed analytic work throughout Europe, and his private practice is full. He is not angry about his relationship to Britain, though he concedes that notwithstanding his achievements, he is regularly "identified in the street as some kind of wog or Paki." Strictly speaking he is neither; he is a Parsi. His parents were born to Bombay's upper-middle-class Parsi community and came to London in the 1950s after completing their university education in India. His grandfather was a prison warder in India who was killed in a riot, dying a hero.

Upon arriving in Britain, Phiroze's parents saved every penny they earned to send him to elite British schools, where he was bullied and beaten, as Zia was. This experience appears to be universal among British immigrants, although as Orwell made clear, this has long been a tradition among native Britons, too. Phiroze recalled that the ring-leader among his tormentors, curiously, was another Asian. He now supposes that the boy "was beating up a part of himself—the Asian, black, nonwhite part."

Although his experience of Britain has been in some ways similar, Phiroze, unlike Zia, pronounces himself satisfied with the progress immigrants have made. "It seems not too difficult for blacks and Asians in Britain to advance in law, medicine, politics," he said. "I'm quite satisfied with the way Asians have been penetrating senior echelons in the past forty years. It would be greedy to want more MPs, more judges, more bishops. I think it's going quite nicely; I have no complaints."

The first Parsi was elected to the British Parliament in 1892. By 1922, there were three seated Parsis. Even now, there are no more than 5,000 Parsis in Britain, so this achievement can only be considered remarkable—particularly considering that only two Muslims have ever been elected to Parliament, and both of them only in the past five years. "Admittedly," said Phiroze of his sanguinity, "I'm such a sheltered, middle-class public-school boy."

To have middle-class parents changes neither Britain's racism nor its unemployment rate, but it appears to change a child's attitudes toward those obstacles to success, and to spare him from a schizo-phrenogenic internal conflict about upholding his ethnic and religious identity. Phiroze's parents, unlike Zia's, were not conflicted about their son's assimilation. "My parents came over thinking, 'We want Phiroze to be a good little European. We won't teach him our language, we'll send him to public school, we'll give him a taste for European art, culture, and literature'—which is exactly what happened; look around." He gestured toward the sculptures on his wall. "'And then he will become a kind of middle-class, Jaguar-driving fellow—a very posh-sounding, well-spoken guy.'

"My parents wanted me to have almost nothing to do with their culture. They didn't show any interest in taking me back home. It seems to me fundamentally foolish to go to a new country and refuse to have anything much to do culturally with the people who live there. It's going to be a recipe for neurosis and disaster and intergenerational conflict. It's a terrible thing. I'm really glad my parents didn't put me through that experience."

"My heart goes out to them, really," he said of children whose parents resisted their assimilation. "It must be very painful to exist like that. You see the parents saying, 'We don't want you to marry a white girl, we don't want you to go to McDonald's, we don't want you to hang out on the corner with those smoking, glue-sniffing white boys. You'll stay at home, you'll marry a nice girl from our community, and you'll maintain a bloodline and a tradition that means that we will somehow be here even when we are not here.' And their kids hate it and they resent them, and most of their kids rebel, and hang out on the corner and smoke cigarettes and have white girlfriends, and sometimes— this was in the press recently—sometimes the fathers will kill the daughters." Just seconds before, he had said that he had "no complaints" about the way immigrants were adapting to British life. I asked him: Surely this was cause for complaint? "Yes. But this isn't just about integration—it's about crazy, mad, murderous parents as well, which is a separate issue."

I wasn't convinced. I'm not sure he was either. But I think it was the first time he'd given the question much thought.

If you are an immigrant in Britain, it seems, the education level of your parents will determine your likelihood not only of professional success but of sexual success as well. Phiroze has never had a relationship with an Asian woman. All of his romantic partners have been upper-middle-class white women. This is also true of his Asian friends, who come from similar backgrounds. "All my middle-class Asian friends have married white girls. But their parents already had degrees, were already doctors. . . . All my friends are Indians, Parsis, Bahá'ís. The three Bahá'ís I know are superb achievers. Parsis are the world's most highly educated community—on average they have three degrees each. Every Parsi I know in this country is highly educated."

But no degree is protection against prejudice. His own practice, Phiroze remarked, would have grown twice as quickly had he advertised under the name Jack Stevens. "I wanted to succeed as an Asian. I wanted to raise the esteem profile of my group. There are Asians in medical practice in Britain, but they tend to be seen as eccentric doctors who trained abroad, in places like Calcutta and Bangalore and Madras. Many of them still have very strong Indian accents and many of them are disrespected by their white colleagues." He himself has a public-school accent, just as his parents intended. "I wanted to succeed as someone of that genetic stock and skin coloring, while maintaining standards of excellence that would be the equal or better of any white man here.

"And no, I don't feel like a white man and I never shall."

## WHY AMERICA SUCCEEDS WHERE BRITAIN FAILS

Why is it that Bangladeshi and Pakistani immigrants to America tend to be less alienated, economically marginalized, and emotionally anguished than those in Britain, and why do they show less inclination to antisocial behavior, including Islamist violence?

American immigration policy certainly accounts for this to a degree. The United States gives immigrants with high levels of educational and professional achievements priority in the immigration queue. In the United States, immigrants from Bangladesh and Pakistan are on average far better educated than those in Britain, which deliberately encouraged unskilled laborers to emigrate. Nonetheless, many rural refugees and economic migrants from the Indian Subcontinent have come to America—uneducated, unskilled, and unprepared for modernity—and have succeeded nonetheless.

About 38 percent of Bangladeshi men are unemployed in Britain; fewer than 10 percent are unemployed in the United States. British unemployment rates are generally higher than American ones. This, too, accounts for some of the difference. But even when figures are adjusted to reflect general rates of unemployment, Pakistanis and Bangladeshis are much more likely to be jobless in Britain than America.

A key reason for the difference is Britain's class structure, a stubborn relic of the feudal era. Few manage to escape from Britain's underclass: Young people of all races from lower-class backgrounds are extremely unlikely to enter higher education. According to the 2003 Education and Child Poverty Report, educational success in Britain is more determined by social class than in any other country in the developed world.[18]

Unlike America or other European countries, Britain never experienced an outright revolutionary assault on its feudal social hierarchy. America's founding fathers declared titles illegal. This did not, of course, eliminate inequality, but at least this declaration enshrined the *ideal* of classlessness. No social group in Britain has had its privileges forcibly removed. In Britain, you tend to stay where you are born—or in the case of immigrants, you stay as you arrived.

The United States, moreover, has always been a country of settlers. The idea that an immigrant may arrive penniless on Ellis Island and become, through his thrift and industry, a millionaire is a central and defining trope of American national mythology. Even when it is not true, it is widely *believed* to be true, which doubtless gives hope and comfort to immigrants who are in fact destined to pack supermarket shelves at minimum wage for the rest of their days. (The propagation of this myth, it is interesting to note, owes much to a particular set of immigrants—American Jews in Hollywood—for whom it has been particularly true.[19]) Immigration in Britain is a more recent phenomenon. Although foreigners have come for centuries from its Celtic periphery and from Europe, only recently has Britain experienced mass immigration from vastly *different* cultures.*

A much longer historic tradition of relying on immigrant labor makes American employers less likely than their British counterparts to discriminate against immigrants. Moreover, the American legal system punishes discrimination more vigorously than the British one. British laws prohibiting job discrimination were put in place in 1976, some twelve years after the U.S. Civil Rights Act and more than a century after Reconstruction. These laws have resulted in only a few convictions, and compensation to victims has been extremely modest. In the United States, plaintiffs in race-discrimination cases regularly receive handsome legal redress. Britain has no official affirmative action policy. Furthermore, the cost of hiring and firing is higher in Britain than in the United States: British law, for example, requires employers to compensate employees made redundant after two years of service. Such labor market rigidities heighten employers' unwillingness to take a chance on employees they view as unreliable, reinforcing any tendency to discrimination.[20]

But most important is something less easy to quantify: Immigrants to America have always *wanted* to become American.

Not long ago, I discussed the difference between immigrants to the New and Old Worlds in an exchange of letters with the Brazilian poet Nelson Ascher. His response perfectly captures my sense of this:

> Can it perhaps be that American assimilationist traditions and American sexual practices are two sides of the same coin on which *E Pluribus Unum* is written? Choosing America usually implied accepting Rilke's dictum "You must change your life,"

---

*There are, of course, debates about the ability of certain groups to assimilate successfully in America, but these have focused on Hispanics, not Muslim Asians. Even Hispanics, it should be noted, have high rates of military enlistment and rank well on other key indices of identification with the host country.

didn't it? It used to be a decision to become someone else, even to change names: a break with the old countries. It seems most Muslims who went to Europe didn't really want to become something else, nor did the Europeans want them to become Europeans: That wasn't written on their mutual social contract. If America is the land of second and third opportunities, where people can reinvent themselves professionally and in other ways many times over throughout their lives, intermarriage and divorce are so many other possibilities in this process. You move to another state, change professions, remarry, convert to another faith, leave the Democrats and start voting Republican, trade the *New York Times,* say, for the *Washington Post,* make or lose money. That's not how things happen in Europe, is it? My dad was born Ferenc Ascher, but for almost 50 years now he has been Francisco. People came to Brazil in order to forget, to erase the past, to get out of history (we have geography, no history). Thus, possibly, many Muslims who opt for the U.S. do it because they are tired of being Muslims and want to keep in the long run, at best, only some culinary habits. Not so in Europe. Half a century ago the Europeans might have convinced their recently arrived Muslims to do the same, but that simply wasn't the European way, not since the times when the newly arrived barbarians converted to Christianity in order to become Europeans. Western Europe didn't really want to incorporate the 1 percent of Jews who dressed in the same way as they did, spoke their languages, looked like them and were proud to be Britons, Frenchmen, Germans. How can it cope with 10 percent of Muslims who do not even want to assimilate anymore? Sometimes I think that maybe contemporary Europe has a problem on its hands.

It is tempting to imagine Zadie's relentlessly funny London, a pluralistic society of Indians, Pakistanis, and Afro-Caribbeans, as analogous to New York at the turn of the century, with its immigrant culture of Jews, Irish, and Italians. But the analogy is not correct. In the United States, men are encouraged to believe that money and power might come to them at any point in their lives. Not so in Britain, where the idea of upward economic mobility, the ideal of the self-made man, has been subordinated to ancestral hierarchies and the leveling principle of social justice. No wonder certain immigrants— poor, frustrated, socially and sexually alienated, seeing little hope that this will change—are angry. This may not be the *source* of Islamic radicalism, as Zia imagines, but it's definitely not the cure for it either.

## WHAT DOES THIS MEAN FOR US?

Within days of the September 11 attacks, British prime minister Tony Blair pledged to stand "shoulder to shoulder" with the United States. He has done so. Britain has committed far more troops and resources to Afghanistan and Iraq than any other allied power. At every turn, Blair defends the United States both literally and rhetorically.

According to a 2004 Harris poll, Americans view Britain as our closest ally. The admirably defiant British response to the London Underground bombings suggested to many that this affection was not misplaced. "If these murderous bastards go on for a thousand years," wrote the *Mirror* tabloid, "the people of our islands will never be cowed."[21] The *London News Review* addressed the terrorists directly: "What the fuck do you think you're doing?" they asked. "This is London. . . . Do you have any idea how many times our city has been attacked? Whatever you're trying to do, it's not going to work. . . . So you can pack up your bombs, put them in your arseholes, and get the fuck out of our city."[22]

It is tempting, after displays of resolve like this, to believe Britain to be immune to the enmity borne toward America by the rest of Europe. Tempting, but wrong. Two influential segments of the British population, its intellectuals and its Muslim immigrants, loathe the United States with a vitriol that must be appreciated when assessing the solidity of the Anglo-American alliance and its future. This problem is only likely to grow. Indeed, it is perfectly conceivable that

Britain could, like France, become a quasi-hostile power within one election.

This is what al Qaeda hopes. It is what they were striving to achieve by setting off bombs in London. The authors of *Jihadi Iraq: Hopes and Dangers*—an Islamist strategy document published on the Internet prior to the bombing in 2004 of Madrid's Atocha train station—theorized that a well-timed terrorist attack could precipitate a British withdrawal from the Gulf. Tony Blair and his supporters strenuously denied that Britain's presence in Iraq precipitated the terrorist attacks, noting that al Qaeda emerged long before the Iraq War. Indeed, it is quite possible that the bombings would have occurred even had Britain refused to send troops: On September 27, 2005, French counterterrorism police arrested nine Islamic militants planning a similar attack on the Paris subway system, and France, of course, opposed the war in Iraq.

Nonetheless, it's absurd to think that al Qaeda does not number among its aims British withdrawal from the Gulf, just as it numbers among its aims the restoration of the caliphate, the global imposition of Islamic law, the veiling of women, the destruction of Judaism and Hinduism, and the beheading of blasphemers, among other ambitious objectives. With Britain standing in the way of all these aims, the attack on London was what historians would call an overdetermined event. It is puzzling that Blair feels the need to deny this. It is equally puzzling that critics of the war see in this obvious connection an argument *in favor* of British withdrawal from Iraq, rather than against it. They haven't asked me, but if they did, I would give them this advice: When in doubt about the proper orientation of your moral compass, point it *away* from the people who want to behead you. If al Qaeda is disturbed by the presence of British troops in Iraq, this is a sign that the troops are where they should be.

Al Qaeda's strategy for changing Britain's regime and precipitating its flight from the Gulf remains viable, as has already been established in Spain. A few more bombings in London, particularly if they involve chemical, radioactive, or biological weapons, might do the trick. While the United States could weather the loss of Spain from the coalition, the loss of Britain would be a political and military disaster. British troops constitute more than half of the non-American multinational force there and are by many accounts (and for obvious historic reasons) more gifted military administrators than we are.

While it is consoling to think that the British would never appease terrorists, this has not, historically, been the case. The IRA is thriving. Its bombers have been amnestied. Its political wing, Sinn Fein, has been integrated into mainstream politics. There is a great tradition of courage and defiance in British history, but there is also a significant tradition of appeasement—indeed, the British invented the term—and the recent swelling of British anti-Americanism is not an encouraging sign.

## THE ANTI-AMERICANISM OF BRITISH INTELLECTUALS

Britain's intellectual elites, in particular, are gripped by an anti-Americanism unremitting in its petty prejudice, sheer ravening ignorance, awesome self-contentment, and utter lack of critical acuity. In 2002, for example, the British playwright Harold Pinter, having survived an operation for cancer, remarked,

> I found that to emerge from a personal nightmare was to enter an infinitely more pervasive public nightmare—the nightmare of American hysteria, ignorance, arrogance, stupidity and belligerence: The most powerful nation the world has ever known effectively waging war against the rest of the world. . . . The US administration is now a bloodthirsty wild animal. Bombs are its only vocabulary.[23]

Pinter recently won the Nobel Prize for literature despite having written nothing worth reading since 1959. The subtle Swedish sense of humor, I am told, is quite difficult for outsiders to grasp, and this would seem to be a case in point.

In a 2003 opinion piece in the *Telegraph* subtly headlined "I Loathe America," the novelist Margaret Drabble offered these sentiments:

My anti-Americanism has become almost uncontrollable. It has possessed me, like a disease. It rises up in my throat like acid reflux, that fashionable American sickness. I now loathe the United States and what it has done to Iraq and the rest of the helpless world. . . . There, I have said it. I have tried to control my anti-Americanism, remembering the many Americans that I know and respect, but I can't keep it down any longer. I detest Disneyfication, I detest Coca-Cola, I detest burgers, I detest sentimental and violent Hollywood movies that tell lies about history. I detest American imperialism, American infantilism, and American triumphalism about victories it didn't even win.[24]

The reelection of George Bush erased any remaining restraint among British journalists. Americans, wrote Brian Reade of the *Mirror,* are "self-righteous, gun-totin', military lovin', sister marryin', abortion-hatin', gay-loathin', foreigner-despisin', non-passport ownin' red-necks, who believe God gave America the biggest dick in the world so it could urinate on the rest of us and make their land 'free and strong.'"[25]

Please pause to admire the man's exquisite command of the cliché.

The *Guardian* features a column in which readers write to ask questions about curious everyday phenomena. Why, for example, does water drain counterclockwise in the Southern Hemisphere? When a reader wrote to ask, "Is there a reliable way of telling the difference between Americans and Canadians? I don't want to take an instant dislike to the wrong person," the comment passed without remark. It is a useful thought exercise to imagine any of these words written about blacks, Jews, or in fact *any* other nationality or ethnic group: it would be unthinkable. Had the editors of the *Guardian* published the same question about Indians and Pakistanis, they would have been the targets of fatwas and firebombs.

Salman Rushdie, a man well acquainted with fatwas and firebombs since the publication of *The Satanic Verses,* reproachfully reported the new climate in London: "Night after night, I have found myself listening to Londoners' diatribes against the sheer weirdness of the American citizenry. The attacks on America are routinely discounted. ('Americans only care about their own dead.') American patriotism, obesity, emotionality, self-centeredness: these are the crucial issues."[26] Before spending years cowering in a cupboard following the death sentence pronounced upon him by the Ayatollahs, Rushdie himself was rather a lusty critic of the United States. As Dr. Johnson remarked, however, the prospect of being hanged in a fortnight concentrates the mind wonderfully.

Less than a month after the bombing in London, British MP George Galloway toured the Arab world. "Two of your beautiful daughters are in the hands of foreigners—Jerusalem and Baghdad," he told audiences there. "The foreigners are doing to your daughters as they will. The daughters are crying for help, and the Arab world is silent. And some of them are collaborating with the rape of these two beautiful Arab daughters. Why? Because they are too weak and too corrupt to do anything about it. . . . It's not the Muslims who are the terrorists. The biggest terrorists are Bush, and Blair, and Berlusconi, and Aznar, but it is definitely not a clash of civilizations. George Bush doesn't have any civilization, he doesn't represent any civilization. We believe in the Prophets, peace be upon them. He believes in the profits, and how to get a piece of them."[27] Stirring words, those, although rather hard to reconcile with the conclusions of the final Volcker Report on the oil-for-food scandal. The committee's investigators were persuaded that Galloway received some 18 million barrels of oil allocations and hundreds of thousands of dollars in cash payments from the former Iraqi regime.[28] Given Galloway's notorious litigiousness (peace be upon you, George!), I should mention that he denies these charges and that I have not seen the evidence against him with my own eyes. That said, were I an Arab parent, I would not let that man anywhere *near* my daughters.

Opinions such as Pinter's and Galloway's inevitably filter into the mainstream. A February 2003 poll commissioned by Britain's Channel 4 discovered that Britons viewed the United States, not Iraq or North Korea, as the nation that posed the greatest threat to world peace. The British teachers' union has passed referendums condemning America, so we may assume anti-Americanism is taught in British schools. Americans in Britain have reported vulgar harassment on buses, in the streets. The expression of unqualified hatred for America has become socially acceptable.

This anti-Americanism is not a new phenomenon. Like anti-Americanism throughout Europe, it antedates the invasion of Iraq and the presumptively clumsy diplomacy of the Bush administration. The sentiment has historically come in waves. Edward Wakefield, in the 1830s, described Americans as

> [a] people who, though they continually increase in number, make no progress in the art of living; who, in respect to wealth, knowledge, skill, taste and whatever belongs to civilization, have degenerated from their ancestors . . . who delight in a forced equality, not equality before the law only, but equality against nature and truth; an equality which, to keep the balance always even, rewards the mean rather than the great, and gives more honour to the vile than the noble. . . . We mean, in two words, a people who become rotten before they are ripe.[29]

More recently, there were massive protests against Ronald Reagan's deployment of Pershing II missiles in Europe, and before that, against the Vietnam War. Even after the Second World War, hostile sentiment toward Americans was widespread.

But this recent outbreak has a new demographic element. Traditionally, Britain's anti-American elites have been vocal, but they have generally been marginalized as chattering donkeys: They have never been able to exert sufficient influence to unravel the Anglo-American alliance. There are now, however, some 1.6 million Muslim immigrants in Britain, and more worshippers at Britain's mosques each week than at the Church of England. These immigrants form a highly visible and powerful anti-American vanguard and voting bloc, and their sentiments are particularly hostile toward America.

Anti-Americanism is a key and inextricable tenet of political Islamism, as is anti-Semitism—just as anti-Semitism was crucial, not incidental, to Nazi ideology. The problem of Islamic radicalism in Britain and the anti-Americanism to which it gives rise will not be solved anytime soon: its historical roots are far too deep. Through the unlikely alliance of the Muslim Right and the British Left, anti-Americanism has escaped its circumscribed association with privileged, self-enamored sophisticates, permeated Britain's underclass, and become inextricably conflated with a raw strain of racial and religious resentment.

This is a particularly unfortunate development. It would be naïve to assume it can have no consequences for the Anglo-American relationship.

# CHAPTER 4

# THE HOPE OF MARSEILLE

ICI VERS L'AN 600 AVANT JC DES MARINS GRECS ONT ABORDE, VENANT DE PHOCEE, CITE GRECQUE D'ASIE MINEURE. ILS FON-DERONT MARSEILLE, D'OU RAYONNA EN OCCIDENT LA CIVILISATION*
—INSCRIPTION AT MARSEILLE'S VIEUX PORT

COMPARED WITH THOSE OF OTHER European countries, French policy has in one way been a success. It has been a full ten years since the last wave of Islamic terrorism on French soil, a circumstance in large measure owed to the sheer ruthlessness of French antiterrorism prosecutors and investigators, who are Europe's most draconian. Terrorist suspects detained in France disappear for years without trial; they are interrogated under circumstances that make Guantánamo seem like Disney World, and when they are put away, they are put away for good. So far, these policies have worked.

But in other respects, France has no more successfully assimilated its immigrants than Britain or the Netherlands. When the suburbs of Paris went up in flames in November 2005, no one who knew those neighborhoods was surprised. The proximate cause of the riots was

---

*"Here, some six hundred years before Christ, debarked Greek sailors from Phocaea, a Greek city in Asia Minor. They would found Marseille, bringing the light of civilization to the West."

91

the electrocution of two teenagers of North African extraction who had clambered into a power substation to hide from the police. But these areas—populated chiefly by North African immigrants and their descendents—had long been on the verge of complete anarchy; it did not take much to push them over the edge. Even before the riots broke out, an *average* Saturday night's entertainment in the suburbs of Paris involved immolating 100-odd cars and an unveiled woman or two for good measure. No one in his right mind would enter those neighborhoods if he didn't have to, at least not without an armored tank. In the wake of Hurricane Katrina, a great many clucking French editorialists pronounced themselves scandalized by the state of American race relations. To those of us familiar with the state of French suburbs, their animadversions really did seem a bit rich.

Although recently the riots have been dominating global headlines, France's failure to assimilate its immigrants has given rise to a related crisis of equally serious dimensions. In late 2000, the commencement of the second Palestinian Intifada ignited the most extensive outbreak of anti-Semitic violence in France since the Holocaust. It continues to this day. The crimes have been perpetrated almost entirely by the *beurs*—Arab immigrants. The political alliances forged between Jewish and Arab leaders during the rise of the right-wing National Front have broken down. Both the most recent riots and these events suggest that the French have coped no more successfully with large-scale Muslim immigration than the British or the Dutch.

France's model of immigration, the so-called republican model, rests upon the demand that immigrants become culturally, intellectually, and politically assimilated. Like assimilation by the Borg, this process is *complete:* immigrants are asked to abandon their native cultures and adopt a distinct set of mental habits, values, and shared historic memories. Taken as a whole, these habits, values, and memories—*not* shared religion, race, or blood—are held to be the essence of France, the glue that binds French citizens together.[1]

The core values of France, inherited from the French Revolution, are based on the idea of individual rights. For official France, it is the citizen who is recognized, never the ethnic group to which he belongs. When the French Revolution emancipated Protestants and Jews, it emancipated them as individual citizens, not as groups defined by their religious membership. Related to the republican model is the doctrine of *laïcité,* a strict form of secularism that derives historically from the bitter rejection of France's authoritarian Catholicism. By this doctrine, all reference to religion must be excluded from the public sphere. In theory, *laïcité* guarantees equality before the law for all French citizens, and militates against anti-Semitism.

*In theory,* I stress.

The republican model of immigration has until recently allowed France to assimilate, successfully and completely, wave upon wave of Celtic, Germanic, Latin, and Slavic immigrants. The process is characterized by the state's refusal legally to recognize cultural and ethnic minorities, the official denial of the very idea of cultural identity. Similar principles were applied as well in the former French colonies, often to peculiar effect: I have spoken to Cameroonians who recall opening their first history text as children and reading with bewilderment the book's opening lines: *Nos ancêtres, les gallois . . .*

Integration in France implies a contract between the immigrant and the nation. The immigrant agrees to respect the universalist values of the republic, and the republic in turn guarantees his children full integration and social standing. Interior Minister Nicolas Sarkozy, the son of a Hungarian immigrant, is an excellent case in point: In one generation, Sarkozy—who is of Jewish extraction—has come to dominate French political life. He has done so by being *more* French, more committed to republican values, even *sounding* more French than any of his adversaries. He has held multiple cabinet positions and been head of his party, the conservative UMP (Union for a Popular Movement). He was the leading candidate for the presidency in 2007 until recently, when he called the suburban rioters "scum" and proposed cleaning out their neighborhoods with a Kärcher—an industrial-strength waterhose. (It is possible, apparently, for a politician to sound a bit *too* French.)

The American and Anglo-Saxon models of immigration rest on

significantly different principles and traditions. Britain and the United States emerged as federations of smaller states, and in both societies there is a looser and more pragmatic relationship between citizens and the center, a greater devolution of authority to local governance. In consequence, Britain does not merely tolerate immigrants speaking their own languages and worshipping their own gods, it encourages them. London's Muslim Welfare House, for example, subsidized by a grant from the British government, offers Koranic study and lessons in Arabic. The United States enforces multiculturalism with affirmative action programs backed by the full weight of the law. At every level of society, Americans are exhorted to celebrate diversity.

The French government vigorously rejects this kind of cultural separatism, which it terms "communitarianism." The word connotes the intrusion of unseemly religious or ethnic particularism into the public sphere, a refusal to be assimilated. The French hold—correctly—that Britain's extreme communitarianism contributes to a climate in which British Muslims do not consider themselves Muslim Britons. The debate over the veil is emblematic. The French government has banned students from wearing the veil in the classroom. In Britain, the issue is viewed as a matter for schools to resolve individually and independently of the government. In the United States, the Justice Department has intervened to protect the right of students to wear the veil.

When Arab immigrants in France insist on sending their daughters to school in a veil—or when they torch synagogues, for that matter—the French government views these unwelcome events through this ideological prism. The malefactors, they sense uneasily, are not taking a shine to republicanism.

## MARSEILLE: THE EXCEPTIONAL CITY

Marseille, France's second-largest and oldest city, was initially not exempt from the wave of anti-Semitic violence. In September 2001, the Gan Pardes School in Marseille was set alight. The words "Death to the Jews" and "Bin Laden will conquer" were spray-painted on the walls. Over the next year, Jewish cemeteries were defaced and swastikas painted on Jewish homes. During demonstrations in support of the Palestinians, marchers shouted, "All Arabs are Palestinians. We are all suicide bombers."

On March 31, 2002, a series of coordinated anti-Semitic attacks throughout France drew comparisons to Kristallnacht: Masked assailants smashed cars into a Lyon synagogue and set it on fire; a shotgun was fired into a kosher butcher shop in Toulouse; arsonists attempted to burn down a synagogue in Strasbourg. A Jewish couple was assaulted in a small village of the Rhône. In Marseille, the Or Aviv Synagogue in the quiet northern neighborhood of Les Caillols was reduced to ashes by arsonists and the Torah scrolls charred.

To the bewilderment of French Jews, the Palestinian Intifada has attenuated, but the so-called French Intifada has not—except in one city. The violence in Paris, Lyon, Strasbourg, and other major French cities has continued, and in some places worsened. In these cities, anti-Semitism appears to be uncontainable. But in Marseille, the animus has fizzled out. The city reacted with revulsion to the burning of the Or Aviv Synagogue. Citywide protests against anti-Semitism were immediately organized; Arabs participated in the demonstrations. The leaders of Marseille's Islamic community firmly condemned the attack. By contrast, after similar violence in Toulouse, Muslim community leaders offered not one single gesture of solidarity.*

---

*It is difficult to establish, statistically, the degree to which Marseille differs from other French cities. Groups that compile statistics on anti-Semitism in France use different methods, and moreover compile these figures to different political ends. Consequently, numbers vary wildly: For example, in 2001, SOS Racisme claimed there were 405 anti-Semitic incidents in France, the Representative Council of Jewish Institutions of France reported 330, the Interior Ministry found 163, and the Consultative Commission on the Rights of Man discovered 146. To confuse the methodological issue further, statistics generally reflect absolute numbers of incidents in a city, rather than per capita incidents, and do not take into account the size of a city's Jewish population. A city with 10,000 Jews is apt to report more anti-Semitic crime than a city with 10 Jews, but this does not necessarily mean Jews in the first city are in greater danger. Finally, it is particularly difficult to distinguish between a crime wave and a crime-reporting wave: The French government, in its campaign to combat anti-Semitism, has encouraged Jews to report even the smallest incident of aggression; this policy has been pursued vigorously in Marseille. But an increase in *reported* crime does not necessarily mean that *real* crime has increased. My claim that anti-Semitic violence is less

Marseille is not now free of anti-Semitism, by any means; this, after all, is the political base of the National Front, whose campaigns are driven by a furious anti-immigrant and anti-Semitic sentiment. But by comparison with the rest of France, Marseille has been calm. Until recently, there have been no burned cars and urban riots, as in Strasbourg, Paris, and Lyon. Even in the latest, massive outbreak of rioting, which quickly spread to every major city in France, Marseille was scarcely disturbed—a gang of kids tried to break into a supermarket; the police stopped them, and that was that.

In the rest of France, the violence against Jews appears to be organized. Some Jewish leaders believe it to be centrally planned and directed, perhaps by al Qaeda cells; they note that as on March 31, 2002, similar attacks often occur in separate cities on the same day, and find improbable the claim that this is mere coincidence. In Marseille, however, what violence there is seems to be spontaneous, disorganized, and largely committed by disaffected, economically disadvantaged juveniles who spend too much time watching al-Jazeera via satellite dish.

Marseille is a city of immigrants. Fully a quarter of Marseille's population is of North African origin, and demographers predict that Marseille will be the first city on the European continent with an Islamic majority. Its Jewish community is the third-largest in Europe. The most ethnically diverse city in France, then, has paradoxically been the most successful in containing this outbreak of ethnic violence.

When I went to Marseille to investigate this curious anomaly, my operating assumption was that Marseille's calm must be attributable to particularly vigorous police work. But I spoke to cabdrivers and waiters, to the police chief and his deputy, to street cops and officials at City Hall, to regional historians and archivists, to right-wing and left-wing community leaders. Everyone insisted that the efficacy of the

---

prevalent in Marseille than elsewhere in France is largely based on anecdotal evidence, but it is strong anecdotal evidence: Everyone in France accepts it as a given, and it can be confirmed by even a casual perusal of French newspapers over the past several years. Horrible things just don't seem to happen in Marseille as often as they do elsewhere.

police was only one part of the story, and everyone also agreed that Marseille's calm was no accident. There is something unique about the city that protects it from extreme cyclones of ethnic unrest.

Few social phenomena have monocausal explanations, and of course there is more than one reason for Marseille's comparative tranquillity. But one aspect of the answer is a surprising one: It is Marseille's approach to ethnic community politics, an approach that is unlike that of any other city in France.

Marseille's approach, in fact, challenges the core principles of the French republican ideal and the historic concept of what it means to be French. Marseille's success, in turn, suggests that if the exaggerated tolerance of Britain and the Netherlands has permitted Islamic radicalism to flourish, so too has its inverse.

## "IN MARSEILLE WE GET ALONG"

I arrived in Marseille on a sweltering summer afternoon. From the train station I could see Marseille's roseate castle glowing against the sunbaked Provençal hills. It was siesta time, and too hot to move quickly. I walked slowly down the hill to the Canebière, the tree-lined street that leads to the old port. The cafés were filled with dark-skinned men, their faces lined from the sun; they were recent immigrants, to judge from the sartorial clues. They wore clothes few native Europeans would wear—button-down shirts with short sleeves, dress slacks pressed with unfashionable care. Some had missing teeth and some had gold teeth; many had mustaches. They were sitting quietly with their hands folded, marking time, or filling in racing forms while drinking their coffee and chatting in Arabic. There were few women in the cafés, although there were many on the streets, dark-skinned and sloe-eyed. Some were veiled, but most were wearing skimpy tank tops and low-rise jeans. They were, after all, in France, and it was the revealing dress of the women, above all, that made Marseille feel more like a European city than an Oriental one.

I found a hotel on the Canebière, run by a family of Maghrebis, then took a taxi to the industrial northern neighborhood where I was to meet Zvi Ammar, the president of the Jewish Consistory of Marseille. "It's true that in Marseille we get along," my cabdriver told me. "I'm a Jew, my neighbors, they're Arabs, we understand each other fine. . . . It's not like the rest of France; we're cosmopolitan here, everyone understands everyone else." But when I asked him why, he couldn't tell me. "I'm not very political. I don't know. It's just the way it is. We have the sunshine here, the port." The sunshine and the port: Everyone mentioned that. But if sunshine and ports were a recipe for peace, Lebanon would be a paradise.

Zvi Ammar was born and raised on the island of Djerba, Tunisia, but betrayed the influence of the French educational system the moment he opened his mouth. The clue was his love of the schema. He approached the problem of anti-Semitism in France by breaking it into subsets; he labeled and defined those subsets, then presented his conclusions in a well-rehearsed lecture. "For four years," he told me, "the Jewish community of France has suffered from acts of an anti-Semitic character. These acts have two forms: There are acts against the dead, and there are acts against the living. Acts against the dead are committed by the extreme right. Neo-Nazis attack cemeteries and blaspheme tombs, defacing them with swastikas, Celtic crosses, and references to Hitler. The forensic signature of a neo-Nazi attack is the artwork. Their swastikas are carefully drawn and perfectly even."

We were interrupted by his mobile phone. Ammar is fluent in French, Hebrew, and Arabic, and during our conversation took calls in all three languages. After hurling rapid-fire Arabic down the phone for a few minutes, he hung up and returned to his exposition. "The attacks against the living are committed by Maghrebis—mostly youths. They now commit about ninety percent of the anti-Semitic crimes in France. When Maghrebis draw swastikas, they are careless. Their artwork is sloppy and childish."

The French intellectual system, I thought while listening to him, has a striking power to take over the souls of men and women whose native culture encourages forms of reflection as far from the French model as it is possible to get. When a man becomes French, when he is educated in the French manner, he begins to think like a Frenchman. *The problem has three parts, the solution has four. State, expand, schematize, analyze, conclude.* It has been so since Descartes.

It is interesting to imagine—but hard to demonstrate—the effect this system of thought must have on French political culture. It is clearly very useful for paper shuffling and the kind of analytic work done by the police. The same system, however, must make it very hard for anyone in a position of power or authority to think informally, or react spontaneously. This, perhaps, is one reason the French authorities are such sticklers for protocol. They need rules to tell them what to do. Without them they would be lost.

Ammar agreed that Marseille had been spared the worst of the four-year-long French Intifada. "We've been a bit luckier here," he said. One reason for this is that Marseille has benefited from vigorous police work. This is not unique to Marseille, but has been particularly effective in Marseille. The French government is so highly centralized that all law-enforcement initiatives are coordinated at the national level, not the city level. The government of President Jacques Chirac, under Prime Minister Jean-Pierre Raffarin, took aggressive measures to combat anti-Semitism. Following the attack on Marseille's Or Aviv Synagogue, the government deployed riot troops to every place in Marseille where Jews congregated. Outside Marseille's synagogues, a heavy and visible police presence remains to this day. The police have worked in close coordination with the domestic intelligence services, which have ramped up their surveillance of mosques and Islamic radical cells. The government has set up a toll-free number for Marseille's Jews to call; they have asked Jews to use it to report even the smallest aggression, such as casual insults on the street, so that officials may better spot trends and deploy resources to emerging hot spots. The police have been instructed to treat complaints of harassment with the utmost seriousness.

Foreign intellectuals and journalists have been quick to charge French officials with pusillanimity in responding to domestic anti-Semitism, arguing that the government has chosen to appease France's large, left-leaning Muslim population rather than protect its numerically smaller Jewish constituency. The Jewish leaders with whom I spoke in Marseille dismissed this suggestion. They considered Chirac's response to domestic anti-Semitism appropriate and forceful.

While France's socialists and leftists, I was told, had been "in denial" about the problem, the current administration was not. All agreed that Lionel Jospin's Socialist government, which lost power to the conservative UMP party in 2002, had responded tepidly to the mounting crisis. They had been ideologically blinkered, Ammar reasoned. "They didn't believe we could speak of racism that came from the Maghreb community, which was itself victimized by racism. For the Left, this was an earthquake." The Left held France's Jews and Arabs to be natural class and ideological allies. Until recently, this was not as absurd as it sounds: In response to the rise of the National Front in the 1980s, Jews and Arabs united to form the pressure group SOS Racisme. Although allegedly apolitical, its leaders were close to important politicians of the Socialist Party. "No one else in France," Ammar said, "had helped the Muslim community more than us, the Jews, through organizations like SOS Racisme—all the founding members of that organization were Jews. We were highly sensitive to their suffering."

The national, coordinated violence on the day of the torching of Marseille's Or Aviv Synagogue was a turning point, proof that the violence was not, as the Socialists believed, a transient problem or an expression of trivial juvenile delinquency. After this, the Chirac government moved swiftly and aggressively. Pierre Lellouche, a member of the National Assembly and senior figure in Chirac's UMP, sponsored the Lellouche Law, which came into effect in February 2003. The law called for the doubling of punishments for crimes committed with a racist or anti-Semitic motive, and was approved with rare unanimity in both the National Assembly and the Senate. French police delegations were sent to New York to study Mayor Rudy Giuliani's zero-tolerance policy. Sarkozy, then the interior minister, briefed police officials on the Lellouche Law. Referring to its double-punishment proviso, he announced that France would now adopt a *double* zero-tolerance policy toward anti-Semitic crime, a forceful if mathematically meaningless declaration. He formed a new police unit to investigate these incidents. Demonstrators were banned from displaying swastikas or other anti-Semitic symbols.

I was surprised that not one person in Marseille complained to me that Paris or the police were indifferent to attacks on Jews or that official policy was tainted by any kind of anti-Semitism, subtle or unsubtle. "France is not an anti-Semitic country," Ammar insisted. "An anti-Semitic country has anti-Semitic policies, like Vichy, with its anti-Semitic laws. Here it is the contrary. *The contrary.* We must speak the truth. You cannot say that because there are anti-Semitic acts, France is an anti-Semitic country." Ammar did note, however, that the judiciary had been slow to implement the Lellouche Law and to incarcerate offenders. This, he believed, was because the judiciary, reflecting the views of the French public at large, was not yet prepared to accept the gravity of France's problem. Others to whom I spoke in Marseille had a different perspective on the judiciary's apparent faineance: Officials within the police force and at City Hall held that the likely explanation was not indifference to the seriousness of the crimes; rather, most of the offenders have been juveniles, and the French legal system, in a long-standing tradition, is particularly protective of minors.

Ammar lunches regularly with members of Chirac's inner circle. Official France, Ammar believed, was shaken to the core by the rise in anti-Semitism. "We, the Jews, we're used as a kind of barometer. We may only be one percent of the population, but they know that if they are allowed to attack us, tomorrow they will go much, much further. A politician told me last week, 'You, the Jews, you're French here in France, it's your country, but if there's trouble tomorrow, you have Israel. Us? Where will we go? Nowhere. We don't know where to go.'" Even ministers widely seen as sympathetic to Arab grievances were profoundly alarmed by the anti-Semitic violence. Ammar told me of meeting Dominique de Villepin, who at the time was minister of the interior and was "responsible for security, boss of the French police," as Ammar put it. Villepin, he said, had remarked, *"Monsieur Ammar, le pire n'est pas derrière nous. Il est devant nous."* The worst is not behind us. It is ahead of us.

The government was doing all it could, Ammar believed. But the problem, he thought, was insoluble. The minds of Arab youths in France had been bathed in ravening hatred by broadcasts from the Middle East, from al-Jazeera and from al-Manar, the Hezbollah propaganda TV station. Ammar understands these Arabic broadcasts only too well. "The images, the music, the speeches—they are all designed to incite to the maximum, to make you want to go out in the street and find Jews to kill." In almost every Arab home, there is a satellite dish. "Sincerely, I am telling you: There are no solutions. I don't see how you can put a policeman behind every Jew: It's not possible."

Two months after our conversation, the French government banned al-Manar. "No one," said a Foreign Ministry spokeswoman, "should doubt France's determination to combat all aspects of racism and anti-Semitism." Shortly thereafter, it granted al-Manar a reprieve, subject to its willingness to ascribe to France's code of media conduct. The tidal influx of anti-Semitic propaganda from other Arabic-language stations and from the Internet remains unstanched, and short of entirely abrogating freedom of speech in France, not much can be done about it.*

Ammar is right. It is not possible to put a policeman behind every Jew. Yet, as he agreed, France's new law-enforcement initiatives had been more successful in Marseille than the rest of France. So clearly, there *are* solutions. But why should police tactics that have failed in other French cities be more effective in Marseille?

Seeking an answer, I took this question to those I thought might know—Marseille's police.

## LIKE NO OTHER CITY

I spent the following day at the National Police Equipment Convention of France. Some thousand-odd police officers had arrived for

---

*Al-Manar proved unable to resist the temptations of on-air Jew-bashing and has now been banned again.

the outdoor event, held in a leafy Marseille suburb under a bright Mediterranean sky. Street cops in sharp blue uniforms milled about the convention grounds, mingling with captains sporting embroidered military insignia and epaulettes, hostage-rescue specialists in camouflage gear, riot police in flak jackets. More cops were serving up espresso and croissants at the refreshment stand. After lunch, they began passing out shots of whiskey.

White tents had been set up over booths displaying police gear. Attendees could examine the new SIG Sauer semiautomatic and a snaking coil hose with an eye at the tip, designed to provide visibility around corners. Delegates from the former French colonies had flown in for the event: a bald man in mirrored sunglasses, his military uniform sagging with medals, displayed an odd, solemn interest in a tripod-mounted automatic weapon the size of a small motorcycle and useful, according to the manufacturers, for crowd control. It was something like a French Amway convention sponsored by *Soldier of Fortune,* the surreal effect amplified by the Brazilian lounge music piped in all day over the loudspeakers—syncopated accordion renditions of "The Girl from Ipanema," "Mucha Muchacha."

A team of hostesses in identical filmy tan dresses, their shoes and necklaces perfectly matched, handed out programs. At nine o'clock the drug-sniffing Labradors would be taken through their paces, then an officer would shoot his partner in the chest à la William Tell, displaying his marksmanship and the efficacy of the force's bulletproof vests. I was told I shouldn't miss the fashion show: the Interior Ministry had recently commissioned the design of a new national police uniform, a gesture said to have considerably improved morale.

I wandered over to the outdoor auditorium to watch the hostage rescue. A team of sinewy, iron-jawed men in flame-resistant black coveralls was limbering up at the edge of the crowd, pulling on gloves and balaclavas, adjusting their knee pads, strapping pistols to their legs. A bus had been positioned on the staging ground. The master of ceremonies called for volunteers to play the hostages. The women in the crowd volunteered frantically.

The hostages were escorted onto the bus. We were told that

negotiations had broken down. The situation was very grave. At the signal, the team streaked in and took cover behind a car. Shots were heard, then screams. The pyrotechnicians set off a gigantic purple flare as a distraction. Half the team stormed the bus, smashing in the windows, clambering through, and pumping the terrorists full of bullets. The other half spirited the hostages away, protecting them with their bodies. Everyone applauded.

Afterward, I asked one of the rescuers why they wore the black balaclavas.

"Because they're so scary-looking," he said, dabbing the sweat from his brow.

Between the demonstrations, I sat at a lawn table shaded by a parasol, amid big bushes of pink flowers, and spoke to the cops who patrol Marseille's streets. I started by speaking to two of them, but soon others, overhearing our discussion, sat down: They all wanted their say. Before long, a dozen cops were sitting at the table. Marseille, they agreed, was different; it was cosmopolitan; it was a port; ethnic conflict was not as much of a problem as it was in other cities. But that didn't mean the place wasn't a mess. "There are neighborhoods we can't even enter," one told me.

"There's no respect for the police anymore," another added.

"Kids these days don't have a good upbringing. They don't respect anything."

"It used to be that everyone respected the police. Now they know we're not allowed to do anything. If you give someone a smack, it's on the front page the next day. They never show what happened *before* that smack, though—just the smack."

"We don't have enough money. We need more money."

"Are you going to talk to Sarkozy? Tell him we need more money."

Cops, everywhere—always the same complaints.

I asked them why they'd gone into police work.

"Idealism," said one.

"Job security," said four more.

Of the cops at the table, about half were white. There was one black man, and the rest looked as if they might be of North African origin. There were two women. I asked whether the police force made an effort to hire ethnic minorities, as they did in the United States.

"Oh yes, of course."

"But not officially. You can't do that officially. That's against republicanism."

"But unofficially—of course!"

Everyone in official France, from top to bottom, knows the party line: *We are a republic. There are no ethnic groups.* But everyone, I discovered, also knows that this is a fraud.

I spent the rest of the day looking for Marseille's police chief, Pierre Carton. I spotted him just as a gigantic, flame-red police helicopter swooped down from the sky: The special forces had arrived to rappel down the side of a four-story building. I had to shout to make myself heard, because the loudspeakers were now blasting the theme from *The Ride of the Valkyries.* The chief was beaming: he was proud of his men. He kindly suggested that we might be able to talk more comfortably in his office, and invited me to join him there later in the afternoon.

The police station was massive, with the atmosphere and architecture of a Saracen fort, and the chief's office was spacious and sunny. He invited his deputy to join us. The secretary brought in cups of strong espresso. "There's been tension since the beginning of the Second Intifada in Israel, yes," said Carton in response to my question, "but not a *débordement*—an overflow. It's not like other cities." He was modest about this achievement: "If we've had any success, it's very relative. It's owed, in part, to the geography and sociology of the city. Marseille is a city with space. It's an agglomeration of what we call village nuclei, small neighborhoods that form a complete fabric. What's particularly important is that the *banlieue* is in the city itself." In every other sizeable French city, the *banlieues*—the suburbs—form menacing rings of criminality and unemployment around the city. This was a common theme of my conversations in Marseille: The city owes its peace, in part, to the fact that immigrants have not been shunted off into suburban slums as they have been in other large French cities.

Marseille is particularly spread out: its 800,000 inhabitants enjoy a city twice the size of Paris, with a coastline that spans more than thirty-five miles. The population of greater Paris, by contrast, is 10.5 million. During the 1960s and 1970s, when France launched huge collective housing projects, Marseille benefited from its low population density. Immigrant neighborhoods are now distributed evenly throughout the city, and young people, whatever their ethnic origin, congregate in the same neighborhoods: the Vieux Port, the Canebière, St. Ferréol Street, the beaches of the Prado, the Vélodrome. This use of urban space is uniquely Marseillais. In Nice, Montpellier, Bordeaux, Paris, and other major cities, youths of foreign origin and the native-born do not socialize in the same places. This, clearly, is an important reason for Marseille's comparative calm.

His deputy agreed: "This is important: The projects aren't detached from the rest of the city or from its traditional structures. The fact that the projects are sprinkled through the city means the inhabitants don't feel cut off from civic life or the traditional life of the city. If they use public transportation, kids from the projects can be in the center of town within five minutes."

I asked the chief whether Marseille's policing tactics, at the street level, had changed significantly under Chirac. Absolutely, he said; under the Socialists they had been crippled, but now the power of the police had been unleashed. Encouraged by signals from the Chirac government, he now responded to minor anti-Semitic crimes with a "furious" display of force—something he had felt unable to do in the political climate of the Jospin era. "During the Socialist era, between 1981 and 1995, the organization of the police was a bit different. We had less power at our disposal for a strong reaction—police power was spread out. Now it's been regrouped. Now we have forces that can respond quickly and forcefully. This was a national initiative, but it suits us well here.

"The mentality is different now. We try to be visible. We try to be very present in difficult areas. That frightens the delinquents and reassures the honest people. That's been our policy for the past few years. Now even small aggression, verbal aggression, is punished. Because that's where it starts. We try to react quickly. If you leave it, if you don't react, it degenerates rapidly. We want to avoid having others get the same idea, because here you have young people watching things on television, images of the Intifada. . . . We make arrests to show it won't be tolerated." He was quick, however, to specify that these were *republican* arrests, not communitarian arrests: "In France we arrest individuals—it's *you* who threw a stone at me, not the group to which you belong."

"Our model here isn't repression, though," he added. "It's permanent contacts among groups, in the schools, among associations. The police have a permanent dialogue with neighborhood associations— when there's a problem, we go directly to the source. We have personal relationships with the Jewish community, with the Islamic community. We have personal contacts at many levels: Not only the chiefs but the cops on patrol have regular meetings with community representatives. Not only with religious leaders but with ethnic leaders." He caught himself: "But we keep this within the republican framework, not the communitarian one."

His deputy interrupted; he wanted to be sure I understood this: "It's not the French tradition to be communitarian. It's the inverse. It's not like Britain, for example. We have very different traditions—we support integration. We strenuously avoid communitarianism."

It was not at all clear to me what this might mean: How can you have relations with the Islamic community without acknowledging that there *is* such a thing as an Islamic community? As I was later to conclude, the remarkable thing about Marseille is that its politics are in fact highly communitarian. Everyone simply insists vocally that they aren't, as if this made it so.

Marseille's success in avoiding the extremes of ethnic tension seen in other French cities was not, Carton freely offered, entirely attributable to his aggressive police work. "There's the climate. There are lots of leisure activities. The beach is free. Hiking is free. You don't have to spend money to enjoy yourself. If you're in Paris and you don't have money to go to restaurants, you're excluded. We're unique here. We have youth centers for kids from difficult neighborhoods— sports, boating. And then there's the football team: that really unites people. All colors, they call out, 'We're Marseillais.' It crosses all borders. They don't say, 'We're *beurs*'; they say, 'We're Marseillais.'"

Quite a few people mentioned this to me. Marseille has many free leisure activities, particularly sporting clubs for youths—boxing, judo, gymnastics, football. After hearing this over and over, I began to wonder whether the skepticism I'd felt about Midnight Basketball in America was warranted. Maybe these programs work?

"We have normal delinquency," the chief reflected, "but yes, ideological crime is marginal. We have traditional crime—*French Connection* crime."

I was later to realize that Marseille's tradition of *French Connection* crime had more relevance to its present calm than one might suspect.

There are some untraditional problems in Marseille as well. Like the panther. That is how the police in Marseille spent the summer: hunting a panther. The chief deployed dozens of officers after residents reported spotting the animal. "For fifteen days we looked for the panther, but he turned out to be just a big fat cat. Here, we have a tradition of exaggeration. It's prettier to say 'a panther' than 'a big fat cat.' You know, there are lots of stories about people who find these animals when they're young, and then when they grow up they don't know what to do with them. So we took it seriously. We applied a lot of police power to that."

"It's what we call the principle of precaution," his deputy added gravely, a finger resting against his nose. "You just can't be too careful."

## MARSEILLE'S GIFT

There is strong law enforcement, the wide geographic distribution of housing projects, activities for the young, the sun, the port, and the soccer team. But the remaining key to Marseille's civility is the most interesting.

A historical interlude. Marseille is a merchant port, northern Europe's natural outlet to the Mediterranean and the Suez Canal, a corridor between Orient and Occident. Its identity is and has always been intimately bound with immigration. In the seventh century B.C., the chief of the landing Phoenician galleys—a man said to be as handsome as a god—married the daughter of the king of the local Ligurian tribe. The city's origins are thus with a mixed couple, one native, one foreign.

According to Herodotus, Phoenician inhabitants took refuge in Marseille, then Massilia, when the Persians destroyed Phocaea. Then as now, the city was a haven for immigrants. Greeks, Romans, Genoans, Spaniards, Levantines, Venetians—all have come to Marseille and stayed. Each decade since the beginning of the twentieth century has seen the arrival of tens of thousands of new immigrants, most of them refugees: Armenian survivors of the Turkish genocide, German and Polish Jews, Republicans escaping the civil war in Spain, Vietnamese, Cambodians. The decolonization of the Maghreb brought a massive influx of North Africans to the city, giving it its nickname: the capital of Africa.

The exact religious composition of Marseille is unknown, for French law prohibits census taking; the very act is considered antithetical to republicanism. By informal estimates, there are 190,000 Muslims, divided among 70,000 Algerians, 30,000 Tunisians, and 15,000 Moroccans. There are nearly 70,000 Comorians, making Marseille the second-largest Comorian city in the world. Muslims from black Africa number between 5,000 and 7,000. There are at least 65,000 Armenian churchgoers, 20,000 Buddhists, and tens of thousands of Orthodox Greeks.

Marseille's 80,000 Jews constitute 10 percent of the total population, their ranks swollen by Algerian repatriation. The presence of Jews in Marseille can be traced at least to the sixth century: Jews arrived in 574, fleeing forced conversion in Clermont-Ferrand. In 1484 and early 1485, shortly after the incorporation of Provence into France, the Jewish quarter of Marseille was plundered. Jews were murdered and the survivors fled, only to return again after the expulsion of Spanish Jewry in 1492. In the seventeenth century, Jews were expelled. They returned in 1760.

Between 1940 and 1942, Europe's Jews again sought sanctuary in Marseille, then in the Free Zone. My grandparents were among them. Under the Occupation, the Jews were viciously hunted, arrested, and deported; my grandparents escaped with the help of their relatives in America. The dapper New York intellectual Varian Fry came to Marseille to lead the most successful private rescue operation of the Second World War, saving as many as 2,000 Jews, among them Marc Chagall, Max Ernst, Jacques Lipchitz, Hannah Arendt, Heinrich Mann, Franz Werfel, and Alma Mahler Werfel. Of course, he could not save them all. The synagogue on the rue de Breteuil was pillaged and its façade destroyed, the prayer books and the Torah scrolls burned. When the Germans left the city, perhaps 5,000 Jews remained. They rebuilt the community and the synagogue.

Observers have long found Marseille's flamboyantly diverse population alarming: In 1936, the violently anti-Semitic journalist Henri Béraud remarked in *La Gerbe* that inroads to the city had been

> transformed into giant sewers, a growing, crawling, fetid bog running over our land. It is this immense flood of Neapolitan filth, of Levantine rags, of sad, stinking Slavs, of dreadful, miserable Andalusians, the seed of Abraham and the asphalt of Judaea . . . doctrinaire ragheads, moth-eaten Polacks, bastards of the ghettos, smugglers of weapons, desultory *pistoleros,* spies, usurers, gangsters, merchants of women and cocaine, they arrive preceded by their odor and escorted by their germs.[2]

But the inhabitants of Marseille have historically taken pride in the city's vulgar cosmopolitanism, and its immigrants have always been politically powerful. The city has 2,600 years of experience with ethnic diversity, and it has developed strategies to cope with it. These strategies have not always been pretty, but they have worked.

The strategies have not conformed to any legal doctrine of republican France. Far from it. Marseille, autonomous until conquered by Charles of Anjou in the thirteenth century, was not bequeathed to the French crown until 1481 and has in some ways *never* become a fully assimilated French city. It is no great secret that its central political tradition, the one that sets it apart from the rest of France, is its exceptional corruption. Particularly, Marseille has notoriously tolerated crooked alliances between its city officials and its ethnic community leaders. Immigrant groups have flourished under this system of patronage and clientelism, one that has shored up rigged electoral agreements while governing the distribution of subsidies and favors.

Local politicians have traditionally cultivated strong personal relationships with the leaders of Marseille's various ethnic groups. During the Depression, for example, the mobsters Paul Bonnaventure Carbone and François Spirito—a Corsican and a Sicilian—achieved an understanding with Marseille's fascist deputy mayor, Simon Sabiani. By making Carbone's brother the director of the municipal stadium, Sabiani opened municipal employment to Marseille's Corsicans and Sicilians. In return, the enterprising mobsters organized a shock corps to lead Fascist street demonstrations and, when asked, to publicly pummel leftist dockworkers and union members. Curiously, this corrupt and personal political tradition appears to have evolved into a mechanism for managing contemporary ethnic conflict. It is called Marseille Espérance.

Marseille Espérance—the Hope of Marseille—was inaugurated in 1990 by former mayor Robert Vigouroux and formally institutionalized by the current mayor, Jean-Claude Gaudin. Funded by City Hall, Marseille Espérance unites the city's religious leaders around the mayor in a regular discussion group. Everyone I spoke with in Marseille, unanimously, pointed to the organization as key to the city's social harmony. "Marseille Espérance is *very* important," the police chief said. "For unity. As soon as there's a crisis, they calm things, they issue communiqués—they are seen together. It's symbolic, seeing them together, the rabbi, the preacher, the mufti."

Vigouroux created the group in 1990 specifically to stave off ethnoreligious conflict between Jews and Muslims. The extreme Right had recently placed strongly in the polls. Conflict was mounting over the construction of a central mosque in the city. Passions were inflamed by the crisis in the Persian Gulf. The idea behind Marseille Espérance was simple: Each of the city's religious communities would send a delegate to the group, which would meet regularly to discuss civic problems, to "combat intolerance, ignorance, and incomprehension," and to "promote respect for one another."

In the tradition of the city, the mayor maintains strong personal relationships with each member of the group. Whenever tension threatens to rise—for example, after the burning of the Or Aviv Synagogue in 2002, and at the beginning of hostilities in Iraq in 2003—the group meets and at the mayor's urging makes some kind of very public display of solidarity. Islamic leaders were present for the burial of the charred Torah scrolls; they were photographed comforting Jewish religious leaders, standing with them arm in arm. This occurred in no other French city. Members of Marseille Espérance have taken trips to the Wailing Wall. They have hosted conferences and visits from such figures as the Dalai Lama, Elie Wiesel, and the Patriarch of Constantinople. An intercommunity gala is held annually. The organization is so widely held to be effective that government delegations from Brussels, Antwerp, Sarajevo, Barcelona, Naples, Turin, and Montreal have come to study it.

It is entirely counterintuitive that Marseille Espérance should work at all. I would never expect a symbolic and powerless group dedicated to "combating intolerance and ignorance" to be so effective, or, if not effective, to be *perceived* as so effective. But the faith placed in this group by everyone in Marseille was surprising and touching. It was the first thing everyone mentioned to me in our discussions, held out as a model for other cities, offered as proof that if only people would just get together and listen to one another respectfully, strife and violence around the world could be resolved.

I am chary of bodies that, like the League of Nations, appeal to noble principles with no will or mechanism to impose their fine ideals at the barrel of a gun, and refused at first to believe that this group could truly be any kind of key to the city's comparative exemption from ethnic tension. But presented with example after example of Marseille Espérance's civilizing influence, I was forced to conclude there must be something to it. When Ibrahim Ali, a young Comorian, was killed by neo-Nazis, the mayor gathered the delegates of Marseille Espérance and enjoined them to pacify the community. They did so. They did so again when a young Frenchman, Nicolas Bourgat, was stabbed to death by a Moroccan immigrant. Marseille Espérance convened at City Hall after September 11. Standing by the mayor and the chief of police, the group issued a passionate communiqué denouncing religious fanaticism; again, tensions in the city subsided. They convened at the commencement of recent hostilities in Iraq; afterward, at the urging of the mayor, the Muslim delegates returned to their mosques and called for calm. Other Muslim clerics throughout France used this occasion to incite a frenzy of anti-American and anti-Semitic bloodlust.

The crucial point is not whether it works—it does seem to—but why it works. Although no one will admit it, Marseille Espérance is a political sleight of hand. It is, in effect, an end run around the government's anticommunitarian principles. The violence now emerging from Islamic immigrants and directed toward Jews represents a breakdown in the republican scheme: certain Muslim immigrants are proving unassimilable; ethnic identity politics are proving stronger than the republican ideal. Of course, only a fraction of France's Muslims are committing these crimes; most are peaceful citizens, prepared and even eager to be assimilated. But a stubbornly unassimilable rump remains, and it is causing a great deal of grief. Part of the problem, certainly, is that Islam's teachings constitute a political program as well as a religious one: secularism and *laïcité* are not readily reconciled with Islam's insistence on the convergence—the identity, even—of the political and devotional realms.* The French government has no real idea what to do about this; no one in Europe does. There is no tradition, in France as a whole, of managing immigrants who cannot or will not assimilate. But in Marseille, there is.

Since the law forbids the recognition of ethnicity, the city recognizes religions—ethnicity by proxy. Marseille Espérance facilitates the emergence of personalities who represent whole ethnic groups and who forge links between their communities and the rest of the city. It affords Arabs—as Muslims—representation *as a group* in city politics. By means of their strong connection to the mayor's office, community leaders have been able to promote an Islamic agenda effectively. They have secured, for example, elaborate slaughter facilities for the ritual animal sacrifice of Eid-el-Kebir and grave sites for Muslims in the Aygalades Cemetery. Negotiations for the construction of a central mosque and an Islamic cultural center in Marseille are under way. In return, the mayor demands that Islamic leaders keep the extremists in their community in check. Here we see the old Marseille tradition: One hand washes the other.

---

*It would be intellectually indefensible to propose this as a complete explanation for Muslim separatism in France or elsewhere. Islam obviously gives rise to both radical and moderate interpretations; in its moderate interpretations, the acceptance of secular state sovereignty is perfectly admissible—and the great majority of Muslims in France adhere to the moderate view. One question, then, is why the radical element has in recent years gained ground. The growing influence of Saudi Arabian Wahhabism surely plays a sinister role: Saudi Arabia now provides 80 percent of the funding for mosques and Islamic centers in France. Another reason, as Zvi Ammar pointed out, is the explosive proliferation of radicalizing Arab media, disseminated through French cable and satellite television providers. France's perennially high structural unemployment rate does not help matters; economically marginalized youths who see no prospect of advancement in French society will obviously find more to admire in radical separatism than those who view integration as a sure path to social advancement. Finally, most of France's previous immigrants came from Europe, and therefore from cultures more similar to France's own. It is simply easier to bridge the gap between, say, Polish culture and French culture than it is to bridge the gap between Algerian and French culture. If nothing else, consider the subjugated status of women in most Islamic countries, one that is rightly repellent to European sensibilities. Islam has always seen in Christian Europe a rival, not an analogue. It requires a *much* greater stretch for someone born and raised in the Islamic world to become French than it does for someone born and raised in Portugal.

Nothing like Marseille Espérance exists in other French cities. Whatever community leaders and politicians may say—and all will deny it; it is heresy to endorse communitarianism in France—Marseille Espérance institutionalizes and strengthens communitarian politics, and by bringing religion to the forefront of the political sphere, directly contravenes the ideal of *laïcité*. It affords official recognition to personalities who act publicly in the name of their cultural and ethnic communities and who have the power to bring the members of those communities into line. In other words, a system born of Marseille's traditions of patronage and corruption—a tradition entirely antithetical to France's republican ideals—now helps to keep the peace.

It's a gift to Marseille from the mob.

## A DELICATE BALANCE

The mayor, as a personality, is central to this delicately balanced communitarian ecosystem. In an adroit piece of political jujitsu, Jean-Claude Gaudin defeated the National Front in 1995 while simultaneously putting the Left out of power for the first time since 1953. He is notably one of the most philo-Semitic politicians in France, and a committed Zionist. His official visit to Israel in early 2004 took him to Tel Aviv, Jerusalem, Haifa, and Maale Adumim, the largest settlement in the West Bank. There he declared that "Israeli land must not be given to others." "Speak not of colonies," he added, "but of constructions." On the same trip, he remarked that he had come to appreciate the strategic significance of the Golan Heights. Later, on French radio, he insisted that the settlements were "villas, not shantytowns." He stressed to assembled Israeli reporters that he favored the transfer of the French embassy from Tel Aviv to Jerusalem. His philo-Semitism has carried over to the city's politics: He is known for his alacrity in responding to anti-Semitic incidents; when hostile graffiti is reported, for example, he sends his own services to remove it, usually within the hour. This is not the case in other French cities; recently, for example, in Perpignan, I found fading anti-Semitic graffiti—*Juden raus!*—

scrawled on the walls of a children's playground; it had clearly been there for quite some time. I have seen many similar messages in Paris.

Was the mayor a sincere Zionist, I wondered, or was this mere posturing, a quid pro quo in exchange for the electoral support of Marseille's Jews? I put this question to his adjunct mayor, Daniel Sperling, who is also a prominent member of Marseille's Jewish community. "When a mayor takes an interest in Israel," he replied, "of course it's because he's interested in Jews in France. But the mayor is sincere. First of all, he's a practicing Catholic; he comes from the Christian Democratic tradition. . . . The mayor, like Chirac and other members of the Right, has always sincerely admired Israel, the way it was created, the way it works, as a political project, how they transformed the land given them after the Balfour Declaration by means of a strong ideology. . . . The mayor has always been, how to say it, more than respectful. Impressed by the way the Jews have always conducted themselves."

A sincere Zionist, then.

"But until a certain time, he confused Israel and the Jews. Up to a point. It's okay, he understands now. He's an old politician; he's seventy-five years old, he's been in politics for twenty-five years, and for him, Israel *was* the Jews. A few times, talking to Jews of Marseille, he called Israel 'your country.'"

This is quite a fundamental error. To suggest that French Jews are not fully French is not republican at all. Even the mayor of Marseille—and perhaps especially the mayor of Marseille—seems something less than completely committed to this principle.

I wondered to what extent the mayor's public kinship with Israel and Jews was related to Marseille's comparative calm. Had he set the tone for the city? Had he obliquely sent a message to its Arab population that violence against Jews would not be tolerated? "Of course," Sperling said. "The mayor is impressed by zero tolerance, by the example of New York." But he seemed to think the key point was not so much that the mayor had reached out to Marseille's Jews, but that the Jews had reached out to the mayor. "I organized the mayor's last trip to Israel. I'm a member of the many Jewish associations here. For more than thirty years I've been part of the community. I know it by heart.

"But," he quickly added, "my power isn't about lobbying, like in the United States. We don't have anything like AIPAC [the American Israel Public Affairs Committee]. That doesn't exist here; it's not organized like that. It's *more* effective here because it's more discreet, and secret." Sperling presents himself as a superbly articulate, polished politician, so I was surprised that he was willing so freely to admit that Jews exercise covert control over Marseille's politics. The claim seemed both indiscreet and inconsistent with the principle of republicanism—although consistent with everything else I was learning about Marseille. "There are many people here who want to kill me for it, of course." I chuckled politely, then realized he wasn't joking.

Sperling held that despite the way it sounded, the fashion in which he represented his community to the mayor was *not* a form of communitarianism. "Jews aren't a lobby group here the way they are in the United States. That's not in the statutory law of France, of the republic. I am *against* communitarianism. I am a French elected official who happens to be Jewish. But I fight communitarianism. I am part of the French republic. I am elected for all the citizens. That's my personal path. When there are Jewish demonstrations in Marseille, I send a non-Jew to talk to them. Always. So that non-Jews see." What Sperling seemed to be saying, then, was that community politics are only community politics if they take place *in public*. In private, obviously, it's another story.

In any event, the mayor's determination to stamp out anti-Semitism—whether motivated by his sincere idealism or by the Jews' persistent but officially nonexistent lobbying—is clearly relevant to his interest in and commitment to Marseille Espérance.

Of late, Sperling allowed, there has been a bit of a problem. Local Muslims recently elected the radical cleric Mourad Zerfaoui to the presidency of the Regional Muslim Council, and Zerfaoui is not much of a team player. In fact, Zerfaoui is such an extremist—he has condemned Marseille's other Muslim leaders as "puppets who move in the hands of the West and America"—that the mayor's office has no idea how to deal with him, and thus does not. I seized upon this tidbit with interest, wondering if it suggested the limits to the mayor's patience with community politics. I asked Sperling if I might be permitted to speak to the mayor himself. He told me that I could submit my questions to the mayor in writing. I did so, asking—innocently enough, I thought—whether the mayor's refusal to engage with Zerfaoui contravened the spirit of Marseille Espérance.

After several days I had received no answer. I called Sperling to ask whether the mayor had ever received my questions. To my astonishment, I received a ferocious scolding: My question had been, he said, impertinent and inappropriate, and particularly offensive given the time he had generously devoted to discussing Marseille's political life with me. To propose that the mayor was snubbing Zerfaoui, he said, amounted to a declaration of *war,* suggesting as it did that the mayor might be *un raciste.* I am not exaggerating here. He really said this.

I was flummoxed: What on earth was he talking about? At last, after discharging a great deal more spleen, he suffered himself to pass me to the mayor's spokeswoman, Marie-Noëlle Mivielle. She, too, was in a lather about my impertinent question. "It's not the mayor who refuses to speak to Zerfaoui!" she insisted, hysteria creeping into her voice. "It's Zerfaoui who will not return *his* calls!" She stressed to me that the mayor had done *so much* for Marseille's Islamic community, had made *such efforts* to organize planning for the construction of a central mosque, had lent *such support* to the enlargement of existing mosques, had even made available a multipurpose room for Muslim cultural activities! Of course, I said soothingly, of course. Of course he cares. I would never dream of suggesting otherwise.

At that point, I just wanted to get off the phone alive.

This bizarre incident, I suspect, signifies the degree to which communitarian politics have come to dominate Marseille's civic life. The mayor so fears the appearance of excluding *anyone* that I managed to violate six thousand kinds of protocol just by suggesting that he might be. I have never before witnessed such defensiveness about an official's commitment to ethnic outreach—not even on an American university campus. And that's saying something.

## CO-OPTING THE MODERATES: EUROPE'S ONLY HOPE

I stopped in the Internet café below my hotel each morning to check my e-mail. Ads in the window advertised cheap long-distance rates to Algeria, Morocco, the Comoros. When I entered the address of my e-mail server, I looked at the sites checked by patrons before me: www.aljazeera.com. The home page of the Islamic Association for Palestine. These addresses were intermingled with pornography: www.swapyourwife.com. No one looked at anything else. This vivid illustration of the chief concerns of Marseille's exogenous population made the city's harmony seem all the more striking to me. It could so easily be otherwise.

Of course, Marseille is not some kind of pluralistic utopia. While there is less anti-Semitic tension in Marseille than in comparable French cities, there is tension nonetheless. Yet the fact remains that in Marseille, unlike other French cities, the worst of the tension has been dampened. A show of force from the cops, a few calming words from the local mufti, a symbolic meeting of the local religious leaders, and Marseille returned to its usual preoccupations—the football team, the sun, the sea, panthers on the loose. However tempting it is to ridicule the exaggerated political correctness emanating from the mayor's office, it is only honest to concede that they are doing something right, at least for now.

Could these solutions be applied elsewhere? The curious case of Marseille raises important questions for the rest of France, and indeed for much of Europe. As Europe's demography changes, ethnic conflict in its cities will continue to grow. What can be done? Marseille's success in coping with such conflict is, obviously, an advertisement for strong police work—a strategy combining New York–style zero tolerance with personal relationships between police and ethnic community leaders. Marseille is a rebuke to a housing policy that in the rest of France has shunted immigrants to the city periphery. It is an endorsement of social programs that give kids something benign and inexpensive to do.

But most significant, Marseille suggests that the French republican ideal is dying. It was a noble experiment. But its days are over. Marseille functions in large part because its constituent ethnicities, particularly its Arab immigrants, are recognized, organized, courted, and given voice in a formal system. Although everyone in France extols the principle of republicanism, Marseille, by compromising that principle, is the only city in France that has kept the French Intifada at bay.

Now let me make one thing clear: In admiring this achievement, I am in no way endorsing the kind of freewheeling multiculturalism that is, in effect, a moral relativism that often shades into nihilism. Nor am I applauding the self-extinguishing form of tolerance that results in state sponsorship of radical mosques. There is a difference between observing that it is good idea to give ethnic groups a vehicle by which to express themselves politically and declaring that *anything* these ethnic groups want or do is acceptable. But perhaps there is a compromise— one rooted in pragmatism, not ideology. An absolutely uncompromising attitude toward ethnicity, it would seem, disheartens moderates and encourages extremists. When certain groups are given a formal means to express a reasonable and moderate ethnic agenda, the violent and immoderate elements of that group may more readily be contained by the moderate ones, who have been co-opted into the system.

Indeed, France's innovative interior minister has already happened upon this idea: Sarkozy has negotiated with France's moderate Muslim leaders to create the French Muslim Council, the first representative body of French Muslims to be formally recognized by the government. The council will, among other things, secure chaplaincies in the army and prisons, acquire Muslim burial sites, deliver halal meat certificates and build—with the government's financial support—new mosques and prayer halls. "What we should be afraid of," Sarkozy has said, "is Islam gone astray, garage Islam, basement Islam, underground Islam." His implication, obviously, is that there is another kind of Islam, one that can be domesticated, Westernized, co-opted. I hope he is right.

A tradition of corrupt politics is certainly *not* a necessary precondition for the establishment of systems like Marseille's in other cities. All that is required is civic leaders committed to creating and strengthening the city's relationships with ethnic community leaders. Organizations modeled on Marseille Espérance could be created and maintained, with relatively small investment, in any European city. They might work. They might not. They are certainly worth trying.

Anything is worth trying. If immigrants cannot be assimilated and they cannot be sent back—and they can't—Europe must find some way to make its peace with them. If not, as Villepin remarked, the worst is not behind them. It is ahead of them.

CHAPTER 5

# WE SURRENDER!

THE REJECTION OF ALL MORAL ABSOLUTES, Chantal Delsol argues, is the source of the profound risk aversion of the modern European. "In general," she writes, "our contemporary cannot imagine for what cause he would sacrifice his life because he does not know what his life means."[1] Though Delsol does not explicitly say so, this is as good an explanation as we are apt to find for the willingness of the Spanish people instantly and obediently to capitulate to the demands of the terrorists who last year slaughtered some 200 of their countrymen.

On March 11, 2004, three days before Spain's legislative elections—exactly six months after the anniversary of the attacks on the World Trade Center and the Pentagon—terrorists linked to al Qaeda bombed four commuter trains in Madrid, killing nearly 200 men, women, and children and injuring 1,600 more. The bombs had been timed to detonate during the morning rush hour. They exploded with such force that severed limbs were thrown through the windows of nearby apartment buildings.

On the following day, authorities retrieved a videotape from a trash basket near a Madrid mosque. "We declare our responsibility for what happened in Madrid," said the man on the video, who claimed to be issuing a statement from the military spokesman for al Qaeda in Europe. "This is a response to the crimes that you caused in the world, and specifically in Iraq and Afghanistan, and there will be more if God wills it." He added the obvious: "You love life, and we love death."

Hours before the polls opened on Sunday, demonstrators filled the streets of Spain. The focus of their outrage was not al Qaeda but Spanish prime minister José María Aznar, who had committed Spanish troops to Iraq and had, the demonstrators believed, obfuscated evidence that the bombings had been committed by Islamic radicals, not Basque terrorists. The prime minister had been expected to win reelection with a large majority, but the voters responded to the massacre by voting into office the opposition candidate, José Luis Rodríguez Zapatero, who pledged to withdraw Spanish troops from Iraq immediately.

This was precisely what the perpetrators of the massacre intended. Four months before, an entity with ties to al Qaeda called the Media Committee for the Victory of the Iraqi People had used the Internet to publish a document titled *Jihadi Iraq: Hopes and Dangers*. The premise of the document was that the United States could not be defeated by direct military action. Its allies, however, could be pared away, leaving the United States isolated. The committee recommended attacks on the less resolute coalition partners—specifically, "painful strikes" against Spain before its election.

The document was notable for the sophistication of its analysis of Spanish domestic politics. "We think," wrote the author, "that the Spanish government could not tolerate more than two, maximum three, blows, after which it will have to withdraw as a result of popular pressure. If its troops still remain in Iraq after these blows, then the victory of the Socialist Party is almost secured, and the withdrawal of the Spanish forces will be on its electoral program." If Spain was forced out of Iraq, the committee theorized, pressure on the other coalition partners would mount, "and hence the domino tiles would fall quickly." The use of the phrase "domino tiles" suggests that the author was a student not only of contemporary European political culture but also of American foreign policy and its history: It was President Eisenhower who advanced the Domino Theory to justify American support for South Vietnam. It is odd that even in excoriating the United States, militant Islam looked to America for analytic inspiration. It suggests that the author studied at an American or European university.

The following Monday, the prime minister–elect vowed to withdraw Spain's 1,300 troops from Iraq. The Spanish forces there had not been cosmetic; they had been playing an important role in the flashpoint Shia holy city of Najaf and could not readily be replaced. In a statement that passed nearly unnoticed, Zapatero added that he hoped to nurture closer ties between Spain and Morocco. Three of the five men arrested in connection with the bombings were Moroccan. Imagine how the American people would have responded had President Bush announced, following the September 11 attacks, that he hoped to *strengthen* U.S. ties to regimes that harbored terrorists.

By capitulating to the terrorists' demands, the Spanish electorate proved that a well-timed bloodletting could achieve better results than the perpetrators of the slaughter had dared to hope. In doing so, they condemned many more of us to death. Why wouldn't the murderers repeat such a successful experiment? Is it any surprise that they did, in London, in July 2005?

It is painfully obvious that the people of Spain either fundamentally misunderstand—*or do not care about*—the nature of the threat posed to Western civilization by Islamic radicalism. They are not alone, obviously. Shortly after the bombings, Romano Prodi, then president of the European Commission, declared that "using force is not the answer to resolving the conflict with terrorists." In a joint press conference with French president Jacques Chirac, German chancellor Gerhard Schroeder said of terrorism, "Military force is not the only solution. One needs to look at the roots of it, including lack of development in the developing world."

This is an extraordinary thing to say in the aftermath of such an event. For one thing, it's nonsense: The world's fifty least-developed nations rarely produce terrorists. Who has ever died at the hands of a terrorist from Upper Volta? Samoa? Equatorial Guinea? Consider UNESCO's list of the world's forty-nine least-developed countries: So little are they known for exporting terrorism that one might with equal logic conclude that the *remedy* for terrorism is lack of development.* The nineteen hijackers who took 3,000 human lives on September 11 were mostly educated, upper-middle-class Saudis, citizens of one of the most developed countries in the Middle East. The terrorists who attacked London came from Britain.

But more important, what the Spanish voters and European leaders seem *unwilling* to comprehend—surely not *unable,* for the concepts are not complex—is that this, like the battles against fascism and communism, is an ideological conflict, not an economic one, and it is a conflict against a pitiless enemy that seeks the destruction of modernity and nothing less. This point may readily be confirmed by consulting Osama bin Laden's multiple fatwas to this effect, which conspicuously lack clauses offering an end to the unpleasantness in exchange for an infusion of development aid. These documents, much like Hitler's *Mein Kampf,* tell the world exactly what the author has in mind and how he plans to achieve it. One need only read them to understand the terrorists' program completely; they are available on the Internet. The goal is the worldwide establishment of a medieval caliphate—a global Taliban regime. No one can say we were not warned.

## WHETTING THE ALLIGATOR'S APPETITE

If the Spanish believe their conflict with Islamism to have been resolved by their withdrawal from Iraq, they are living in a fantasy. The

---

*The list: Afghanistan, Angola, Bangladesh, Benin, Bhutan, Burkina Faso, Burundi, Cambodia, Cape Verde, the Central African Republic, Chad, Comoros, the Democratic Republic of the Congo, Djibouti, East Timor, Equatorial Guinea, Eritrea, Ethiopia, Gambia, Guinea, Guinea-Bissau, Haiti, Kiribati, the Lao People's Democratic Republic, Lesotho, Liberia, Madagascar, Malawi, Maldives, Mali, Mauritania, Mozambique, Myanmar, Nepal, Niger, Rwanda, Samoa, Sao Tome and Principe, Senegal, Sierra Leone, Solomon Islands, Somalia, Sudan, Tanzania, Togo, Tuvalu, Uganda, Vanuatu, Yemen, and Zambia. Of this list, only Afghanistan and Sudan notably export terrorists. Terrorists tend to come from Chechnya, Lebanon, Libya, Iran, Iraq, the Israeli Occupied Territories, Pakistan, Sudan, Syria, and Uzbekistan. These places obviously have something in common, but it is not underdevelopment.

terrorists themselves explicitly placed their attack in the larger context of Islam's expulsion from the Iberian peninsula in the fifteenth and sixteenth centuries. In the videotape discovered after the bombing, one of the terrorists can be heard referring to Spain as "the land of Tarik ibn-Ziyad," the first Arab leader to cross the Strait of Gibraltar in 711. Another said, "You know the Spanish crusade against Muslims, the expulsion from al-Andalus and the tribunals of the Inquisitions, that was not so long ago." These are not isolated statements. The corpus of Islamist doctrine is clear on this point: The expulsion from Spain was the most bitter of historic grievances visited upon Islam. This is a living memory, one that vitalizes the terrorists' quest for vengeance, a humiliation they fully intend to reverse.

Given the choice between war and dishonor, the Spanish chose dishonor. They would have war as well. Two weeks after the election, another massive bomb was discovered on Spain's high-speed train line, forty miles south of Madrid. Had it detonated, the carnage would have considerably exceeded that of the previous bombings. The promise to withdraw from Iraq predictably did no more than whet the alligator's appetite. Clint Eastwood's creation, Dirty Harry, was asked why he was so sure the freed murderer of a little girl would continue to kill. "Because he likes it," he replied. Exactly so. *They like it.*

In the succeeding months, Spanish security services narrowly foiled plots to blow up the Spanish High Court and the Madrid soccer stadium. In September 2004, Spanish police arrested a cell of Pakistani drug dealers and extortionists with links to al Qaeda. The cell had been sending money to the group of Islamic radicals who killed journalist Daniel Pearl in 2002 in Pakistan. Their video collection suggested their keen interest in the architecture of unusually large buildings in Barcelona. From this alone, it would seem that Spain's new Iraq policy has not worked as planned.

It is possible for reasonable men to argue that the war in Iraq was a misguided step in the battle against Islamic fundamentalism. It is not possible, however, for reasonable men to believe that the Spanish withdrawal from Iraq *at that moment and in that context,* coupled with comments like Prodi's and Schroeder's, would not thrill and embolden terrorists around the world, confirming to them their belief in the decadence and pusillanimity of the West, bringing even graver jeopardy upon Europe, the United States, and their allies. Again, this point can readily be confirmed at the source: Bin Laden himself has spoken, often, of the delirious exhilaration and inspiration he derives from each instance of Western capitulation to terror. In this 1996 fatwa, for example, he considers the American withdrawal from Somalia:

> When tens of your soldiers were killed in minor battles and one American Pilot was dragged in the streets of Mogadishu you left the area carrying disappointment, humiliation, defeat and your dead with you. Clinton appeared in front of the whole world threatening and promising revenge, but these threats were merely a preparation for withdrawal. You have been disgraced by Allah and you withdrew; the extent of your impotence and weaknesses became very clear. It was a pleasure for the "heart" of every Muslim and a remedy to the "chests" of believing nations to see you defeated in the three Islamic cities of Beirut, Aden and Mogadishu.

Can there really be any doubt about how the Spanish withdrawal from Iraq would have been perceived by Bin Laden and those who share his ideology? Can there be much doubt about how they understood Prodi's and Schroeder's comments?

Of course it is true that military force is not the only solution. *Overwhelming* military force is the only solution. If Prodi does not believe force to be the answer to resolving the conflict with terrorists, how does he propose combating terrorists who believe force to be the answer to resolving their conflict with us? They have demonstrated their willingness to kill us by the thousands and have clearly stated their ambitious plans to kill as many more of us as possible, preferably with chemical, biological, and nuclear weapons. One of the Madrid bombing suspects, not incidentally, was found with floor plans to Grand Central Station on his computer. Why would Europe's leaders seek to diminish this dreadful truth while the blood of their compatriots was not yet dry, rather than morally and psychologically preparing their citizens for a long military conflict against a depraved enemy—a conflict brought to European soil only days before?

Schroeder's comments were not merely an abdication of leadership, they were astonishingly insensitive to historic resonance. Confronting in the Nazis a similarly murderous, anti-Semitic, and expansionist ideology, British prime minister Neville Chamberlain happened upon the identical response. "We should seek," he said, "by all means in our power to avoid war, by analyzing possible causes, by trying to remove them, by discussion in a spirit of collaboration and good will." The consequences of his posture have now passed into infamy. Yes, yes, I *do* keep bringing up the Nazis. Those who would argue that this is not the correct historical analogy are challenged to find one single relevant place where the analogy fails.

Had the Spanish government responded to the Madrid bombings by announcing that in light of this irrefutable confirmation of al Qaeda's connection to Iraq, Spain would now not only refuse to withdraw but *quintuple* its troop strength, the more rational calculators among those tempted to emulate the bombers might have been given pause to ponder. Imagine Schroeder speaking thus: *Never give in— never, never, never, never, in nothing great or small, large or petty, never give in except to convictions of honor and good sense. Never yield to force; never yield to the apparently overwhelming might of the enemy.* That, of course, is what Churchill said—and it is Churchill, not Chamberlain, whom history has vindicated—but it is impossible to imagine any contemporary European leader saying any such thing.

How is it possible that Europeans could fail to see in Spain's flight, to hear in the rhetoric of its leaders, the echo of Neville Chamberlain? How is it possible that Europe could *again* be embracing appeasement? Why are Europeans so unwilling to fight for their civilization and so willing to surrender to wicked, bloodthirsty ideologues who despise every value and freedom Europeans profess to cherish? Chantal Delsol's answer makes sense: They cannot imagine fighting for a cause because they no longer believe a cause may be worth a fight.

# CHAPTER 6

# NO PAST, NO FUTURE, NO WORRIES

R ECENTLY, WANDERING THROUGH PERUGIA, in Italy, I stopped in the Pasticceria Sandri, a ravishing, high-ceilinged pastry shop built in 1871. I took in the pyramids of chocolates on filigreed silver platters, wrapped in sparkling blue-and-silver foil; the extravagant platters of pastries made from raisins, spices, figs, walnuts, apples, cocoa powder; the boxes of panettone, wrapped in thin golden paper, piled high on the countertops. The air was fragrant with anise and almonds and the whole bakery seemed to sparkle, as if dusted in spun sugar. The exuberantly frescoed walls were decorated with toys—glassy-eyed antique dolls and marionettes, cheerful wooden drums, soldiers, brightly painted figurines, music boxes. I am sure that every Italian in Perugia has nostalgic memories of that shop, of the way Mamma took them there for a *sfogliatelle* with hot chocolate after school, as a special treat. The place was, clearly, designed to delight children.

But there were no children in the Pasticceria Sandri. Not one. Nor were there any on the streets of Perugia. I looked carefully, in the evening, when the crowds poured into the Corso for the *passeggiata*. The city's twelfth-century aqueduct culminates at the piazza in a marble fountain with sculpted panels depicting animals and mythological creatures. There were no children examining them, no parents gently explaining, *Now, that is a unicorn, Bruno, and that, that is a faun.*

The piazza is framed on one side by an opulent palace built of travertine and local stones, on the other by the high Gothic windows and Baroque façade of the Cathedral of San Lorenzo, where Urban IV is buried, and where, under the portico, a section of the city's original Roman walls endures. There were no parents pushing strollers past the palace, no grandparents coaxing hesitant toddlers down the cathedral stairs. I saw thousands of Italians walking, shopping, gabbling with friends, taking *aperitivi,* sitting on the San Lorenzo steps and watching the other people passing by—but I did not see one single child.

On my flight to Italy, I had noticed an article in the in-flight magazine about a long-limbed woman in her thirties, evidently at her leisure at a beach resort. Wearing a gauzy white dress, she stood at the edge of the sea, gazing into the horizon, alone. She lounged in the solarium, alone. She sipped a tropical drink, alone. On the next page, a sidebar translated the text into crude English:

The portrait of a generation in skirt that rides a new philosophy of life: gathering in urban tribes and—above all—escaping from marriage. About thirty years old, with good education and a medium-high income, good looking, single for choice rather than for need, they are an army of women living in solitude as a period of their life, maybe transitory, certainly positive. A portion of the existence suspended among the dependence upon the parents, the complications of life in pair and the responsibility towards the family. A privileged moment to live alternating happy hours with friends to evenings at home, with a cucumber mask on the face, watching a movie and weeping, eating a light single-portion dinner, wearing an old sweater and wool unmatched socks. Spinster, therefore, has no more a negative meaning.

I looked up at the flight attendant who was pouring my coffee. She seemed remarkably cheerful for a spinster who had spent the past night weeping alone in her unmatched socks with a cucumber mask on her face, whether that had a negative meaning or not.

The sociological developments so cheerfully celebrated in that magazine are in fact an utter catastrophe for Italy, as they are in the rest of Europe. Not since the Great Plague has Europe's population been so dramatically gutted. Italian women are, as the magazine correctly noted, postponing marriage. When they do have children, late in life, they are having very few of them—rarely more than one. Over the past twenty-five years, Italy's birthrate has plummeted. It is now the lowest in Western Europe.*

If a society has modern standards of medical care, the inevitable correlate of a decline in births is a rise in the elderly proportion of the population. Italy is now the first country in human history with more people over the age of sixty than under the age of twenty. If current trends continue, according to the UN's projections, the next fifty years will see Italy's population drop from 57.5 million to 45 million. The youngest generation, children under the age of fourteen, will shrink by 14 percent. The cohort of people between fifteen and sixty-four—working age—will shrink by 44 percent. The aged population, over sixty-four, will grow by 50 percent. There will be a 160 percent increase in the population of Italians over the age of eighty.[1] Imagine the state of Italian universities, music, literature, theater, the arts when its population comes to be distributed in that manner.

The contraction of Italy's population has had drastic economic repercussions already. Italian industries are suffering severe labor shortages. Italy's extensive welfare system—funded through workers' wages—is going bankrupt. Ten years ago, Italians who had worked for twenty-five years could look forward to retiring at the age of forty-three with a pension that amounted to 80 percent of their salary. The narrowing tax base has forced the government to raise the retirement age to fifty-seven. In 2008, it will be raised again to sixty.[2] The government recently proposed raising it to sixty-five, a suggestion that triggered labor unrest and strikes.**

---

*There is some debate whether this distinction belongs to Italy or Spain. It's more or less a tie.

**In fairness, strikes cannot necessarily be taken as important indicators of popular opposition. Italians are known to strike at any provocation, and work stoppages have a remarkable tendency to coincide with important football matches.

The Italian case is the most extreme, but throughout Europe the birthrate has been declining since the Second World War. Demographers speak of the total fertility rate, or the number of children the average woman is apt to have over the course of her reproductive life span. That rate is now about 1.5 in Europe. Scandinavia, Britain, and the Netherlands are slightly more fecund—total fertility rates there are slightly above 1.7. But Ireland and France are the only countries in the European Union where fertility approaches the so-called replacement rate of 2.1, the level required to keep population levels stable.* When total fertility rates drop below a certain point, a shrinking population will enter a sudden, steep spiral of decline. Demographers call this phenomenon negative momentum, and Europe is on the verge of it. Gross domestic product will drop commensurately. Imminent depopulation means that no one need worry about Europe's aspirations to become an economic superpower, or any kind of superpower, for that matter.

Unless these trends reverse themselves—and there is no reason to imagine they will—European countries will soon be unable to make payments on their extensive pension and health care programs. No serious economist disputes that at this rate, barring reform, Europe's pension schemes, along with the rest of its costly social welfare programs, will bankrupt the Continent within a generation. Immigration is Europe's only hope. There *is* no alternative, unless Europeans are prepared to give up on the welfare state, and they are not. Whenever pension reform is proposed in France, Germany, Spain, and Italy, protesters immediately take to the streets in numbers sufficient to bring civic life to a halt and cause swift, devastating economic damage. It does not seem to trouble them that the economies they are damaging are the source of the welfare payments they are trying to protect. Labor unrest and demonstrations routinely cripple French transportation and public services. Italy—all of it—is more or less permanently on strike.

But immigration in numbers adequate to rectify the population de-

---

*This assumes the mortality rate is a constant. In Western Europe these days, it is.

cline will come at a huge cost in social stability, particularly if the majority of immigrants are Muslims, as they are now. Immigration levels are nowhere near high enough now to offset the diminution of Europe's native population: to do so they would have to be five to ten times higher still. Particularly given Europe's high rate of unemployment—some 15 to 20 million Europeans are jobless—it is hardly likely that so many immigrants could easily be culturally, politically, or economically integrated.

The latter point is so obvious that it hardly needs to be argued, but if in doubt, consider this: Shortly after September 11, the Italian journalist Oriana Fallaci published a passionate and undisciplined polemic called *The Rage and the Pride*. In passages that infuriated anti-discrimination activists—who sought to have the book banned—Fallaci castigated her countrymen for permitting immigrants to overrun Italian cities. Here she describes a tent erected in the center of Florence by Somali vagrants:

> Mothers, fathers, brothers, sisters, uncles, aunts, cousins, pregnant sisters-in-law, and if they had their way, their relatives' relatives as well. . . . A tent placed in front of the cathedral with Brunelleschi's cupola and by the side of the Baptistery with Ghiberti's golden doors. A tent, finally, furnished like a sleazy little apartment: seats, tables, chaise-lounges, mattresses for sleeping and for fucking, ovens for cooking food and plaguing the piazza with smoke and stench. . . . Thanks to a radio tape player, enriched by the uncouth wailing of a muezzin who punctually exhorted the faithful, deafened the infidels, and smothered the sound of the church bells. Add to all this the yellow streaks of urine that profaned the marble of the Baptistery. (My, these sons of Allah sure have a long range! However did they manage to hit the target when they were held back by a protective railing that kept it nearly two whole meters away from their urinary equipment?) And along with the yellow streaks of urine, the stench of the excrement that blocked the door of San Salvatore al Vescovo: that exquisite Romanesque church (year 1000) that stands at the

rear of the Piazza del Duomo and that the sons of Allah transformed into a shithouse.[3]

Fallaci was of course immediately condemned by Europe's politicians, clergy, academics, and journalists as a hysterical bigot. This she may be—I'm staying out of this one—but here is the point: *The Rage and the Pride,* a violent, uncensored anti-immigration manifesto, was also the most successful book ever published in Italy. The entire first edition, 200,000 copies, sold out within hours. For months, the publisher printed 50,000 new copies a day. Italians who had never before visited a bookstore waited on line for copies. It was also the number one best-seller in Germany, France, and Spain. The success of Fallaci's book should be a hint that Europeans are not adjusting well to immigration, nor are immigrants adjusting well to Europe.

Anti-immigration parties are gaining strength across the Continent. If immigration rises to ten times the current levels, Europe will explode. If it doesn't, Europe will implode.

## "ITALIANS HAVE, YOU KNOW, BEEN AROUND FOREVER"

However uneasily Italians view immigration, few seem fully to appreciate that the only alternative, if their country is to avoid terminal decline, is reproduction. When I was last in Rome, a friend introduced me to two Roman girls, both from distinguished Roman families. Giulia Arceri is twenty and Cristina Rossi is twenty-one. We sat on a bench beneath a spreading Roman pine in the courtyard of a villa on the crest of the Janiculum, Rome's highest hill, where the shadows cast by the sharp light made the courtyard look like a chiaroscuro painting by a Renaissance master, and discussed Italy's future. "Are you worried," I asked them both, "about the decline of Italy's population?"

Giulia looked at me as if I had asked whether she was alarmed by the remilitarization of Alpha Centauri. "No," she said finally.

"Does anyone in Italy worry about it?" I asked.

They both giggled. At last Cristina spoke up: "I don't *think* so."

"Why not? After all, if current trends continue, there will be no Italians."

They soaked that thought in for a while. Giulia waved her hand in the general direction of the Coliseum, the Arch of Constantine, the Forum. "I guess we think," she said, "that Italians have, you know, been around forever."

They *have* been around forever, that's what's so mystifying about it, and that's what makes all the explanations generally on offer for this demographic transformation seem so inadequate. Some attribute the decline of Italy's population to rapid industrialization, which, accompanied by urbanization, has broken up traditional family networks. They note that rural Italians traditionally viewed children, who provided farm labor, as an economic asset, whereas urbanized Italians see them as an economic burden. Some note that better medical services, and a resultant decrease in infant mortality, have led Italians to bear fewer children in the expectation that more will survive.

It is not just Europe. Virtually every advanced industrial democracy is suffering from population decline. But there is one enormous exception: the United States. If industrialization, urbanization, and medical advances necessarily led to population decline, one would expect the American population to be declining fastest of all. During the 1970s, American fertility briefly dropped below the replacement rate. But in the 1990s, the trend reversed itself. The United States now has an annual population growth of 1.1 percent, higher than China's and by far the highest of the developed countries. There are 3 million new Americans born each year. The population of the United States is about 293 million. If the total fertility rate stays at current levels, there will be about 600 million Americans by the end of the century.

Some see the cause of Italy's population decline in the diminished role of the Church and the loss of traditional Catholic values. (Italy's Catholics have been vigorous lobbyists for solutions to save the Italian family from extinction, but they have not been particularly successful, and Rome, as it happens, has the lowest fertility rate in Italy.) Others place the blame on the Italian government, which has taken few measures to provide child care or social support to mothers. Some fault Italy's high housing costs, which encourage children to live with their parents well into middle age. The Italian rental market is over-regulated, making it difficult to find a house or apartment. It is nearly impossible to get a mortgage to buy a home: The Italian banking sector, which runs on a complex, antique system of family cross-shareholding that protects banks from competition and takeover, is Europe's least competitive and least responsive to market demand.

Quite a few commentators point to the near-congenital immaturity of Italian men, who, Italian woman complain—and complain, and complain, and complain—are lazy, spoiled, self-indulgent, unfaithful, slovenly, and swinish, unwilling to help with household chores, incapable even of dressing themselves without their mother's aid. Italian women, evidently, consider them unfit for reproduction.[4]

All these theories doubtless have some explanatory power. But none is fully satisfying. If a woman badly wants to have a baby, she will go to great lengths to do so, whatever the economic obstacles and the inconvenience, even if she has no partner at all. One need only spend a day at a fertility clinic to see that this is so. So why do Italians—and Europeans generally—now need to be coaxed, forced, cajoled, or bribed into doing something that has always been viewed as the central imperative of existence, the act that most lends meaning to people's lives?

## THE LOSS OF A VISION

Something else about Italy immediately strikes the visitor as odd. Again take Perugia: The city center is an ancient, melancholy maze of arched caverns and twisting alleys, built on a jutting hill that dominates the Tiber Valley. In the winter, fog snakes over the rooftop gardens and pours into the narrow streets. Perugia was the capital of the Etruscan empire, and an imaginative spectator can inspect the original Etruscan gates, thousands of years old, and for a flicker of a moment see ghostly Etruscans passing below, then scuttling off through the misty, narrow streets, fretting about the prospect of imminent obliteration by the Romans.

But if you descend that hill to the outskirts of the city, you will see housing projects made of clapboard and cheap, cracking cement. The buildings are tall and unornamented. They are not made of local stone and they do not use local colors. They look like giant tombstones. The squat concrete shopping malls on the outer rings of the city are sprawling, unplanned developments completely antithetical in spirit to traditional Italian architecture and civic design. If historically the Italian city was contrived to draw city dwellers into the streets in a kind of daily communal celebration, these suburbs seem designed to foster anomie and indifference to civic life. All the suburbs around Italy's great cities—Rome, Venice, Florence, Naples—look like this.

These gloomy suburbs are where Italians live now, not the picturesque city centers, which have become too costly for all but the most successful urban elites and the handful of ancient families who pass their apartments from one generation to the next. Ordinary Italians visit the city center as an outing, or to shop, then return to their modern neighborhoods. They no longer live on charmingly haphazard streets scaled to a pedestrian size—they live on streets laid out in rectangular grids, where the traffic and pollution are nearly overwhelming. In the winter, when it rains, the oppressive concrete buildings turn dark and glowering. The long concrete blocks form wind tunnels. In the summer, there are no shady alleyways. To save heat or to keep out the sun, the windows are always shuttered, and the shutters are made of ugly metal, giving the impression that the buildings have no windows at all—they appear to be nothing more than concrete and metal walls.

The streets are decorated not with frescoes but with trash cans and billboards featuring vaguely pornographic advertisements for Italy's three competing cell phone companies, or for competing funeral homes (funerals with honor, or funerals at the lowest prices, guaranteed).

There are few trees in the suburbs, no public spaces—and where there are public spaces, they are nearly empty, with no cafés, no churches. The piazza is no longer the center of civic life. And while the architecture in the historic city centers is carefully preserved by diligent curators, their streets and walls are covered with graffiti. No one cleans it off.*

Italy's coastlines, too, have been desecrated from end to end with urban sprawl, industrial parks, landfills, and unremittingly ugly tourist resorts. The waters have been polluted, often by sewage. This is *not* the inevitable consequence of economic development: The California coastlines are by comparison pristine, and California's economy is roughly the size of Italy's. This is a monument to greed, and shortsighted greed at that: by permitting the beauty of the coasts to be destroyed, Italians have ensured that in due course they will cease to be tourist attractions.

But it is not just greed and shortsightedness at work here—Italians have not become *more* greedy and shortsighted than they were when *The Merchant of Venice* was written. Italy has clearly experienced a change in some kind of collective cultural vision. In the age of Michelangelo and Leonardo, the city planners of Florence supervised the development of the city in minute detail, concerned, above all, to cultivate the absolute value of absolute beauty. When Stendhal visited Florence, he reported that

> the tide of emotion was as intense as a religious feeling. My soul . . . was in a state of trance. Absorbed in the contemplation of sublime beauty, I could perceive its very essence close at hand. . . . I had reached that most high degree of sensitivity in which the divine intimations of art merge with the sensuality of emotion. . . . I was seized by a fierce palpitation of the heart. I walked on fearing that I might fall to the ground.[5]

---

*The Italian tradition of political graffiti dates from the Roman era, so perhaps this is not remarkable.

In the late 1970s, the chief of psychiatry at Florence's Santa Maria Nuova Hospital described a phenomenon she termed Stendhal's syndrome—an intoxication with Florence's high Renaissance beauty so intense as to inspire dizziness, fainting, even outright madness. It is still quite common among visitors, apparently.

How is it that the inheritors of Italian culture have lost the genius for creating this kind of beauty? And what does it mean that they have? I had filed this question in its own mental category, but while I was thinking about Italy's declining population, I received a letter from David Hazony, the editor of *Azure,* a journal published in Jerusalem. David immigrated to Israel from the United States as an adult. He is in his mid-thirties and the father of eight children. I had asked him why he had undertaken willingly to raise so large a family, wondering if his response might help me to understand why Italians, by and large, no longer feel this impulse. I had expected him to say something about his religious beliefs, but his answer made no reference to religion.

> People who live in civilizations with a strong sense of history are more likely to want to have more kids. If you are encouraged to think of your culture as something important within the flow of human history, something that is handed from one generation to the next, then you will feel a debt to the past and an obligation to the future, and you are more likely to relate to the project of having kids with a certain degree of seriousness. Raising children is hard and mostly thankless, so you need a good reason to do so, even if it's to some extent instinctive or intuitive. It is through kids that people express a certain fundamental loyalty to something greater than themselves. Conversely, societies that discourage reverence for the past, that discourage loyalty in general, will almost automatically undermine any kind of vision for the future—since once you have disregarded the past, you have no reason to think that the next generation will not similarly discard whatever you have done. The result: People are more likely to have fewer kids.[6]

I doubt this is a complete explanation for Italy's declining birth-rate. Clearly the problem is complex and multifaceted. But having seen the architecture of contemporary Italy, I wonder if he might not be on to something.

## ARE THE AXIS POWERS PUNISHING THEMSELVES?

Although strictly economic explanations do not seem adequate to explain Europe's large-scale population trends, countries that invest in policies to make it easier to have and raise children do tend to have higher fertility rates than those that don't. The showcase example is France, which now has a total fertility rate of 1.89, the highest rate in Europe save Ireland. Women in France are entitled to four months of paid maternity leave, with job protection and a range of benefits to offset the costs of education, housing, and transport. The more children a Frenchwoman has, the more benefits she receives. In recent years, France's natural population growth—that is, growth excluding immigration—has accounted for nearly all of Europe's natural population growth. Swedish fertility, too, spiked when the state began offering extensive financial benefits to mothers.

In 2003, Silvio Berlusconi's center-right government introduced a scheme to bribe couples into having a second child with a 1,000-euro bonus. Few have taken it—the amount is considered insultingly trivial by most Italian women, as indeed it is. The Italian government is making no plans to invest in social services needed by working mothers.

Why is Italy reluctant to take steps that might reverse, or at least slow, its declining birthrate? Because these schemes instantly call to mind Mussolini's campaign to raise the Italian birthrate. Mussolini, believing a nation's dominance to be tied directly to its population, sought to increase Italy's population by 20 million people. "Fertile people," he declared, "have a right to an Empire, those with the will to propagate their race on the face of the earth."[7] To encourage marriage, he decreed a tax on all bachelors. He implemented a scheme of financial aid for large families, offering bonuses to the families of soldiers and civil servants for each new child. Childbearing contests were held: the winners were applauded as national heroes, reviewed on parades, given medals, and sent on promotional tours of Italy; their faces beamed from the covers of Italian magazines and newspapers. Abortion and contraception were severely criminalized. Italian women were inundated with unrelenting propaganda encouraging domesticity and maternity. It is no surprise that schemes for increasing fertility are now, in the Italian mind, intimately associated with the memories of Fascism.

This was also true in Germany and Spain, the two other European nations where birthrates are now declining most precipitously. Franco, too, equated a people's influence with the size of its population and took measures much like Mussolini's to increase birthrates. The Nazis were obsessed with German population growth. Central to Nazi ideology was an emphasis on traditional gender roles, and from the time the Nazis came to power, their propaganda focused intensely on German women, urging them to stay at home and bear as many children as possible. Grants were awarded to "hereditarily healthy" German families with four or more offspring. Mothers of large families received the Cross of Honor of the German Mother. Fathers received cash awards. Whenever aggressive schemes are now proposed to raise the German birthrate—which is in steep decline, and lowest, interestingly, among German academics[8]—vehement objections are raised, and these objections inevitably make reference to the Nazis.

It is enormously suggestive that birthrates are dropping faster in the former powers of the Axis than anywhere else in the world. It is tempting to wonder whether, in some way, the experiences of the Second World War convinced people in these countries, at a deep, inarticulate level, that they do not deserve to exist.

When one accepts (if only unconsciously) the precept that one's life is essentially meaningless, and that one's own culture and values are in no way so commendable that they deserve perpetuation, the impetus to risk one's life or sacrifice one's comfort to defend that culture and those values is strongly diminished in favor of seizing temporary daily pleasure and gratification. The impulse to replicate oneself becomes starkly attenuated. Contemporary man, writes Chantal Delsol,

> no longer seeks any joy he cannot have in the present. If he dismisses eternity and immortality, it is because he is tired of seeing the present sacrificed for an uncertain future. Too often duped, like someone whose hovel has been expropriated on the promise of a palace that never materializes, he now only wishes to take advantage of his brief but sure duration on this earth. . . . He will hear nothing of sacrificing his own inclinations in order to perpetuate a family business or preserve material things. . . . He has seen so many inherited certainties, institutions and behavior patterns turn out to be indefensible that it is without regret that he abandons all of these obligations.[9]

Without regret, perhaps—but surely not without consequences.

## CHAPTER 7

# BLACK-MARKET RELIGION: THE NINE LIVES OF JOSÉ BOVÉ

If anything ail a man so that he does not perform his functions, if he has a pain in the bowel, even . . . he forthwith sets about reforming—the world.

—HENRY DAVID THOREAU, *Walden*

YET IT IS DIFFICULT TO BELIEVE in nothing. European men and women still confront the same existential questions, the same mysteries, the same suffering as everyone who has ever been born. They are suspicious now of the Church and of grand political ideologies, but they nonetheless by nature yearn for the transcendent. And so they worship other things—crops, for example, which certain Europeans, like certain tribal animists, have come to regard with superstitious awe. If asked, they will not say that they are *worshipping* their crops, of course. Officially, they do not worship anything. But in practice their activities take a particular and recognizable form, their rhetoric employs a distinct and familiar vocabulary, and their beliefs form part of a European religious tradition no less ancient than the Papacy.

As a case study, let us look now at one particular purveyor to Europe of black-market religion, José Bové. The charismatic anarchosyndicalist was born—most recently—in 1953 in Bordeaux, in the southwest of France, where he is usually born, although he has been born, from time to time, in Flanders, and in Westphalia, and sometimes he has been born in Hungary. He has occasionally been born in Holland, and he has been particularly apt to be born in the Rhine Valley. The most recently born Bové is a great folk hero in France, a modern Robin Hood, they say, or when they are being more Gallic about it, a modern Vercingetorix, who in 53 B.C. raised an army against the Roman legions wintering in Gaul.* Bové is applauded for standing up against what he calls "the totalitarianism of capitalism." The founder of the powerful French farmer's union, the Confédération Paysanne, and the leading spokesman for the international peasant movement Via Campesina, he advocates agriculture based on the family farm and what he terms "food sovereignty," which he defines as a nation's ability to grow, rather than import, its own crops. Bové seeks strict government controls on agriculture, as well as high subsidies and tariff barriers to protect the kind of local farming he favors. He has become one of the most vivid and visible spokesmen of the antiglobalization movement, and a leading critic of genetically modified organisms, or GMOs.

Bové speaks English fluently, having at the age of three accompanied his impeccably bourgeois parents—who have no traditional farming roots whatsoever—to the United States, where they conducted research in agricultural chemistry at the University of California at Berkeley. Few of Bové's followers realize that his father leads French research into GMOs, and has notably saved Brazil's orange industry by creating a transgenic orange immune to the insect-borne disease that once destroyed 300 million Brazilian trees. The elder Bové was until recently director of the French National Institute for Agronomic Research near Bordeaux, and his infrequent but exasperated public comments about his son's activist agenda suggest that he wishes he had taken the time to genetically modify his own organism. It is tempting to

---

*When this analogy is made, it is for some reason always forgotten that Vercingetorix ultimately permitted himself to be given up to the Romans. The Gallic chieftain languished in the Tullianum at Rome for five years before his public beheading in 46 B.C.

view the younger Bové's career entirely through the obvious oedipal prism. But there is more to the story.

Bové attended a Catholic secondary school near Paris, from which he was expelled—significant enough, as we shall see—for rejecting Catholic doctrine. He declined a university education, instead joining a group of conscientious objectors to military service. This led him to the protests against the militarization of the Larzac, a limestone plateau in the south of the Massif Central, where French farmers fought against the extension of military camps between 1971 and 1981. Arrested for invading a French army base during a 1976 protest, Bové spent three weeks in prison. Following this, he attended a "direct action" training camp in Libya sponsored by Muammar Qaddafi. ("Direct action" is a common leftist euphemism for violence or, in fact, terrorism, as in the French Leninist terrorist group of the same name, Action Directe.) No one has any idea what he did there, or if they do, they are not saying.

Bové formed the Confédération Paysanne in 1987, becoming one of its three principal spokesmen, and certainly its most telegenic. He led the destruction of GMO rice plants at the Nerac research lab early in 1999, then pillaged a Novartis seed production facility and the greenhouses of a public research center. He has been credited with hijacking shipments of biotechnology-grown corn.

The Larzac is where Bové now lives, and the Larzac was the site of a massive demonstration against the World Trade Organization in August 2003. It was in the Larzac that Bové learned the fundamentals of sheep farming. In between public appearances and prison time, Bové produces what I am told is an excellent Roquefort.

## THE FIRST LIFE OF JOSÉ BOVÉ

It is not clear when exactly the first José Bové was born. The year, perhaps, was A.D. 560. The place was Bourges, we believe, in the Loire Valley. The man first came to the attention of St. Gregory, Bishop of Tours, in 591; he writes of him in his *Historia Francorum*.[1] We do not know the man's name, so let us call him the ur-Bové. The ur-Bové, afflicted by madness induced by a swarm of flies, made his way to Arles, where he became a hermit devoted to prayer. When he emerged from his ascetic seclusion, he pronounced himself possessed of the gifts of healing and prophecy. Indeed, he declared, he was Christ himself. His unlettered contemporaries agreed, flocking to him in great numbers to be healed by his touch. He displayed such powers that Gregory sensed the hand of the Devil.

His followers brought him gifts, which he distributed to the poor. He insisted that his followers worship him, and they did. Later, he organized them into an armed band; he led them through the French countryside, ransacking and pillaging, ultimately arriving at Le Puy, where his stark naked messengers streaked into the city, vaulting and somersaulting, to announce his arrival to the bishop. The bishop sent a party to meet the ur-Bové: they chopped him into pieces.

Gregory was much dismayed by these events; connecting the advent of the false prophet with the occurrence of famine, he concluded that the end was nigh.

That is all we know of the ur-Bové.

## THE DARK ANGEL OF THE ANTIGLOBALIZATION MOVEMENT

The Great Peasant Revolt of 1999 began in August after the United States imposed tariffs on French cheeses and pâté de foie gras as a reprisal for the European Union's ban on American hormone-treated beef. To symbolize his vexation, Bové took his tractor and, in the term he favors, "deconstructed" a McDonald's in Millau, near his home in the Larzac. Some 300 people joined him, and a good time was had by all, except, of course, by the owners of the McDonald's (who were French, not American). All present reported a festive atmosphere. The day concluded agreeably in Millau's outdoor cafés.

Today, McDonald's; tomorrow, the world. Bové instantly became the new darling of the antiglobalization movement. The sack of the McDonald's was not, he hastened to explain, an anti-American action per se. "This is a fight," he explained, "against free-trade global capitalism. It's about the logic of a certain economic system. . . . It can be a struggle against any country, this one or that one."[2] Those around him have not necessarily understood this subtlety; since then, wherever he has appeared, effigies of Uncle Sam have gone up in flames.

Bové was sentenced to three months in prison for his role in the uprising. He was photographed, famously, on the steps of the courthouse, handcuffed arms above his head, beaming broadly, his extravagant mustache fanning out from his face like a revolutionary banner. "This image," writes a Bové admirer, the French journalist Gilles Luneau, "has become a historic symbol; it illustrates a world where we live in chains, where revolt is both necessary and legitimate."[3] Bové refused to pay bail to escape going to jail, but supporters the world over sent checks to free him. The Confédération Paysanne set up an office in front of the prison gates. Hundreds of visitors came every day to sign petitions on Bové's behalf. Daily, demonstrators throughout France demanded his release. On Bastille Day, Bové was pardoned by President Jacques Chirac, and in the end served only forty-four days of his sentence. In the spring of 2000, in mimicry of Bové's protest, a bomb was detonated at a McDonald's in Brittany, in the northwest of France. A young Frenchwoman, Laurence Turbec, was killed.

Following his release from prison, Bové adopted a dizzying global schedule of protests and publicity appearances in the service of anti-globalization causes. He attended the 1999 demonstrations against the World Trade Organization in Seattle, where he ate a Roquefort sandwich in front of a McDonald's that was then, inevitably, vandalized. He later described the riots there—which led the governor to declare a state of emergency and call in the National Guard—as "glorious events."[4] My mother, who lives in Seattle, wasn't so sure. Her first taste of martial law left her nonplussed. I believe she described the protesters as "animals."

In 2001, Bové took part in a large-scale destruction of genetically modified crops in Brazil, the land of his father's genetic modification triumph. He popped up again in Porto Alegre for protests during the conference of the World Social Forum, and in Mexico at the end of the

Zapatista March. He was sighted in India, leading an enormous demonstration against a conference on GMO plants organized by the transnationals, and spotted again in France, urinating on a bale of imported wheat. One might wonder how he found the time to farm.

Later that year he was arrested again for destroying genetically modified rice and maize samples at CIRAD, a government-sponsored biotech research station in Montpellier. His Confédération Paysanne took crowbars and sledgehammers to a CIRAD greenhouse, then pulled up and burned a thousand genetically modified rice plants, simultaneously destroying computer files holding the company's research data. When in response the police yanked Bové from his bed at sunrise and whisked him off to jail by helicopter, the Confédération Paysanne began issuing press releases within nanoseconds: it was outrageous, they protested, to arrest a farmer just before the morning milking.

One of the more inexplicable aspects of Bové's activist agenda has been his agitation on behalf of Yasser Arafat and the Palestinians. In 2002, at the height of the Second Intifada—when the random mass murder of Israelis was a near-daily occurrence—Bové was found in Ramallah, protesting the Israeli occupation. This was not his first visit to the West Bank. A June 21, 2001, story in the *Independent of London* described an earlier confrontation between the Israelis and Bové's international activist colleagues: "'No violence! No violence!' chanted Mr. Bové and his friends. A group of Palestinians nearby took up chanting but maybe misheard the French accent as they shouted, 'No peace! No peace!'"[5]

Throughout France, Bové's devotees have followed his lead on this issue. Not long after Bové's visit to Ramallah, I spent a week at a yoga clinic on a biodynamic farm in Provence run by two members of Bové's Confédération Paysanne. Prominently displayed in the dining room, interleaved with brochures describing the farm's organic pâté, were tracts calling for the interposition of an international police force in Occupied Palestine. The link between pâté and Palestine is at first blush unclear, but Bové explains it thus: The occupation is an *agricultural* issue at heart; the Israelis, he says, are "putting in place—with the support of the World Bank—a series of neoliberal measures intended to integrate the Middle East into globalized production circuits, through the exploitation of cheap Palestinian labor."[6]

It is of course difficult, by means of this ideological framework, to explain why the Israelis keep razing those Palestinian olive groves.

## THE SECOND LIFE OF JOSÉ BOVÉ

José Bové was born again in Antwerp, less than a century after the turn of the millennium. Tanchelm of Antwerp, a failed diplomat for the county of Flanders, entered his second career as a wandering preacher and heretic in 1112. According to the Chapter of Utrecht, his eloquence was extraordinary. He began, like so many *propheta* of the era, by condemning corrupt clerics, then broadened his attack to the Church *tout court*. Churches, he said, were no better than whorehouses. Like other Bovés throughout the ages, he adroitly attached his followers' sense of spiritual unease to their most pressing economic grievance: according to the chapter, "He easily persuaded the populace to withhold tithes from the ministers of the Church, for that is what they wanted to do."[7]

The area from which Tanchelm preached had for many years been swept by communal insurrections. From the Rhine Valley to Utrecht, from Flanders to northern France, town after town had risen up against its feudal suzerains. The historian Norman Cohn tells us that these movements were organized by the merchants, and that the merchants' goals were more worldly than transcendental: they were particularly exercised by high dues and tariffs. When unable to achieve their aims peacefully, they organized insurrectionary societies, setting fire to cathedrals and attacking Church officials. Tanchelm's rhetoric about priestly corruption proved quite a convenient accompaniment to this species of vandalism, much as the present-day Bové's rhetoric about corruption quite usefully matches his followers' frequently violent demands for protective trade barriers against foreign competition. The words the modern Bové uses to describe capitalists, elected governments, multinationals, and the World Trade Organization are from the same lexicon: *Parasites. Vampires.*[8]

But this is not to describe the Bovés's followers—then or now—as ideologically disingenuous. On the contrary. They were and are true believers. Tanchelm's charisma was legendary; his flock, according to the Chapter of Utrecht, was blindly devoted, rushing to make offerings to him, throwing their jewels in his coffers.

Tanchelm, like so many of the Bovés, had a gift with women. Many of the millenarian sects encouraged a kind of sexual libertinism not generally associated in the modern mind with the Christian tradition; Tanchelm's was one of them. Because he was God incarnate, Tanchelm avowed, intercourse with him was a sacred act. It appears that many women agreed. The canons of Utrecht were powerless to put an end to his agitation and troublemaking, so great was his influence, until, at some time around 1115, Tanchelm was helpfully killed by a priest.

Messiahs of this kind, Cohn observes, typically arose in Europe not among the poor as such, but among those in the lower strata of society who faced a challenge to their agrarian way of life, and who had lost their faith in traditional values. Europe experienced just such a social crisis in the late eleventh century, and from this moment, we see Bovés born everywhere; indeed, in the Valley of the Rhine there is an unbroken tradition of revolutionary millenarianism until well into the sixteenth century. The circumstances in which the Bovés thrived appear to have been quite uniform: They arose in areas where economic and social change was rapid, and where living circumstances had come to differ significantly from Europe's customary, settled agricultural life. As the population grew throughout the Middle Ages, so did the cities. The newly urbanized, particularly the displaced peasants, found themselves bewildered by the demands of the primitive capitalism of the town, and disoriented by the loss of their traditional social and kinship networks. To them, the Bovés were irresistible. For these people, Cohn observes, "Any disturbing, frightening, or exciting event—any kind of revolt or revolution, a summons to a crusade, an interregnum, a famine, anything in fact which disrupted the normal routine of social

life—acted on the people with peculiar sharpness and called forth reactions of peculiar violence."[9]

Then and now, the Bovés's followers came from the same class,
and as the present Bové has remarked, the current movement is "understandable, given all the agricultural and workplace traumas that
are happening."[10]

Salvationist cults, led by charismatic, messianic prophets, gave
these lost souls a sense of belonging and a mission—a mission, no less,
of transcendent, global significance: the total transformation of society
into a utopia based on a mythic Christian past.

They still do.

## THE MODERN PROPHET OF CROP WORSHIP

I should put my cards on the table: I am not unsympathetic to José
Bové. The questions he raises about modern agriculture are not trivial
or easily dismissed. I cannot disagree with him when he argues that we
know too little about the long-term environmental and health effects
of GMO crops to permit the corporations that manufacture them—
and stand to profit enormously from them—to be the chief arbiters of
their safety.

Nor am I sure that I trust our governments to make these judgments, either. I lived in England during the Thatcher era, when worried
consumers first began to fear a link between mad cow disease and its
human analogue, the deadly and ghastly variant Creutzfeldt-Jakob. I
distinctly remember the British agriculture minister appearing on television, shoveling a burger into his bewildered four-year-old daughter's
mouth. *See? It's safe.* Several years later, a British health secretary announced the probable link between cattle and the human form of the
illness.

I am sympathetic, too, to Bové's indignation about the cruelty and
inhumanity of modern factory and battery farming, and to his charge
that mass agricultural production techniques endanger both our health
and the environment. The mad cow epidemic appears to have been the

direct consequence of the grotesque practice of feeding unsanitary animal remains to herbivores. Animals' immune systems, Bové holds, are weakened when farmers rely overmuch on antibiotics and growth hormones; disease is easily spread among overcrowded animals. Epidemics are the inevitable consequence. The British were forced to torch more than a million farm animals during the 2001 hoof-and-mouth crisis. It was a revolting spectacle. Bové says he is against that, and I am against that, too. Nor can I disagree with him when he says that mass-produced junk food does not make for an optimal human diet.

The man is charming, I'll give you that. "The first thing you notice about José are his eyes—a luminous blue, full of warmth. His smile is never far away—the lines around his eyes always seem to herald it,"[11] gushes Gilles Luneau. There is that charisma. All the women have a crush on him. He recently left his wife of more than thirty years for a younger woman. (Before then, the media was much taken by the strength of the couple's bond and their long-standing shared passion for activist causes. Now she denounces him as a dangerous demagogue. Journalists have been inclined to ignore this awkward development.)

I am not at all sympathetic, however, to Bové's stance on the Israeli-Palestinian conflict, nor to his enthusiasm for the unfortunately named Kongra-Gel, the newly reconstituted PKK, a loathsome rabble of Kurdish separatists who constitute one of the world's most disgusting terrorist groups, and I say this in full awareness that the competition for claim to this title is stiff. The members of Kongra-Gel are child killers and beheaders with the best of them. Bové recently declared his intention to join Kongra-Gel as a protest against its inclusion on the EU's list of terrorist organizations. Nor have I much sympathy with Bové's clichéd, thoughtless opposition to U.S. military policy in Afghanistan and Iraq, which involves the inevitable wearying collection of neo-Marxist claims. I don't need to spell them out—you've heard them all before.

But it is not through any reasoned position—certainly not on these issues—that Bové has achieved his celebrity. As Eric Hoffer rightly remarks in *The True Believer,* a rising mass movement attracts a following "not by its doctrines and promises but by the refuge it offers from the anxieties, barrenness and meaninglessness of an individual existence."[12] Just so. The real source of Bové's popularity is this: He has managed to transform a scientific question—What is the best and safest way to produce food?—into a quasi-spiritual one. Bové is the modern prophet of crop worship.

Bové is, in fact, a neo-Christian heretic, just like all the Bovés before him.

## A PERENNIAL EUROPEAN PERSONALITY

In the popular imagination of farmers in the developing world, Bové looms large, to be sure, but larger still looms the figure of Norman Borlaug. His name is unknown in the developed world, though he is the greatest hero of the poor in all of human history. Borlaug was the father of the Green Revolution, which dramatically increased agricultural yields in the 1960s and 1970s. In Mexico, India, China, and beyond, Borlaug is credited with saving more than a billion people from starvation. For this, he won the 1970 Nobel Peace Prize.

Borlaug, who is now in his nineties, views GMOs as the future of the Green Revolution, essential to boosting crop production as the world's population—projected to be more than 8 billion by 2025—increases. Without GMOs, he believes, starvation will ensue. He is intensely contemptuous of Bové and his associates, whom he holds to be pampered European imbeciles who know nothing about hunger. According to Borlaug, and to many of Bové's critics, there is so far very little evidence that GMOs are dangerous and much evidence that they are not. Indeed, the development of pest-resistant crop varieties appears to be beneficial to the environment inasmuch as it reduces the need for chemical spraying.

Who knows? I certainly don't. This much is clear, though: As a direct consequence of Bové's activism, France in 1998 pronounced a two-year moratorium on certain types of transgenic plant research and production. The producers of GMO crops have lost the enormous

European market, and it has cost them a fortune. The repeated destruction of their experimental plants has left them hesitant to continue their research. The effect of Bové's campaign has been to delay significantly the development of genetically improved crop varieties. Because of the publicity Bové has generated, consumers in the Third World are intensely fearful of GMOs. Some states of Brazil have forbidden their import. In 2002, as 6 million Zimbabweans faced famine, their government rejected an American donation of 10,000 metric tons of whole-grain corn because the shipment might have contained genetically modified grain.* Farmers throughout Africa are reluctant to plant GMO crops because they cannot be exported to European markets. Bové's critics charge that he has therefore already doomed many in the developing world to hunger and death, and I am not sure they are wrong.

My point here is not to resolve the question. My point is that Bové is an ancient historic figure, a perennial European personality, who has adapted himself splendidly to this modern debate. In this sense, he is much more (and much less) than he seems.

## THE THIRD LIFE OF JOSÉ BOVÉ

José Bové was born again sometime in the first half of the thirteenth century as Jacob, a renegade monk from Hungary. Preaching in Picardy, the Master of Hungary led the Crusade of the Shepherds, the first of the century's great anarchic movements. By all accounts he was a prepossessing and vastly eloquent figure. He declared that God was displeased with the vanity and ostentation of the French nobility and had chosen the shepherds, instead, to carry out his work. (Bovés throughout history have had an affinity for sheep.) Peasants rushed to convene under the Master's banner; soon they were joined by a motley assortment of criminals and rabble-rousers. Together they became

---

*They might well have rejected it anyway, on some other pretext: as in many African countries, the government of Zimbabwe is quite keen to starve its own people as a political weapon.

known as the Pastoureaux—the original Confédération Paysanne; the word means the same thing. They marched, armed with pitchforks and pikes, into the villages of France, intimidating local authorities. When they ran short of provisions, they resorted to pillaging, but often the locals put all their possessions at the crusaders' disposition, for they were much admired. The French singer Francis Cabrel has described the current Bové as "one of the last courageous, natural, honest voices left in a world where the rest are tarnished by compromise," and this is exactly how the Master of Hungary and his disciples were perceived.[13]

Much of the Master's vitriol was directed against the merchant capitalists in the towns. We see now the emergence of a kind of class consciousness the current antiglobalists would readily recognize, particularly in its agricultural angst. Among proverbs and miracle plays written by the poor, we find sentiments that would not have been out of place in Millau or Porto Alegre: "Magistrates, provosts, beadles, mayors—nearly all live by robbery. . . . They all batten on the poor, they all want to despoil them. . . . They pluck them alive. The stronger robs the weaker." "Good working men make the wheaten bread but they will never chew it; no, all they get is the siftings from the corn, and from good wine they get the dregs and from good cloth nothing but the chaff."[14] From the contemporary Bové, we learn something similar: "The multinationals are taking over, denying large numbers of farming families access to the land and the possibility of feeding themselves."[15]

One might wonder if the rhetoric is not the same because the conditions are the same: Is it not the case that then, as now, the poor are exploited by the rich? Not quite. In India and Pakistan—thanks to the same free market and the Green Revolution that Bové deplores—GNP has in fact been rising steadily—by as much as an order of magnitude—since the formation of the World Trade Organization's progenitor, the General Agreement on Tariffs and Trade (GATT), as have per capita income, living standards, and life expectancy. Hunger has markedly diminished. So has infant mortality. If the industries mentioned by Bové are suffering, many more are thriving. In fact, I'll just get this out of my system right now: The free market is the *only* economic system in history that has ever succeeded in providing basic standards of living for large populations, at least without herding the bulk of them into forced labor camps. If in doubt about this point, consult footage of the fall of the Berlin Wall. Notice in which direction the people are running. No, Bové's complaint is not about fact; it is about ancient—and I do mean *ancient*—force of habit.

The Master of Hungary preached against the clergy, attacking them for their hypocrisy and greed. He promised his crusaders they would be received with miracles when they reached the Holy Land. His bands marched through Paris and Tours and Orléans, putting clerics to the sword and drowning them, all to the enthusiastic approval of the watching crowds.

At Bourges, the Master of Hungary preached against the Jews and sent his men to destroy the Torah scrolls. In this regard, he was typical of Bovés throughout the ages; they have traditionally been anti-Semites. In the eyes of the crusading *pauperes,* the final battle against the Prince of Evil—believed to be soon at hand—was to commence with the smiting of the Jews. The popular imagination of the Middle Ages cast Jews as terrifying demons, perverted ingrates who refused to admit the divinity of Christ, inheritors of the monstrous guilt of his murder. Inevitably, then as now, Jews were associated with trade, capitalism, and usury. A particularly venomous and unremitting hatred of the Jew gripped the imagination of the millenarian masses at the time of the first crusades; the eschatology of the Second Coming associated Jews with the Antichrist himself, with the peoples of Gog and Magog, who fed on human flesh and corpses. In popular art Jews were portrayed as lustful torturers who castrated children for sport and ripped babies from their mothers' wombs to drink their blood. Their power was held to be growing, their sins and sorceries more and more untrammeled, more and more outrageous. This was to be expected, for the End was nigh. In the next half century, nearly all the Jews in the southwest of France were to be massacred.

Shortly after his speech at Bourges, José Bové, the Master of Hungary, was pursued by irritated burghers and chopped to pieces.

## A FAMILIAR TASTE FOR VANDALISM AND VIOLENCE

We see in the present Bové's movement, and the personalities of those who surround him, much that is familiar. (Bové, an avid student of European peasant revolts, is well aware of this.) First, there is the remarkable fact that the hero of the peasants has chosen to make his case through vandalism, rather than through legal organs of political persuasion. He justifies this by arguing that the dangers posed by GMOs and by homogenized, modern farming techniques are so vast that he has no moral choice. But again, the dangers of GMOs are abstract and unproved. This does not mean they are not real, but it does suggest that they may not be the true source of the emotive power Bové has managed to harness.

Consider this: We have known for more than fifty years that tobacco will kill some 25 percent of its users. No one in Europe takes to the streets about this, or ransacks the offices of the corporations that promote this lethal product. Bové, populist champion of the public health, is rarely seen without his pipe, which he is forever stoking and tamping and puffing. His followers find this very charming. If Bové were concerned above all about disease and health, putting that pipe away would be the more rational place to start. There are no protesters rioting about France's rate of vehicular homicide, one of the highest in the First World. We see no protesters in Europe demanding greater public (or private) funding to combat AIDS, even though AIDS is the biggest threat to global health in the history of the human race, particularly in the developing world. Clearly, this isn't *just* about rational fear and real risk.

And why, precisely, does Bové believe that he has no means of political expression beyond the destruction of private property? "When," he asks, "was there a public debate on genetically modified organisms? When were farmers and consumers asked what they think about this? Never."[16] But this is patently untrue: The public debate on genetically modified organisms has been endless; a quick search on Google will prove this. In 1999, for example, scientists extensively debated the dangers of GMOs in *Nature* and *The Lancet*. Throughout Europe,

GMOs have been discussed in newspapers, in scientific journals, in women's magazines, in government commissions convened specifically to investigate the issue. They have been discussed on television; they have been debated on the floor of most European parliaments. And throughout Europe, people have been given a chance to vote for candidates who champion their views about GMOs, in regular elections that are generally agreed by observers to be relatively free and fair. The fact that voters have not elected candidates who embrace Bové's philosophy would suggest that they don't agree with him.

Bové hasn't much use for the franchise. "I myself wonder whether one should vote at all," he says. As for the suggestion that he himself might run for office, and use the power of persuasion to pursue his agenda democratically and legally, he replies, "Never."[17]

In the courtroom in Montpellier, Bové concluded, "Yes, the action was illegal, but I lay claim to it because it was legitimate."[18] He did not, however, specify the source of this legitimacy, and it is certainly not clear what it might be, if it is not the popular will. French voters may be wrong about GMOs—even catastrophically wrong—but surely it is an error to suggest that the remedy for this is the rule of the mob. We *know* what lies at the end of that tunnel.

"It was the Americans who led the way in all this," Bové says. "They were the ones who threw the tea overboard in Boston Harbor because they were fed up with taxation without representation. That was an American example."[19] The comment contains its own rebuttal. The Boston Tea Party was a response to taxation *without* representation. France has enjoyed universal manhood suffrage since 1944. Bové, like every man and woman in France, has the right to vote. His is most certainly *not* the American example.

But it is quite a good French example, as we are seeing.

## THE FOURTH LIFE OF JOSÉ BOVÉ

José of Flora, or Joachim, as he is more commonly known, was born in Calabria in 1145 to a middle-class family, as Bovés are usually born.

Joachim was the most significant apocalyptic thinker of the Middle Ages—a more intellectual Bové than most. He began his career unremarkably as an official in the Sicilian court of Palermo. After a spiritual conversion, he set off on a pilgrimage to the Holy Land; when he returned, he lived as a hermit for a number of years before joining the Cistercian Order. (It is striking that so many of the Bovés were hermits before they were activists; the current Bové, at the age of twenty-one, hid from the police in an isolated farm high in the Aspe Valley, part of the Basque region, for nearly a year. There he made yogurt.)

Joachim's linear theory of history was the most complete known to Europe until the advent of Marxism, and was in many ways Marxism's precursor. His inspiration was to find in the Scriptures concealed clues to the pattern of history itself, which was to unfold in three progressive stages, the Age of the Law, the Age of the Gospel, and the Age of the Spirit. The final age would be a utopia of enlightened consciousness and freedom. This inadvertently subversive doctrine—he was not consciously heterodox—has been the clear inspiration for Continental theories of trinitarian historical evolution ever since; it has reappeared, for example, among the German Idealist philosophers, and in the theory of historic progress espoused by the French proto-fascist Auguste Comte.

From the Scriptural clues, Joachim determined, the future could be predicted, and that future was the Apocalypse, near at hand (it was due in 1260, he thought). By the late twelfth century, he had become known throughout Europe for these views, which acquired by the end of his life a decidedly anticlerical luster. Joachim prophesied the replacement of the Roman Church by a universal monastery to which all men would belong. This egalitarian, anti-elite vision of the future proved particularly inspiring to a new generation of revolutionary millenarians. Widely circulated throughout late medieval Europe, his texts furnished a vocabulary by which to indict the increasingly corrupt bureaucracy of the medieval Church. Joachim himself never attacked the papacy directly, but others, particularly radical Franciscans, drew from his writings the conclusion that the pope was none other than the Beast.

Was Joachim truly a Bové? At first glance it might seem not—no rabble behind him, no sheep to speak of—but his sense of history is Bové through and through. The recent Bové, too, sees inevitable, sequential phases of history characterized by particular institutional structures, all leading to a final, universal expansion of consciousness. "History shows," says the new Bové, "that each phase of political development has a corresponding institutional form: France's response to the Industrial Revolution was the nation-state; the WTO is the expression of this phase of the liberalization of world trade."[20] His manifesto, cowritten with his confrere in activism, fellow farmer François Dufour, is titled *The World Is Not for Sale: Farmers Against Junk Food*. One section is titled "A New Consciousness." That new consciousness, the authors believe, is now dawning. If José of Fiore saw the portent of the new era in the emergence of Saladin, the current Bové sees one in the events in Seattle: "Seattle was a historic event, marking the emergence of a new awareness on a world scale." As Joachim predicted, this new consciousness heralds a clearer apprehension of the Antichrist. "In Nice, Prague, Genoa, there has been a real sense of a different sort of consciousness," says José of Millau. "With the movement against a monolithic world-economic system, people can once again see the enemy more clearly."[21]

As Joachim insisted, the new consciousness will not be restricted to the elites. "We are witnessing the rise of a new awareness on a world scale," echoes Dufour, and "confronting issues hitherto only dealt with by experts."[22] If Joachim's followers were heartened by his message, so are the contemporary Bové's: "The struggle is giving them renewed confidence in the possibility of changing things," says Dufour. "They were waiting for a sign."[23] A sign from what? It is as if this vocabulary were programmed into the genome.

"Each new rally," Dufour adds, "holds out hope, is proof that the worldwide challenge is being maintained. . . . It's an odd sort of militancy, with no specific political project."[24]

Of course there is no political project. That is because this is a spiritual project.

## RITUAL, RELATIONSHIP, FAMILY, LOVE, TRADITION

The foreword to *The World Is Not for Sale* is written by the prominent antiglobalization activist and author of *No Logo* Naomi Klein. "José Bové and François Dufour," she writes, "have come to stand for a way of life in which our relationship to food and nature is grounded in respect. For them, food is more than bodily fuel; it is ritual, relationship, family, love, tradition, and so much else."[25]

It is?

*Ritual, relationship, family, love, tradition.* A potent aphrodisiac for people longing, if obviously unconsciously, for the revival of ancient social and kinship bonds, for a religious tradition they have lost. In the same book, interviewer Gilles Luneau lowers the level of discourse, theologically speaking, to the frankly neopagan: "Wheat, maize and rice are more than just crops. They are the outcome of a fusion of sun, water, and soil. In eating, humans inscribe themselves in the cycles of the universe, and this is far more profound and basic than making money." Bové agrees that his activism represents a quest for some kind of sustenance beyond the material: "We eat," he laments, "but don't nourish ourselves, even on the farm." He mourns "the vacuity of much of modern life," and the way even "our deaths, like our food, have become standardized." His program, he admits, goes "beyond the defense of working conditions, incomes or jobs to challenge the social and ecological purpose of work and human activity." The spiritual yearning in these comments is palpable.

Bové does not really deny that the free market and the globalization he deplores have brought unprecedented prosperity to Europe. The downtrodden of Europe are not *physically* oppressed, he says. They are *mentally* oppressed. "These days, in our post-industrial society, social awareness against alienation is more likely to come from *thinking things through* than from experience of more traditional overt exploitation."[26] The emphasis is mine.

I know what he's talking about. I, too, sometimes find myself uneasily thinking things through, late at night, when everyone else is sleeping. I wonder what it all means. I suppose you could call it alienation. If I cannot really bring myself to believe that the cure for this is the purification of the food chain, it is perhaps because I am not a natural mystic.

## THE FIFTH LIFE OF JOSÉ BOVÉ

Sometime in the middle of the fifteenth century, Bové was born again in what is now southern Germany. Hans Böheim, the Piper of Niklashausen, was—again—a shepherd. Before his visitation by the Virgin Mary, in 1476, he had also been a popular entertainer, hence his name.

The Virgin conveyed to him a message: God was greatly displeased, but would suffer Himself to give the people one last chance. The Piper was to abandon his pipes and burn his drum, then bring the pure Word of God to the people. All men were to journey on a pilgrimage to the Virgin of Niklashausen. A dreadful punishment awaited those who failed to heed the summons.

The formerly half-witted and inarticulate peasant found himself suddenly possessed of unnatural eloquence. Adoring crowds streamed from great distances to hear him preach. He claimed miraculous powers for himself, teaching that his intercession had prevented God from killing all the corn and vines. Inevitably, he turned against the clergy, pronouncing them worse, in their corruption and avarice, than Jews. He enjoined his followers to withhold from them all taxes and tithes. This message was, as usual, well received.

The Piper's innovation was his vision of the coming Kingdom, which would not be a heavenly Jerusalem but a return to an imaginary past, a primal and egalitarian State of Nature. Wood, water, pasturage, fishing, and hunting would be enjoyed equally by all in this earthly paradise, as they had been, he imagined, in ancient times, before they were usurped by the nobility. Rulers of every stripe would be overthrown. All would live as equals and brothers.

Vast hordes of the urban poor and peasantry abandoned their

workshops and their flocks to follow him. Camps sprang up around his village, with tents. The bishop and town council, greatly alarmed, plotted to have the Piper arrested, seizing him in the early hours and whisking him off to prison on horseback, no doubt outraging the peasants by disrupting a farmer before the morning milking. The next day, thousands of his followers marched to the castle where he was imprisoned. They drove off the bishop's emissary with stones, then tried to storm the town, shouting the Piper's name. As in Seattle, their protests provoked a violent response from the authorities, who brought out the cavalry and responded with cannon shots. Some forty demonstrators were killed. The rest fled in a panic.

The Piper was tried and found guilty of heresy and sorcery. He was burned at the stake. The current Bové, recalling with nostalgia the "shining crowds" in Millau, has remarked that "our journey from the farm to the court on the tractor trailer was like a trip to the scaffold."[27]

Bovés in the past, I imagine, also found themselves likening their journeys to trips to the scaffold, probably because they *were* taking trips to the scaffold. By the standards of his predecessors, the current Bové must surely count his sentence lenient.

## THE GREAT EUROPEAN AFFLICTION

*Malbouffe.* This concept is important. Bové coined this neologism. As Gilles Luneau correctly observes, there is no word in English that captures its full meaning. It is generally translated as "junk food," but that dismissive, vaguely ironic Americanism does not capture the full *horror* of bad *bouffe,* with its intimation of contamination, pollution, poison. The word *mal* in French should in this case should be translated as *"evil,"* as in Baudelaire's *Fleurs du Mal.* "The sound of it provokes a feeling of nausea," writes Luneau. The word, adds Bové, has "become universally accepted to express a confused unease, a mixture of guilt and accusation."[28]

I know that feeling, too, although again, I am not convinced it has anything to do with impure food.

There it is, in example after example: To his followers, Bové stands for meaning in a meaningless world. "In its rush to make life as fast, efficient and wealthy as possible, many overlooked humanity's hunger for dignity and a way of life that fills oneself with something other than meaninglessness," writes one of Bové's admirers on an Internet webzine aimed at students.[29] From another admirer on the Internet:

> Jose's battle is not merely a battle of farmers. Jose's battle is one of people and the earth. Tracy Chapman once wrote a song with the line, "All you have is your soul." Now we have the makings of a political alignment. The 50,000 people who came to the trial in Millau, following on Seattle, represent a global search for meaning, a global need to live in our hearts and bodies, grounded in the soil and sun, using our intelligence to re-create modern society as respectful of us and our sustenance.[30]

Just look at this vocabulary! Souls, global searches for meaning, the re-creation of the earth itself! Clearly in using these metaphors of food and hunger, of sustenance and nurturance, Bové has tapped a deep mine in the collective unconscious, a profound longing for something that *combats meaninglessness*—the great European affliction. But what, precisely, does Bové propose as the remedy? I have no doubt that anyone who believes an abundance of local sheep farms will cure his sense of aching emptiness will think again after inspecting a herd of sheep at close range over a period of several months.

Curiously, these very same people, according to survey after survey, are apt to declare themselves *deeply* concerned that George W. Bush prays a lot.

## THE SIXTH LIFE OF JOSÉ BOVÉ

The next Bové's name has, like the first, been lost in the mists of time. The antique madman has come to be known as the Revolutionary of the Upper Rhine. This Bové, I'm afraid, is distinctly unpleasant. He lived in the beginning of the sixteenth century in the Alsace (we think), and wrote in German. His *Book of a Hundred Chapters* was the most complete expression of the millenarian eschatology of the Middle Ages.

As usual, it all began with a personal visitation from God, who as usual was vexed with man's sinfulness, but had as usual decided to give him one last chance. God charged the Revolutionary with the task of organizing an association of pious laymen; soon, God assured him, a savior would come to establish a messianic kingdom, where bread, barley, wine, and oil would be distributed at low prices. First, however, the Revolutionary's association, the Brethren of the Yellow Cross, must stamp out sin, which in practical terms meant slaughtering sinners, a prospect that aroused the Revolutionary greatly: "Go on hitting them!" he urged. "From the Pope to the little students! Kill them all!"[31]

The Revolutionary was clear upon this point: the Brethren were the poor; the sinners were the rich, and the Millennium was to put an end to capitalism. Church property would be seized and distributed among the poor. Income derived from property or trade would be confiscated. Private property would be abolished. All goods would be held in common. The emperor (whom he hints would be himself) would urge his subjects to inform on sinful neighbors; sinners would be enjoined to come forth and criticize themselves at special tribunals, to be established in each parish. The judges would punish them with "cruel severity." Jews, of course, would be annihilated.

The Revolutionary was a passionate German nationalist. He envisioned the restoration of Germany to what he imagined was its utopian past, from which it had fallen as a consequence of capitalism and a conspiracy among the inferior, non-Germanic people. He prescribed a complete program for the purification of the German race, to be followed by German conquest of the globe. It has been remarked that his vision did not die with him.

He is a dark Bové, to be sure. But he is a Bové nonetheless.

## BRINGING MEANING TO AN INDIFFERENT UNIVERSE

And what, exactly, does the current Bové's objection to "globalization" signify? It is hard to say just what he means by *globalization,* or what anyone means by the term, which has come to comprise more or less every complaint one might have about modernity, and certainly has nothing to do with that which is global per se, since the movement itself is both quick and proud to describe itself as global. As Bové has said, though, his is a fight against free trade and global capitalism, and that, probably, is as precise a definition of *globalization* as we'll get from him.

Here, too, some of the specifics of Bové's lament are not thoroughly unreasonable, or at least, earnest people of good will might debate them. For example, he opposes the United States' unfettered agricultural dumping—the practice of exporting commodities produced under high levels of government subsidization, which in turn drives farmers in developing countries out of the global market and destroys local agricultural traditions. And indeed, dumping *is* a real problem, and it *does* jeopardize food security in developing countries. That is precisely why Article VI of the GATT allows countries to take action against dumping, and why the WTO's Anti-Dumping Agreement clarifies and expands Article VI.

So why does Bové view the World Trade Organization as the problem, rather than the solution? It is not as if these international agreements were toothless: Most recently, the WTO ruled with Brazil in its dispute with the United States over the dumping of American cotton. Moreover, the WTO is the only formal, coherent forum in the world that exists for the resolution of these disagreements. How does Bové propose that these disputes be resolved instead? He doesn't, but the strong suggestion—from his example—is that he would prefer them to be resolved on the street, with victory awarded to the loudest and most threatening mob. I urge his followers to think this through with care. A world thus governed may not be one in which you wish to live.

It is puzzling, too, that Bové does not seem to grasp a key theoretical point: Dumping is a violation of the principles of free-market economics, not their logical outgrowth. Dumping occurs because government subsidies distort the mechanism of the market. The practice is fundamentally *anti*capitalist. French farmers are among the most highly subsidized in the world—and Bové likes it just that way—so there is a certain inconsistency in his views.

The peasant uprising, Dufour adds, has come to pass because people are beginning to understand the sinister forces "lurking behind the opacity of these international institutions."[32] These institutions are actually extremely transparent: the deliberations and judgments of the WTO may be consulted by anyone, in paralyzing, minute detail, at www.wto.org. Dufour's comment to the contrary is puzzling, until we see it for what it is—a vestigial anticlerical reflex.

There is, again, a long historic tradition evident in Bové's wholesale denunciation of the WTO. Bovés throughout history have always been intolerant of imperfect, earthly organizations. By the standards of medieval Christianity, for example, the record of the Church was far from deplorable; despite corruption and abuses, most of the clergy led relatively austere lives; they, far more than any other category of medievals, were the caretakers of the poor and the sick. But the revolutionary millenarians, certain of the imminent Second Coming and terrified by it, held the world to higher standards. Norman Cohn writes,

> It was because of their inordinate expectations that eschatological movements could not—as the Church itself could and did—simply condemn certain specific abuses and criticize certain individual clerics, but had to see the whole clergy in all its doings as the militia of the Antichrist, bound by its very nature to strive for the spiritual and material ruin of Christendom and striving all the more ferociously now that the End was at hand.[33]

Substitute global capitalism for the Church (or in the case of the Revolutionary of the Upper Rhine, substitute global capitalism for global capitalism), and think of the clerics, perhaps, as the modern government officials who are presumptively in the pockets of the multinationals. You'll see that the result sounds very similar.

I do not wish to resolve an argument about agricultural dumping here. I mean only to suggest that the degree of emotion that accompanies this debate reveals an underlying agenda that goes well beyond the ostensible message. For all his concern about food security, after all, Bové gives nary a thought to what is overwhelmingly the single greatest cause of hunger today: the use of famine as a military weapon. The Sudanese government has been attempting systematically to annihilate the inhabitants of the Darfur region not by flooding them with underpriced food but by intentionally starving them to death. This is a deliberately conceived, carefully planned, explicitly genocidal, man-made famine. Crises like these are the globe's greatest threat to food security, but where is Bové, and where are the antiglobalization protesters? Their eerie silence suggests, again, that feeding the world may not, in fact, be their chief concern, and is certainly not the source of their passion.

Considered in this context, certain comments made by Bové's admirers seem particularly unhelpful. Following Bové's arrest, one antiglobalist organization called Food First declared in a manifesto that Bové's "only 'crime'" was fighting "for the rights of consumers to have access to food that is adequate, culturally appropriate, and produced in a sustainable way."[34] If recent history is anything to go by, the "culturally appropriate" food of Sudan is no food at all. Perhaps a graduate student in the school of Edward Said would like to have a look at the grotesquely patronizing idea of "culturally appropriate" food. I leave it as an exercise.

"Cooking is culture," Bové says. "All over the world. Every nation, every region, has its own food cultures. Food and farming define people. We cannot let it all go, to be replaced with hamburgers."[35] I'd readily agree that the global caliphate of the hamburger would be a terrible thing, fiercely to be resisted, but I have to say it is not a particularly realistic fear. I have lived in New York—the city that defines globalization, if anything does—and I have lived in Paris. As anyone who has lived in both cities will tell you, the cuisine available in

New York is vastly more diverse. It is also generally much better and much cheaper. There are only a handful of restaurants in Paris with first-rate Japanese, Chinese, Thai, Indian, or Ethiopian food, and these restaurants are prohibitively expensive. Most of what purports to be Thai or Indian food has been homogenized into something quite bland and recognizably French. There are not even very many good Vietnamese restaurants in Paris. There is—literally—not one single good Mexican restaurant in Paris, and trust me, I have looked. In New York, you can find excellent examples of each of these cuisines more or less on every block.

So what do they really want? Again, look at their own rhetoric. Donella Meadows, who was an adjunct professor of environmental studies at Dartmouth College and author of a column, "The Global Citizen," admiringly interpreted Bové as an enemy of the "narrow, heartless economics that would have us fill our lives with things produced wherever they can be made most 'efficiently.'"[36] This woman could not seriously have objected to efficiency; I am sure she did not go out of her way, when driving her Volvo to her Dartmouth office in the morning, to take the route with the *most* traffic. So her words make no sense. But she did not really mean what she seems to be saying. This is a case, ironically enough, of false consciousness. No, the key words are these: *narrow* and *heartless*. Cold. Unfeeling. Indifferent. Bové, on the other hand, cares. Bové has a heart. He has a soul. He brings meaning into a meaningless and indifferent universe. *That* is why they love him.

## THE SEVENTH LIFE OF JOSÉ BOVÉ

Until the advent of Catharism, heresy had been a sporadic affair, and if the charismatic messiahs who cropped up here and there were a nuisance to the Church, they were never a serious threat to its existence. The efflorescence of Catharism, however, posed for the first time the prospect that the garden of the Church would be overrun by a particularly hardy heretical weed. The dreamy, gentle, and lunatic Cathars flourished—where else?—in Languedoc, now southwestern France, in the late twelfth century. Pacifists, vegetarians, celibates, believers in the equality of women, the Cathars rather resembled the weird but harmless New Age spiritualists who are often found at the fringes of the antiglobalization movement.

Like the Manicheans, the Cathars were dualists who believed in two gods, a sublime god of the spiritual world and a malign god of the material one. All worldly creation could be ascribed to the malign God and was therefore to be disdained. Worldly authority—the Church, particularly—was a fraud; the sacraments, a farce. Jesus was not a gross material being but an apparition; he had come to Earth as a prophet of dualism; his death was incidental, not the central salvific event of history. The cross was an instrument of torture, its glorification perverse. Men and women were one. Reincarnation was a fact. The Crusades were shameful, as was all violence.

The seductive Cathar heresy swiftly overtook the towns of Albi, Toulouse, and Carcassonne. By the reports that remain (most evidence was destroyed by the Inquisitors), the Cathars lived peaceably among the Jews and Catholics. But ideas like these were for obvious reasons unbearable to the papacy. Innocent III resolved to eradicate the Cathar stain and recruited in his cause the military powers of France, eager to annex the independent Languedoc. Thus began the so-called Albigensian Crusade, named for the town of Albi, from which the heresy had sprung.*

Between 1209 and 1229, papal henchmen and French armies systematically exterminated the Cathars and many others besides, for they were unconcerned to distinguish Catholic from heretic. In Béziers, the pope's legate, Arnoud Amaury, issued the orders that have now passed into infamy: "Kill them all. God will know his own." Some 20,000 men, women, and children—loyal and subversive— were slaughtered and the town was burned to the ground. This was the first but not the last massacre; the crusade continued with

---

*Given the Cathars' celibacy, one wonders why the pope did not bide his time and wait for their natural extinction.

undiminished cruelty for years. When subsequently the Inquisition was convened, it was with the purpose of eradicating all remaining traces of the heresy. In the end, as many as a million perished.

The extermination of the peaceable, dopey, endearing Cathars is one of the sorriest and most shameful events in European history, and this is a history in no way short of sorry and shameful events. If the people of southwest France still feel a suspicion of authority and orthodoxy, who can blame them?

The mention of the Cathar genocide—the word sounds queerly anachronistic, but it is exactly the right one—still prompts the residents of the region to defensiveness. Recently I found myself in the great Romanesque cathedral of Toulouse. I asked a guide at the door whether it might be possible for me to inspect the church's archival records about the Albigensians. *Absolutely not,* she said, her face instantly souring. There were none. The Church had nothing to do with it.

It is not possible to say who among the Cathars was the seventh Bové, precisely, but he was surely there, and his spirit lives on.

## THE EIGHTH LIFE OF JOSÉ BOVÉ

And now another Bové is born, this one quite unlike the others, for by this time Christianity itself was dying. Jean-Jacques Rousseau Bové was born in Geneva in 1712. His early life was undistinguished. Moving from Savoy to Turin to Chambéry, he was by turns a notary, a footman, a coppersmith, a dilettante, a composer of music, and a student of the arts and sciences. Biographers have noted that like most Bovés, Rousseau was narcissistic and self-seeking; also like most Bovés, he was unusually attractive to women.

In 1750, having returned to Paris, he achieved celebrity with his prizewinning essay, "A Discourse on the Arts and Sciences," in which he declared the superiority of the primitive life of savage man in the so-called State of Nature and deplored the pernicious effect on the human soul of technology, science, and urbanization. The advancement of the arts and sciences, he held, far from being beneficial to mankind, had in fact served only to crush and alienate the individual spirit.

In this he was both the inheritor and the progenitor of a European tradition of revolutionaries, men who idealized a utopian, irenic past—a pastoral arcadia—and despaired of soulless modernism. German Romantic thinkers of the late eighteenth and early nineteenth centuries were particularly enamored of these ideas; the poet and essayist Gottfried von Herder, for example, condemned the cold sterility of European modernity and found much to admire in the simple, child-like primitives of the tropical zones. The incompatibility of technology and soulfulness has since Rousseau been a standard trope of Continental philosophy.* Not incidentally, that machine-driven soulless-ness is typically associated with America. Heidegger bore a fierce en-mity toward industrial, soul-sapping *Amerikanismus;* Arthur Moeller van den Bruck—father of the phrase "Third Reich"—denounced *Amerikanismus* as something to be "not geographically but spiritually understood," for this was "the decisive step by which we make our way from dependence on the earth to the use of the earth, the step that mechanizes and electrifies inanimate material."[37]

The current Bové espouses precisely these views. We have become embroiled, he says, in "excessive industrialization," turning our backs on the natural rhythms of the land in favor of "the engineer, the tech-nician and the builder." "Technology," he adds, is "stripping meaning from all of life's activities."[38] In a chapter of his manifesto titled "Sub-version in a State of Nature," we learn how Bové cherished the years he spent in the Larzac as a squatter in a primitive shack without a tele-phone, water, or electricity. Bové is nostalgic for the imaginary epoch of "birds, nature, people on the farm." By contrast, he imagines, cardiac problems and hypertension plague contemporary farmers because they are "no longer in touch with their roots." Although farmers' material

---

*These views have not been limited to Europe. As Ian Buruma and Avishai Margalit remark in *Occidentalism* (New York: Penguin, 2004), these ideas have been exported around the globe, resurfacing in cultures as various as that of imperial Japan and the modern Islamic jihadis. Paul Berman makes this point as well in his excellent *Terror and Liberalism* (New York: Norton, 2003).

living conditions, he concedes, have improved, he believes their family lives have deteriorated.[39] (His own family life has certainly deteriorated. Just ask his ex-wife.)

From Rousseau through the Romantics to the present Bové, we see another current of important thought, the disdain for rationality itself. Bové disparages the "rationalization and segmentation of work" and the "scientific organization of work." As Eric Hoffer has noted, the devout are always asked to seek the truth with their hearts and not their minds: "When a movement begins to rationalize its doctrines and make them intelligible," he reflects, it is a sign that its dynamic span is over."[40] Bové's day, it would seem, is not over yet.

No Bové can refrain from outraging the French authorities. Rousseau's views on Christianity should by now be familiar to us: He admired the Gospel for its egalitarianism while vigorously condemning the Church, which, he held, promoted slavery and tyranny. In this regard, it is odd that Rousseau is so often labeled an original thinker. In 1762, the patience of the French parliament was exhausted. Condemning Rousseau's works as antistate and anti-Church, its members called for his arrest and burned his books. He fled to Neuchâtel, in Prussia, where he wrote his *Letters Written from the Mountain,* advocating freedom of religion. He died of apoplexy in 1778. In 1789 came the French Revolution and the frenzied, bloody orgies of the Commune. The revolutionaries clutched Rousseau's works in hand.

I do realize it is a stretch to describe the unquestionably brilliant and subtle Rousseau, one of the great thinkers of modern Europe, as a Bové. To those who would quibble, fine, I cede the point. He was not just another Bové. But his influence on the current Bové is clear. And besides, I needed nine.

## THE ENDURING LEGACY OF MEDIEVAL MILLENARIANISM

It is odd, it is spooky, even, how much of the current Bové's rhetoric descends from medieval millenarianism. Bové's species of crop worship is in essence a neoteric Christian heresy. It is no accident that he was born in Cathar country. His elevation of nature to the status of a surrogate religion recalls the Romantic movement, which itself descends from the same medieval millenarianism. These movements, like Bové's, strived to enact some kind of earthly utopia by restoring some kind of idealized past. Bové's project, like theirs, is essentially spiritual and transcendental. Like all of the leaders of these movements, Bové is intensely hostile toward and suspicious of authority, and also like them, he counters that authority on the street. These movements, it should be stressed, have historically always ended in blood.

Both Nazism and Communism have their origins in the same movements. The frenzy of Europe's incessant *manifs* derives directly from the tradition of the revolutionary millenarians; there are *Blut und Boden* roots below Bové's ecological agenda.[41] Bové's crop worship draws, unconsciously perhaps, on the mysticism of the Vichy Fascists and their call for the "return to earth, to roots." Among Bové's followers, the connection between the literal roots of crops and the metaphorical roots of community are repeatedly stressed: François Dufour, for example, remarks that "you don't have to be a farmer or live in the country to feel rooted in the land. Such roots connect all parts of the country in a unifying whole. . . . People don't want to be uprooted."[42]

The Russian anarchists, too, Mikhail Bakunin in particular, took their inspiration from the same movements; Bové explicitly recognizes his inheritance in this regard, describing himself as an anarcho-syndicalist. (Anarcho-syndicalism, in France, gave rise to one of its oldest trade unions, the Confédération Générale du Travail, historically closely linked to the French Communist Party.)

The passionate terror of *malbouffe*—well founded or not—is also no accident; it recalls the fanatic religious and ritualistic search for purity of the Middle Ages, ethnic purity included. The fear of poisoning was widespread among the millenarians, particularly during the Black Death, when it was concluded that some class of people—most likely the Jews—had introduced into the water supply a deadly concoction of spiders, frogs, and lizards. The Jews were thereupon massacred. (Of course it has also long been a common religious practice among Jews, as well as Muslims, to distinguish themselves from heathens by rejecting unclean food.) The apocalyptic predictions of environmental catastrophe date directly from this era as well, when millenarians confidently foretold the famine, pestilence, and plague that would wipe out sinners and renew the earth for its inheritance by the faithful.

It is all there, and it is all very, very old.

## THE CLASSIC TROPE OF THE MILLENNIAL CULTS

Nor is it any accident that Bové's agenda includes the classic trope of the Christian millennial cults: the demonization of the Jew. This is the real meaning of his activism on behalf of the Palestinians, a classic example of the new European anti-Semitism, one characterized by the irrational and hysterical demonization of Israel.

*Now wait a moment,* Bové's apologists will surely interject. *One can criticize Israel without being an anti-Semite.* Yes, you can. But usually you won't bother. Bové's views on Israel are spelled out completely in an April 24, 2002, interview with Oumma, a popular francophone website devoted to issues of concern to Muslims.[43] The Israeli conflict with the Palestinians, he says, is "a war of a criminal and colonial army against a defenseless civilian population. That exactly sums up the tragedy unfolding in the Palestinian territories." He advocates a complete boycott of Israeli products and the severance of all cooperative ties between the European Union and Israel. "It is at once confusing and unbearable to see this country quietly violating international law, occupying, killing and destroying as long as it can, in all impunity!" He is no great fan of French Jews either: Their attitude is "deplorable," their behavior, "dishonest." For example, he notes,

in Rodez, in Aveyron, the Christians mobilize themselves to denounce the massacres against the Palestinian population, they fast in the cathedral to denounce this injustice. The Muslim community also arrives in large numbers to express their support. Thus the communities join to denounce the evil. The representatives of the Jewish community who oppose the spirit of our activism work against this message of peace. But it is hardly astonishing, because their speech actually camouflages a disguised support for [Ariel] Sharon, a solidarity which, in view of the crimes of that government, seems intolerable to me.

But if he does not find equally intolerable the support—disguised or otherwise—that French Muslims offer to Islamic governments, this surely is not because those regimes commit no crimes.

Nowhere in the interview does he mention—even once—Palestinian suicide bombings. He frequently expressed admiration for Yasser Arafat, "a democratically elected leader," as the hero of a legitimate national liberation movement, but nowhere in public has he mentioned the Israeli army's discovery of documents, signed by Arafat, authorizing cash payments to the families of suicide bombers, or the money systematically funneled from the Palestinian Authority to groups such as the al-Aqsa Martyrs' Brigades, which plans and executes these attacks. He has never commented on Arafat's regular encomiums to the suicide bombers—"Oh God, give me martyrdom like this!"

For a man who so deplores the brutal military occupation of faraway lands, Bové has missed a few easy calls. He has never appealed for a boycott of Chinese goods to protest China's occupation and cultural genocide in Tibet, nor has he lobbied to sever European ties to India in protest of the occupation of Kashmir. (Given his preoccupation with international law and UN resolutions, this oversight is particularly curious.) Nor has he petitioned to rupture the EU's ties to Russia to protest the occupation of Chechnya, even as the rubble that once was Grozny continues to bounce.

That Bové singles out Israel, alone among these nations, suggests his suppressed premises. First, Israel is the world's foremost pariah state and the most deserving object of any right-thinking activist's opprobrium. Second, the occupation of the West Bank and Gaza is manifestly illegal and unjust, and the cause of Arab animus toward Israel, rather than its consequence. Third, no censure or blame for the Palestinians' misery is to be accorded the Palestinian Authority, or any other confrontation state in the Middle East. Fourth, when considering the occupation, there is no need to discuss, no less deplore, the unrelenting and indiscriminate Palestinian terror campaign, on Israeli soil, against Israeli civilians, that began directly after Yasser Arafat rejected an unprecedented Israeli offer for territorial compromise—one that, had it been implemented, would have brought an end to the occupation. These lead to suppressed premise five: It is right and proper for Israelis to be punished collectively for decisions made by their government—but the collective punishment of Palestinians is an abomination. Finally, six, Bové, who was neither elected nor appointed to the task of making foreign policy by an elected government, is doing the world a favor by inserting himself into the globe's most volatile regional conflict. These unspoken premises range from the dubious to the false to the ludicrous.

What can we call this selective and disproportionate animus toward Israel, the state of the Jews, but anti-Semitism? Let's just cut to the chase: Bové, like all the great Christian heretics, simply finds Jews rather distasteful. All things considered, this is not much of a surprise.

## MON DIEU

It is early September 2004, and I am in Perpignan, a small medieval town in the Pyrénées-Orientales. This is the heart of Bové country. I am there for the annual *Visa pour l'image* photojournalism festival. Every night, a slide show of the past year's most newsworthy images is presented in the huge outdoor amphitheater. The photographs are unrelentingly depressing. We see pictures from Darfur of starving mothers with their children, sacks of bones, dying in their arms; refugees who have been raped, tortured, blinded, their last sight on earth that of Janjaweed militias killing their families. We see photographs from Beslan of parents wailing as they discover the bodies of their children. We see a teenage barbarian in Sierra Leone, triumphantly holding up the bloodied, severed head of his rival. The audience—hardened, streetwise photojournalists—watches without comment, applauding only photographs that display unusual technical achievement.

Then we see a photo essay about the Wall—the barrier Israel is building between itself and the Palestinians. A few pictures of a concrete wall flash across the screen. That's it, a wall, a big concrete wall like any other concrete wall. Ugly, sure. But compared with the images that preceded it, hardly shocking. Immediately, though, there is a low hissing in the audience, a collective sucking in of breath. *"Mon Dieu,"* says the Frenchman next to me in a grave, indignant voice. This wall, evidently, is the worst thing on the planet, the worst thing one can imagine seeing. The director of the festival narrates: Everyone, except the Americans, has condemned this wall. But the Israelis persist in their madness. He does not mention that since construction of the wall began, suicide bombings have declined by 90 percent.

The previous day, sixteen Israelis had perished in a Palestinian suicide bombing in Beersheba—one of the few cities not yet protected by the wall. He does not mention this.

## UTOPIA

They have all been much the same, the Bovés. They have all drawn their followers not from the lowest strata of society but from the insecure lower middle classes—urban artisans, journeymen, casual laborers. Particularly, they have drawn their following from the lower tier of the agricultural middle class, who, as a consequence of the growth of towns, had been rapidly losing social stature and wealth. They have all linked the economic anxieties of their followers with their spiritual ones. Their followers have always included society's misfits, criminals, and troublemakers—the current Bové notes that his adherents come "from the extreme right to the extreme left, nationalists, anti-Americans, opportunists of all sorts."[44] They have all been concerned with crops, they have all sought the redistribution of wealth, and they have all hated Jews. They have always appealed to the character described by Eric Hoffer as the true believer: "discontented yet not destitute," electrified by "the feeling that by the possession of some potent doctrine, infallible leader or some new technique they have access to a source of irresistible power."[45] The goals of these movements were never modest: There was always a utopia in sight.

There have been many other Bovés, of course: The pseudo-Baldwin of Flanders, the pseudo-Frederick, the pseudo-Dionysus, Erigena, John Hus, Konrad Schmid, Eudo, Henry of Lausanne, Arnold of Brescia. There were Swabian preachers and Perugian hermits; there were Bovés among the revolutionary flagellants, the Heretics of the Free Spirit, the Taborites, the Hussites, the Utraquists, the Lollards, and the Waldensians. "Ask the rector," as H. L. Mencken counseled, "to lend you any good book on comparative religion; you will find them all listed. They were gods of the highest dignity—gods of civilized peoples—worshipped and believed in by millions. All were omnipotent, omniscient and immortal."[46]

And all are dead—but Bové lives.

# BLACK-MARKET NATIONALISM:
# I HATE

*Denk' ich an Deutschland in der Nacht*
*Dann bin ich um den Schlaf gebracht . . .**

—Heinrich Heine

L IKE EVERYONE ELSE, EUROPEANS long to feel that they are
among their own people—and that indeed their people are a
*splendid* people, a grand and noble people unique unto the world. But
nowhere is this entirely human impulse viewed with more suspicion
now than in Europe, and nowhere is it viewed with suspicion for better reason.

Profound instincts, when repressed, become sublimated. Like the
religious instinct, the instinct to nationalism, when formally denied,
will re-emerge in curious black-market forms. Nowhere in Europe has
nationalism led to greater catastrophe than Germany, and nowhere
has it been more ruthlessly suppressed, thank God. But it has not been
eradicated: it cannot be.

In the case of Rammstein—purveyors of fine black-market nationalism to the German public—it has returned this time as farce rather
than tragedy, but it has nonetheless returned, and this is a warning: It

---

*"When I think of Germany at night, I cannot sleep."

is still there, it has never died, and we may expect to hear more from it in the future, particularly as the social and economic pressures on Europe mount.

Rammstein—the name is a made-up word meaning, more or less, "ramming stone"—is a popular German band. *Very* popular. Rammstein released its first album, *Herzeleid,* in 1995. Within days, it topped the German charts. It stayed in the number one position for five weeks, then remained in the top ten for two years, an unrivaled achievement in Germany's notoriously fickle pop music market. Their next album, *Sehnsucht,* was more successful still: the best-selling album in Germany from the day of its release, it immediately went double-platinum. In 1998, their video *Engel* was awarded an Echo, the German equivalent of a Grammy. In the same year, VIVA, a mainstream German television station more or less like MTV, awarded Rammstein its prize trophy, the Comet, effectively declaring the band the preeminent ambassadors of German popular music. The year 1999 brought Rammstein another Echo for *Sehnsucht.* Their album *Mutter,* released in March 2001, immediately sold a million copies, bringing their total album sales over the 4-million mark. Their album *Reise, Reise,* released in November 2004, surpassed all of their previous sales records. With *Reise, Reise,* Rammstein became the best-selling German-language band in history. Rammstein, in other words, is not a fringe phenomenon.

Let's read Rammstein's lyrics.*

| *RAMMSTEIN* | RAMMSTEIN** |
|---|---|
| *Rammstein* | Rammstein |
| *Ein Mensch brennt* | A man is burning |
| *Rammstein* | Rammstein |

---

*For brevity's sake I have selected a *representative* sample; a complete catalogue of Rammstein lyrics in German and their English translation can be found at http://www.herzeleid.com/en/lyrics.

**Rammstein's name, and this song, allude to the U.S. Air Force base Ramstein, in West Germany, where 69 people were killed and some 500 more injured (most of them burned), when three jets collided above the crowd at an air show on August 28, 1988.

| | |
|---|---|
| *Fleischgeruch liegt in der* | The smell of burning flesh lies in |
| *Luft* | the air |
| *Rammstein* | Rammstein |
| *ein Kind stirbt* | A child dies |
| *Rammstein* | Rammstein |
| *die Sonne scheint* | The sun is shining |
| | |
| *Rammstein* | Rammstein |
| *ein Flammenmeer* | A sea of flames |
| *Rammstein* | Rammstein |
| *Blut gerinnt auf dem Asphalt* | Blood runs on the asphalt |
| *Rammstein* | Rammstein |
| *Mütter schreien* | Mothers scream |
| *Rammstein* | Rammstein |
| *die Sonne scheint* | The sun is shining |
| | |
| *Rammstein* | Rammstein |
| *ein Massengrab* | A mass grave |
| *Rammstein* | Rammstein |
| *kein Entrinnen* | No escape |
| *Rammstein* | Rammstein |
| *kein Vogel singt mehr* | No birds sing anymore |
| *Rammstein* | Rammstein |
| *die Sonne scheint* | The sun is shining |

Here are few more lyrics, from which I have deleted only repetitive passages:

| | |
|---|---|
| *WOLLT IHR DAS BETT IN* | DO YOU WANT TO SEE THE |
| *FLAMMEN SEHEN?* | BED IN FLAMES? |
| | |
| *Wollt ihr das Bett in Flammen* | Do you want to see the bed in |
| *sehen* | flames |
| *wollt ihr in Haut und Haaren* | Do you want to perish in |
| *untergehen* | skin and hair |

*ihr wollt doch auch den Dolch*
*ins Laken stecken*
*ihr wollt doch auch das Blut*
*vom Degen lecken*

You also want a dagger between
the sheets
And to lick the blood
from it

*Sex ist ein Schlacht*
*Liebe ist Krieg*

Sex is a battle
Love is war

*DER MEISTER*

THE MASTER

*Lauft!*

Run!

*Weil der Meister uns gesandt*
*verkünden wir den Untergang*
*der Reiter der Boshaftigkeit*
*füttert sein Geschwür aus Neid*
*es kund zu tun ist ach so bitter*
*es kommt zu dir um zu*
*zerstören*

Called by the Master
Announcing the downfall
The horseman of evil
Stokes the cancer of envy
To herald this is oh so bitter
It comes to you as
destruction

*es wird kein Erbarmen geben*
*lauft, lauft um euer Leben*

There will be no mercy
Run, run for your life

*Die Wahrheit ist ein Chor aus*
*Wind*
*kein Engel kommt um euch*
*zu rächen*
*diese Tage eure letzten sind*
*wie Stäbchen wird es euch*
*zerbrechen*

The truth is a voice in the
wind
No angel comes to avenge
you
These days are your last
And you will be broken like
little sticks

The lyrics of *"Der Meister"* are particularly suggestive. Paul Celan's biographer, John Felstiner, notes that the word *Meister* in German "can designate God, Christ, rabbi, teacher, champion, captain, owner, guildsman, master of arts or theology, labor-camp overseer, musical maestro, 'master' race, not to mention Goethe's Wilhelm Meister and Wagner's *Meistersinger von Nürnberg,* which carries overtones of the 1935 Nuremberg racial laws."[1]

We see in Celan the same association, through this word, of German masters, music, and mercilessness. Consider this passage from Celan's "Death Fugue":

| | |
|---|---|
| *Schwarze Milch der Frühe wir trinken dich nachts* | Black milk of daybreak we drink you at night |
| *wir trinken dich mittags der Tod ist ein Meister aus Deutschland* | we drink you at noon death is a master from Germany |
| *wir trinken dich abends und morgens wir trinken und trinken* | we drink you at sundown and in the morning we drink and we drink you |
| *der Tod ist ein Meister aus Deutschland sein Auge ist blau* | death is a master from Germany his eyes are blue |
| *er trifft dich mit bleierner Kugel er trifft dich genau* | he strikes you with leaden bullets his aim is true |
| *ein Mann wohnt im Haus dein goldenes Haar Margarete* | a man lives in the house your golden hair Margarete |
| *er hetzt seine Rüden auf uns er schenkt uns ein Grab in der Luft* | he sets his pack on to us he grants us a grave in the air |
| *er spielt mit den Schlangen und träumet der Tod ist ein Meister aus Deutschland* | he plays with the serpents and daydreams death is a master from Germany |

Rammstein's lyrics are not comparable in brilliance and mastery to the poetry of Celan, of course, but their preoccupations are strikingly similar. Celan, a Romanian Jew, was raised in a German-speaking household. In 1942, his parents were deported to labor camps in the

Ukraine. The Germans declared his mother unfit for work and shot her in the neck. His father swiftly perished of typhus. Celan himself was interned for eighteen months in a Nazi labor camp. He drowned himself in the Seine in 1970. It is certainly remarkable that the most popular band in contemporary Germany finds itself drawn to the same themes and imagery as Celan. Of course, there is a difference: Celan speaks with the voice of the master's quarry, whereas Rammstein speaks with the voice of his emissaries. Celan, moreover, laments these associations. Rammstein celebrates them.

Here's one more Rammstein song for good measure:

| *WEIßES FLEISCH* | WHITE FLESH |
|---|---|
| *Rote Striemen auf weisser Haut* | Red bruises on white skin |
| *ich tu dir weh* | I hurt you |
| *und du jammerst laut* | And you cry loudly |
| | |
| *Jetzt hast du Angst und ich bin soweit* | Now you are terrified and I am ready |
| *mein krankes Dasein nach Erlösung schreit* | My corrupt being demands salvation |
| *dein weisses Fleisch wird mein Schafott* | Your white flesh will be my scaffold |
| *in meinem Himmel gibt es keinen Gott* | There is no god in my heaven. |

In both form and imagery, Rammstein's lyrics have a distinct history in German poetry. The source is the Neue Sachlichkeit—new concreteness, or New Realism—of the 1920s, of which Georg Trakl is the best-known exponent. These poets aimed to represent reality in concrete images, and their reality, as it happened, revolved around a preoccupation with blood and smashed faces. Trakl's influence is particularly obvious in the band's preoccupation with gore and despair. Consider these lines from Trakl's *"De Profundis"*:

| | |
|---|---|
| *Auf meine Stirne tritt kaltes Metall.* | Cold metal straps on my forehead. |
| *Spinnen suchen mein Herz.* | Spiders search for my heart. |
| *Es ist ein Licht, das meinen Mund erlöscht.* | There is a light that dies in my mouth.[2] |

There are odd parallels between Trakl's life and that of Rammstein's lead singer and lyricist, Till Lindemann. Trakl was a full-blown drug addict, as Lindemann is said to be. Rumors that Trakl had carried on an incestuous affair with his sister pursued him throughout his life, and Lindemann is also quite intrigued by incest. Photographs of Trakl, taken just before his death in 1914, and Lindemann show a spooky similarity.

Rammstein's lyrics also have something in common with the notorious *Morgue* cycle of Gottfried Benn, the Berlin venereal disease specialist who pledged his allegiance to the Nazi Party until it expelled him for perversion. See, for example, Verse IV, "Nigger Bride":

| *NEGERBRAUT* | NIGGER BRIDE |
|---|---|
| *Dann lag auf Kissen dunklen Bluts gebettet der blonde Nacken einer weißen Frau.* | Then the blond neck of a white woman lay bedded on the dark bloody cushions |
| *Die Sonne wütete in ihrem Haar und leckte ihr die hellen Schenkel lang und kniete um die bräunlicheren Brüste,* | The sun stormed in her hair and licked along her light thighs and kneeled at her brownish breasts, |
| *noch unentstellt durch Laster und Geburt.* | not yet distorted by vice or birth. |
| *Ein Nigger neben ihr: durch Pferdehufschlag Augen und Stirn zerfetzt. Der bohrte* | Beside her a nigger, eyes and forehead shredded by a horse's hoof, digging |

| | |
|---|---|
| *zwei Zehen seines schmutzigen linken Fußes* | two toes of his dirty left foot |
| *ins Innere ihres kleinen weißen Ohrs.* | into her little white ear. |
| *Sie aber lag und schlief wie eine Braut:* | Yet she lay asleep like a bride: |
| *am Saume ihres Glücks der ersten Liebe* | at the brink of first love's joys |
| *und wie vorm Aufbruch vieler Himmelfahrten* | as on the eve of many an Ascension |
| *des jungen warmen Blutes.* | of warm young blood. |
| *Bis man ihr* | Until they sank |
| *das Messer in die weiße Kehle senkte* | the knife into her white throat |
| *und einen Purpurschurz aus totem Blut* | and cast a purple garter of dead blood |
| *ihr um die Hüften warf.* | around her hips.[3] |

But while Benn is the passive observer of his early poems, the members of Rammstein clearly envision *themselves* doing the bashing, defiling, and knifing.

Their imagery is suggestive as well of postwar German Expressionist paintings—those of Otto Dix, in particular, who having spent four years in the trenches had a fine pictorial feel for what things looked like after an exchange of artillery. Songs by Rammstein with sado-masochistic sexual themes, such as *"Mein Teil"*—an homage to the German cannibal Armin Meiwes, who in 2002 shared a final meal with his willing victim of the man's severed, flambéed penis—would not have been out of place in Julius Streicher's *Der Stürmer,* a newspaper even many Nazis found excessive in its pornographic obsessions and sensationalism.

At roughly the time "The Master" was topping the German charts, this song, by the Spice Girls, was the number one song on the British charts:

WANNABE

Yo, I'll tell you what I want, what I really really want
So tell me what you want, what you really really want
I'll tell you what I want, what I really really want
So tell me what you want, what you really really want
I wanna (huh), I wanna (huh), I wanna (huh), I wanna (huh)
I wanna really really really wanna zigazig ah

*These* cheerful imbeciles, clearly, are quite unlike Rammstein in their existential preoccupations.* I won't bother you with examples of the French and Italian chart toppers of the late 1990s. Trust me, they're nothing like Rammstein. (They're nothing like music either.)

## INHERITORS OF THE GERMAN MUSICAL TRADITION

Next, let's listen to Rammstein. Much of it can be downloaded from the Internet. Initiates should begin with the song *"Reise, Reise,"* played at top volume. Push your subwoofers to the limit. That is the way it is meant to be appreciated.

Formed in 1993, Rammstein comprises six working-class musicians, all born and raised behind the Berlin Wall: vocalist Lindemann, keyboardist Flake Lorenz, drummer Christoph Schneider, bassist Oliver Riedel, and guitarists Paul Landers and Richard Kruspe-Bernstein.** Their music is extremely sophisticated and superbly orchestrated. They blend metal, industrial, techno, and classical musical techniques, employing a vast range of sound effects—studio-distorted

---

*The song continues for about six more verses in exactly the same vein. The melody itself calls to mind Sir Thomas Beecham's remark that the English may not like music, but they absolutely love the noise it makes.

**Kruspe recently became Kruspe-Bernstein when he married a Jew and adopted his new wife's name. His philo-Semitic marriage has been seized upon with great relief by fans eager to believe that the band's music has nothing to do with what it seems to be about.

guitars, sampled ghostly wailing, Arabic choirs, melodic whistling, string arrangements, chanting crowds of thousands, the sound of marching jackboots, and a full symphony orchestra. The orchestra is one of Germany's best, led by a completely professional conductor.

This point must be made perfectly clear, for it is as important as the observation that Rammstein represents a particularly German and apparently ineradicable strain of utter nihilism: Rammstein is also the inheritor of the German tradition of musical genius. Their rhythmic craftsmanship—unerring and precise—is unmistakably German, as is their intuitive command of musical tension and release. Their bombast, particularly, is reminiscent of Wagner, and so is the music's eerie hypnotic quality. Carl Orff's influence can be heard in Rammstein's use of orchestral arrangements. String passages explode into skull-crushing onslaughts; low, synthesized chords follow and then recede, the effect eerie and thrilling. By comparison, American heavy metal bands seem clumsy, childish, and anemic. In keeping with a long German musical tradition, Rammstein's vocal lines are, like Schubert's, entirely integrated into the musical texture; they are not merely arias with accompaniment. The German language functions almost as an instrument in its own right. With its sibilants, harsh fricatives, unique phonotactics, and stress rules, German lends itself particularly well to powerful, rhythmic song, as it does, of course, to powerful, rhythmic rhetoric.

Themes from Nordic and German mythology appear throughout their videos: *"Sonne,"* for example, features a coke-sniffing, sadomasochistic Snow White.* "Dalai Lama" originates in Goethe's *Erlkönig*. *"Reise, Reise"* is based on a German sea chantey; it represents the master's call to sleeping sailors. Although the words are translated by the band as "Voyage, Voyage," they are also a reference to the Middle High German *Risen, Risen,* meaning "Wake up." The phrase recalls *Deutschland Erwache*—Germany, Wake Up—a Nazi brownshirt slogan. I have seen Rammstein perform this song in concert, in Berlin. It is quite clear that the audience takes the chorus as a verb.

---

*It is instructive to contrast this song, Rammstein's interpretation of "Here Comes the Sun," with the Beatles' original.

*"Reise, Reise"* begins with the sound of lonely waves and gulls, an ominous warlike pounding, and the primitive chanting of sailors in a galley. Suddenly the listener is steamrollered by smashing drums, violent bass, and a full choir, amplified to unspeakable levels. A written account is a pale simulacrum. The song is powerful, stirring, and unbelievably effective—the effect, the *intended* effect, being to engorge the listener with thrilling aggression. If you're in doubt, download the song and play it through your headphones when you next lift weights. Turn the volume up to eleven. Bench-press. You'll be impressed by your athletic achievement.

Most compelling is vocalist Lindemann, a massive former swimming champion from the town of Schwerin. He commands a sinister, low bass rarely utilized in contemporary pop music. His voice is untrained but electrifying. His rolled *R*s are familiar. The members of the band grew up under the Deutsche Demokratische Republik's cheerless tutelage—"We were not even allowed to say Hitler's name," keyboardist Lorenz told me—but somehow Lindemann managed to acquaint himself with that orator's distinctive style nonetheless. He ripples with muscles. He is a man, not a boy, with a voice so powerful and erotic that even women who understand Rammstein's lyrics—or perhaps *especially* women who understand those lyrics—find themselves mesmerized by that voice, by its beauty and masculinity. The first time I heard him sing, the hair on the back of my neck stood straight up.

For some of us, that experience is disturbing, to say the least.

## SPEAKING TO THE HEART

Now let's watch Rammstein perform, in concert.

The performance begins when Lindemann sets himself on fire—literally, not figuratively—then sprays flames into the air with handheld rocket launchers. Soon the entire stage is ablaze. In the band's early days, if fans were insufficiently attentive, Rammstein doused the dance floor with kerosene and set that alight as well. It got them hopping every time. An unfortunate accident put an end to that practice, and now the band's pyrotechnics are coordinated by professionals.

When Lindemann sings *"Bestrafe Mich"*—"Punish Me"—he flagellates himself with a whip. He punctuates *"Du Hast"*—"You Hate"—by firing a gun in the air to a jackhammer rhythm.* During a rendition of *"Ich Will Ficken"*—"I Want to Fuck"—he sports a monstrous black dildo that shoots something viscous over the audience (*what* precisely it shoots is a matter of controversy among Rammstein scholars, with hypotheses ranging from yogurt to yak semen), and follows this drollery with a performance of *"Bück Dich"*—"Bend Over"—in which he simulates the anal violation of his keyboardist, Flake Lorenz, who prostrates himself on the floor with a mask on his face, a prisoner's chain round his neck, and a ball gag in his mouth. Lorenz then smashes a fluorescent light tube against Lindemann's chest. All the while the auditory assault is relentless, machinelike, a musical moving Panzer division. In 1998, Rammstein was invited to the United States to open an event billed as the Family Values Tour. Authorities in Worcester, Massachusetts, watched the show, then threw the two men *directly* into prison on obscenity charges.**

This is martial music. Without the music, the lyrics might be misinterpreted as expressions of adolescent angst. But these are grown men performing: they are in their late thirties and early forties. Separated from the music, the power of the lyrics is severely diluted. Try reading them again, this time nurturing a vivid image of Stuka dive bombers swiftly obliterating the Polish Air Force while eight motorized and six Panzer divisions slice through Poland. Imagine the Wehrmacht marching toward Warsaw as German tanks steamroller Brest-Litovsk and

---

*Du Hast* means "You have." "You hate" is properly spelled *Du Hasst*. But Rammstein translates the song as "You hate." This translation is on their official website; it is the translation they send to fans upon request, and it is the way they sing it when they sing the song in English.

**When a journalist asked whether Rammstein truly represented what most Americans might imagine as family values—particularly since Rammstein's songs are obsessively preoccupied with incest, a dubious family value at best—guitarist Kruspe-Bernstein explained that these were "just love songs from extreme angles." (Paul Gargano, "A Foreign Flair for Family Values," *Metal Edge,* January 1999.)

Storm Troopers slam shut the escape routes across the Vistula. Envision women and children streaming terrified into the roads, attempting to flee the unrelenting, indiscriminate German bombing. Then you can skip the music. You'll already have something of a feel for it.

Rammstein's performance of *"Ich Will"* is particularly evocative. When the insane pounding and relentless march of the drums and the orchestra cease, there is nothing but a hypnotic melody from an acoustic guitar and a warbling, unnerving whistle from the synthesizer. Lindemann hisses:

| | |
|---|---|
| *Wir wollen dass ihr uns vertraut* | We want to be trusted |
| *Wir wollen dass ihr uns alles glaubt* | We want you to believe everything we say. |

Then the hypnotic lull is over, and the musical tanks roar back into action. Lindemann's voice swells to a massive imperative, dominating the thrashing guitars and the booming bass. He thunders to the audience:

| | |
|---|---|
| *Könnt ihr mich hören?* | Can you hear me? |

The enormous crowd roars back, in frenzied but perfect unison, a stadium of synchronous German voices:

| | |
|---|---|
| *Wir hören dich!* | We hear you! |
| *Könnt ihr mich sehen?* | Can you see me? |
| *Wir sehen dich!* | We see you! |
| *Könnt ihr mich fühlen?* | Can you feel me? |
| *Wir fühlen dich!* | We feel you! |

It hardly needs be pointed out what this scene resembles. Joseph Goebbels would have found much to admire in it. "Propaganda," he advised, addressing the Nuremberg Rally in 1934, "must be creative.

It is by no means a matter for the bureaucracy or official administration, rather it is a matter of productive fantasy. The genuine propagandist must be a true artist. He must be a master of the popular soul, using it as an instrument to express the majesty of a genuine political will."[4] The most effective performance and propagandist techniques displayed in the Nazis' mass rallies embodied this appeal to artistry, this aesthetic sensibility—from the grand, theatrical displays of power to the relentless marching rhythms, from the repetitive, emotional sloganeering to the idolatrous celebration of masculinity. Hitler also began his speeches softly and slowly, his voice growing louder, then booming, the masses aroused to an intoxicated frenzy.

Lindemann proclaims himself to be baffled, *hurt* even, by the way certain fans are inspired to respond to these capers with Nazi salutes. "Our tour manager," he has said, "is required to come up on stage as soon as the fascists start using the Hitler greeting."[5] There is not much the tour manager can do about the fans on the Internet, I suppose:

hi ,, im a big rammstein fan ,,, my name is kersten , and is great to share our own feeling about the band ,,,because when u are sad or angry R+ is like my drug ,,,, rammstein means power ,,proud,,nasionalism,,connect my soul to a different world,,,and th e meaning of rammstein is the old germany ,, das reich,, what will happen if rammstein where not germans ,, all that respect will be trash,,, so be proud of rammstein ,of germany ,and our leader adolf hitler¡¡¡

ein volk ein reich ein fuhrer¡¡¡*

Keyboardist Lorenz shares Lindemann's bewilderment about the persistent charges that in Rammstein's performances there is a hint of the old Volk, Reich, and Führer. "How silly can they get," he complains.[6]

---

*Further down in the thread, Kersten receives a dressing down from her fellow Rammstein fans. "Whoa . . . ," says Megan. "Maybe you should chill a bit about that Hitler crap." See http://www.almostrammstein.com/nf/forums/view_thread.html?tid=118.

| | |
|---|---|
| *Du kannst, Du willst und wirst nie vergeben* | You can, you want and will never forgive |
| *und Du verteufelst sein ganzes Leben* | And you condemn his life |
| *treibst in den Wahnsinn von* | You drift in the insanity from |
| *maßlosem Zorn, Vernichtung und Rache,* | Rage, destruction and revenge |
| *Du bist zum Hassen gebor'n* | You were born to hate. |

Lorenz holds—with a straight face, I've seen this—that only silly, joyless martinets would read bloodlust between those lines, or find nihilism in words like this:

| | |
|---|---|
| *Nichts ist für dich* | Nothing is for you |
| *nichts war für dich* | Nothing was for you |
| *nichts bleibt für dich* | Nothing remains for you |
| *für immer* | Forever |

In fact, Rammstein's members proclaim themselves to be *incensed* by the persistent intimations that their music and performances have any political resonance at all, no less a disturbing one. Their publicist has set the matter straight: "There is no political content whatsoever to their music. Their songs are about love."[7]

This rejoinder, the band feels, should have been the end of the matter. Yet some critics seem determined to perceive something sinister in the spectacle of Rammstein performing *"Weisses Fleisch"* before 10,000 drunken Germans, each with his fist raised. "There is a perfect explanation for this," Lindemann has remarked of the critics' animadversions. "Narrow-mindedness."[8] Guitarist Paul Landers shares his indignation. "Absurd," he has exclaimed.[9] But, he has added helplessly, "if some of the journalists want to stick us in the Nazi corner, we can't help it."[10]

Well, actually, Paul, you probably *could* help it, if you really tried. Here's my first suggestion: *Don't use Leni Riefenstahl footage in your promotional clips.* Narrow-minded though it may be, when your videos feature scenes from *Olympische Spiele*—Olympics Games, a documentary commissioned by the Nazis in 1936 as "a song of praise to the ideals of National Socialism"—journalists will be apt to stick you right in that Nazi corner. "We are not Nazis," they protested again in an official statement, adding that they simply chose the film because it was a "visionary work of art."[11] There are a lot of visionary works of art in the world, Paul. But *that* one has a particular meaning. If you're looking for visionary works of arts without those connotations, I commend to your attention Henri Cartier-Bresson's dignified portraits of the elderly Gandhi. If you need any more advice, just give me a call.

Given the musicians' propensity to feel saddened by these hurtful accusations, quite a number of their aesthetic choices seem hard to fathom. For example, the cover art of their debut album, *Herzeleid,* resembles to no small degree a Nazi propaganda poster, the six shirtless band members—enormous, muscular, iron-jawed—looming into the camera lens in what appears to be an archetypal celebration of the Master Race.[12] For the portraits in *Sehnsucht,* the Austrian artist Gottfried Helnwein photographed the musicians in facial bandages, their lips and eyes stretched wide apart by hideous medical instruments. There is an echo of Trakl, again, in these "cold metal straps." But it is unreasonable, the musicians protest, to think that images such as this might evoke obscene historical memories. "It's just reverse discrimination because we are German," says Lorenz. "If we were Spanish or Dutch, there would be no problem."[13]

Then again, it is hard to conceive of a Spaniard or a Dutchman composing *"Links-Zwo-Drei-Vier,"* meaning "Left-Two-Three-Four," and performed, exactly as the title suggests, to the rhythm of a vigorous goose step. A crooning verse is followed by a furious, even apocalyptic chorus, accompanied by the unmistakable sound of metrically precise marching jackboots. A crowd—in perfect synchronicity—screams *"Hi!"* after each refrain. It's quite close to the sound *"Heil."* It's close enough, in fact, that critics on Internet chat sites devoted to restoring pride in the Aryan race find the similarity quite pleasing.*

---

*The *"Hei-Hei-Hei"* chorus in Rammstein's song *"Heirate Mich"* has a similarly agreeable resonance for these fans. See, for example, comments at the Stormfront

Then, in a growling bass whisper, Lindemann urges the audience: *"Mit dem Herzen denken!"*

Think with your heart!

The National-Socialist Speaker's Corps was instructed to use those words exactly when addressing its audiences. Hugo Ringler, for example, an official of the Munich Reichspropagandaleitung, recalls Hitler's rise to power in this essay, published in 1937 for the edification of the Nazi Party's propagandists:

> [*He*] *spoke not to the understanding but to the heart*. He spoke out of his heart into the heart of his listener. And the better he understood how to execute this appeal to the heart, the more willingly he exploited it and the more receptive was the audience to his message. One could not at all at that time persuade the German people by rational argument; things worked out badly for parties that tried that approach. The people were won by the man who struck the chord that others had ignored—the feelings, the sentiment or, as one wants to call it, the heart.[14]

Lorenz has declared that he has no idea how Rammstein has acquired its neo-Nazi reputation. "Just because we play hard German and martial music doesn't make us Nazis. We are definitely not Nazis and the song '*Links*' should help to end this stupid gabbing."[15]

Why he believes this is unclear.

---

White Nationalist Community, http://forum.stormfront.org/showthread.php?t=114116. Members of this community are of varying minds about Rammstein's fellow-kinship: "[I]n the interviews I've read with them," writes someone who calls himself "Panzershrek," "they try to distance themselves from any form of racialism, probably because i"s [*sic*] not good for record distribution deals with the Jew monopolised U.S music industry. Having said that I think they're a great band and even if they aren't racially aware the music certainly sounds like it is, there's something about their music that makes you want to stomp some heads!"

## A FAMILIAR SCENE

Now let's watch a Rammstein video. In fact, let's watch the video that accompanies the song *"Links."* Shot in black, white, and brown, the animated video depicts ants. To the sound of the jackboots, a giant ant pumps his right feeler in the air. We see the giant ant on stage, before thousands of ants, all identical, all returning the salute, like pistons. Ants swarm out of tunnels. The colony surges. For an instant we glimpse something in the background that resembles a storm trooper's helmet. We see a series of insinuated swastikas, although we never see the real thing: What we are seeing are permutations on Rammstein's insignia, which itself is a variant on a Nordic rune, and very much like an Iron Cross.* A pseudoswastika mutates into a headless stick figure. Performer and leader, it conducts the audience, pumping its arm into the air. A massive ant-audience pumps its feelers in unison to the sound of the jackboots. We see two shots—impossibly brief—of white pseudoswastikas mutating against a grainy black background. The effect is like a wartime propaganda film.

We cut to the band members. Swastika-ant becomes Lindemann, his massive swimmer's physique looming. The footage is grainy and stuttering, as if shot in the 1930s. His eyes are full of madman's ecstasy, his body thrashes in time with the music. Flash now to the ants, so closely packed that we see only the tops of their carapaces, like helmets. Flash back to Lindemann—an expression of glee on his face, now for *just one second* sporting a short black mustache, so briefly it could be a trick of the lighting.

The ants organize themselves into columns, pulsing in time to the jackboots. They pour out of tunnels by the thousands, throbbing. We see an image from the sky: The ants converge before a massive tower. They form a giant, pulsating pseudoswastika. They part in columns

---

*Neo-Nazis frequently sport the Iron Cross as a surrogate for the Nazi Iron Cross, which is banned in Germany. The Nazi Iron Cross had a superimposed swastika. The Anti-Defamation League's catalogue of Nordic runes favored by neo-Nazis as swastika surrogates may be found here: http://www.adl.org/hate_symbols/updates.asp.

again. Row after row of ants pump their fists in the air, and the chorus says, *"Hi! Hi!"* Anyone who has seen *Triumph of the Will* will recognize this scene. It is the Nuremberg Rally.

Like Riefenstahl's film, this video is a masterpiece: It is intended to arouse very particular emotions in the viewer, and it does.

## JUST DOING WHAT COMES NATURALLY

Another video. The single *"Mein Teil,"* which may be chastely translated as "My Part," treats the true saga of the cannibal Armin Meiwes, who recently slaughtered and ate a forty-two-year-old Siemens engineer from Berlin. Meiwes videotaped the entire event. The advertisement Meiwes placed on the Internet, searching for a victim, forms the song's epigram:

> „*Suche gut gebauten 18-30jährigen zum Schlachten*"
> —*Der Metzgermeister*

> "Looking for a well-built 18-to-30-year-old for slaughtering"
> —The Master Butcher

The song begins with the sound of a knife being sharpened.

| | |
|---|---|
| *Heute treff' ich einen Herrn* | Today I met a man |
| *Der hat mich zum Fressen gern* | Who'd like to eat me up |
| *Weiche Teile und auch harte* | Soft parts and hard |
| *stehen auf der Speisekarte* | are on the menu |
| *Denn du bist was du isst* | You are what you eat |
| *und ihr wisst was es ist* | and you know what it is |
| *Es ist mein Teil—nein* | It's my part—no |
| *Mein Teil—nein* | My part—no |
| *Da das ist mein Teil—nein* | That over there is my part—no |
| *Mein Teil—nein* | My part—no |
| *Die stumpfe Klinge gut und recht* | The blade good and true |

| | |
|---|---|
| *Ich blute stark und mir ist schlecht* | I'm bleeding heavily and feel sick |
| *Muss ich auch mit der Ohnmacht kämpfen* | I also have to fight fatigue |
| *ich esse weiter unter Krämpfen* | I keep eating despite cramps |
| *Ist doch so gut gewürzt* | It's just so well seasoned |
| *und so schön flambiert* | And nicely broiled |
| *und so liebevoll auf Porzellan serviert* | And lovingly served on china |
| *Dazu ein guter Wein* | A good wine goes with it |
| *und zarter Kerzenschein* | And mellow candelight |
| *Ja da lass ich mir Zeit* | Yes, that still leaves me time |
| *Etwas Kultur muss sein* | It is necessary to be civilized |

The video was directed by the brilliant Zoran Bihac, who also directed the video for *"Links."* Originally, the band had hoped to use Meiwes's own footage of the event, but to their disappointment, the police would not release it from their custody. Several other treatments were proposed and rejected. Here is one rejected concept, according to keyboardist Lorenz:

We also had an idea involving war weapons, some kind of World War I scenario, with a battle going on and people dying and bombs exploding; all that would be happening in the background, whilst up close you'd see these generals bent over a map, dividing up territory, saying "that's my part," "that's my part," "that's my part". . . .[16]

In the end, the band decided upon another approach. Guitarist Kruspe-Bernstein, who founded the band, explained the creative process to me when I spoke to him in Berlin:

The interesting part was, like, people were, you know, how can we do this video? Someone came and said, you know, you know what we do—you guys are getting in there, everyone by himself, and perform, for two hours, whatever you want to do from listen-ing to the song. That was really interesting. We wouldn't know what the other ones were doing, you know? I don't know, for me, it was like . . . well, this is the song, like obviously I could kind of do a dance thing, but I wasn't in the mood to dance, so I thought of masturbation, then you know. . . . I feel like fighting against myself. That's what I did. I was wrestling with myself. That's what I did for two hours. Like a double. Like a wrestler. I was wrestling. And everyone did something else. It was really interest-ing. It was the first time to perform, to act, to do something that we felt. Normally what we do is act. We play-act, in a role. But this time we were really doing something that we felt. It was weird. That was different.

What, then, did the members of the band spontaneously think to do when given this chance to do what they *really* felt? Lindemann, eyes wild with rage and lust, teeth rotting out of his head, sodomizes an angel, then dons a fanged mouthpiece and rips the feathered creature apart with his teeth and bare hands. Lorenz dances in ballet shoes. Schneider dresses as Meiwes's mother and, clutching a handbag, takes the rest of the snarling, snapping, nearly naked men for a walk on leashes. There are brief shots of each of the men howling, their faces contorted with pain and terror. Kruspe-Bernstein shovels the angel's feathers into his mouth and, as he said, wrestles with himself.

The video was controversial in Germany, although not for the reasons one might expect. Critics focused on the grotesque treatment of cannibalism, completely overlooking the far more astonishing im-ages spliced into the film. Shot in black-and-white, they are portraits of Riedel, Rammstein's bass player. He is skeletal and naked but for a filthy rag wrapped around his waist. He is writhing on the ground and screaming in agony. His ribs are protruding, his eye sockets are sunken, and his skull appears hollowed-out. His head is shaved. He appears more dead than alive. When told to "really do something that he felt," Riedel's first impulse was to reenact a nightmare of Auschwitz.

It is hard to say which possibility is scarier—that the makers of this video realized this consciously, or that they didn't.

## "WHAT'S NATURALLY IN THE MUSIC IS WHAT MAKES IT SO GERMAN"

I met the members of Rammstein for the first time, in Berlin, on the day American military action commenced in Iraq. Looking for my hotel, I saw graffiti on the street:

Out, America, occupiers!
Out, America, terrorists!
Out, America, inventors of the atomic bomb!
Out, America, inventors of anthrax!

I saw antiwar demonstrators carrying signs likening President Bush to Hitler. The massive protests had shut down the center of the city.

When I'd called Rammstein's managers to ask whether I might meet them, they were initially enthusiastic. Then Donald Rumsfeld said Germany was part of "Old Europe." Rammstein staged a diplomatic counteroffensive. "Maybe we are all a little over-hysterical these days," their press secretary wrote to me, "but the situation really is bad and going worse. . . . After I learned last week that 'French fries' are no longer 'French fries' but 'freedom fries' I would not be surprised to see German bands banned in the US or whatever. . . . All seems to be possible right now."

I reassured her that as far as I knew, Rammstein had nothing to fear from an enraged American street. Feelings were soothed. Feathers unruffled. I could meet the band as scheduled.

I met the band in a discreet office above a gloomy, anonymous warehouse in east Berlin. This is the neighborhood where Rammstein met and played before the fall of the Wall. To deter fans, there was no sign on their door. In person, they were bland and pleasant, cleanshaven, tall and handsome, dressed in neatly pressed chinos and cotton polo shirts. I had heard that journalists who asked about Rammstein's politics were apt to find themselves ejected from the interview, but after a bit of small talk, they held forth marvelously.

Why, I asked, did *they* think Rammstein's music inspired such controversy?

"People take the lyrics out of context," Kruspe-Bernstein offered. "The romantic, lyric quality gets a bit lost in translation."

A good translation, then, should clear up any confusion? I read out loud, in English:

My black blood and your white flesh
I will always become hornier from your screams
The cold sweat on your white forehead
Hails into my sick brain

Your white flesh excites me so
I am just a gigolo
My father was exactly like me
Your white flesh enlightens me

Well yes, said Kruspe-Bernstein, there is that. But he held that this sounded much more romantic in German. Landers, the second guitarist, wasn't sure. "The lyrics are *scarier* in German," Landers insisted. The two musicians debated the proper translation of the word *geil*. My translator believed it to be correctly rendered as "horny."

"Our music," said Kruspe-Bernstein, "is *German,* and that's what comes through. What's naturally in the music is what makes it so German. We are simply trying to make the music that we are able to make. The classical music, the music of our ancestors, is passed down in a certain way. We have a feeling for it. American music, black music, we don't know how to do that—"

"We have no soul," interjected keyboardist Lorenz.

"And we know how to play on the beat," added Kruspe-Bernstein. "We know how to make it straight, how to make it even."

"Angular and straight," echoed Lorenz with satisfaction.

"We like it heavy, bombastic, romantic. Like the direction that

Wagner takes," said Kruspe-Bernstein. "No other Germans do it the way we do it. We're the only ones who do it the way Germans *should*. The others try to imitate the English and the Americans. We're almost too German for Germany." The thought seemed to pain him. "The Germans are a bit ashamed of their nationality. They've had a disturbed relationship to it since the Second World War. We're trying to establish a natural relationship to our identity."

Would this anthem, I asked, be an example of a natural relationship to German identity?

> The fire purifies the soul
> And remaining is a mouthful of
> Ashes
>
> I will return
> In ten days
> As your shadow
> And I will hunt you down

"Well," replied Kruspe-Bernstein, "one cannot prevent people from interpreting something negatively."

Landers agreed. "It's time to stop being ashamed about what comes out of Germany and to establish a *normal* way of dealing with being German."

> Secretly I will rise from the dead
> And you will plead for mercy
> Then I will kneel in your face
> And stick my finger in the ashes

The *abnormal* way of being German must be mind-boggling. Come to think of it, it was.

Kruspe-Bernstein informed me that the band's essential good nature had been misunderstood. "If people don't understand the lyrics, their interpretations can be more gruesome than is actually the case.

Fantasy can be at work. It can make things more intense, worse than things actually are."

Again, I read out loud, in translation:

You can, you want and will never forgive
And you condemn his life
You drift in the insanity from
Rage, destruction and revenge
You were born to hate

My rage does not want to die
My rage will never die

You ram your hatred like a stone
Into him Ramming stone—
You have pursued, hunted, and cursed him
And he has taken to his heels, crawling

After reading these lyrics, I asked, why might listeners remain concerned? The negative reactions, Kruspe-Bernstein told me firmly, "have to do with the hard sound of the music and the short haircuts."

Lorenz reported himself devastated by the persistent intimations that Rammstein's aesthetic was reminiscent of the Nazi era. "We overestimated the public. The people don't understand it. We thought it was so obvious that we weren't right-wingers that no would see these right-wing elements in what we do."

The members of the band were tired of national self-reproach, they said. "The Americans aren't ashamed about the fact that they killed the Indians," said Kruspe-Bernstein. "If the *Germans* had eradicated the Indians, *we* would have had a bad conscience. *We* would have had to be ashamed."

"The Americans aren't ashamed of what *they* did," Landers agreed. "*Ja.* Our music is about the revival of a *healthy German self-esteem*. When people come to our concerts, they can experience something which they can perhaps otherwise not experience."

"*Ja*, like soccer," said Kruspe-Bernstein. "Soccer is popular because that's the only place in Germany where one can call out *Germany*."

"It's like a Terminator movie," Landers said. "Everyone likes him because he's so strong." I wasn't sure whether he was referring to Lindemann or the Terminator. "At our concerts people can feel *anger*. We feel that Germany is longing for some identity. We had an evil history and everybody is ashamed. 'Our parents or grandparents did *this* and they did *that*.' We just inherited this history. Now we have to live with it and we don't want to. We want to do what we *feel*. Without always feeling responsible for history."

I asked them about the song *"Links,"* and about the way it does seem awfully reminiscent of the old *this* and the old *that*. They appeared profoundly frustrated by my willful determination to misunderstand their intentions. In fact, they said, the suggestion that these lyrics—*Left, two, three, four! Left, two, three, four!*—might evoke a darker moment in German history was frankly defamatory. You see, they explained to me, the song had precisely the opposite meaning. It was all about being on the Left.

The *Left?* Yes, agreed Lorenz firmly, the *Left*. He held that life was better under communism. In what way? "In all ways. I could live without worries about life. No one wanted to do evil to anyone. There was nothing to win or gain."

What about the Stasi, I asked?

"The secret police? Every country has that."

*"Links,"* said Lorenz, was written to clear up all this misunderstanding about Rammstein. "We intentionally show that one can be evil and be on the Left. People say that right-wing music is hard, and we're saying, 'We too can be hard.'"

I'd had no doubt that one could be evil and on the Left. At their extremes, actually, the Left and the Right look very much alike. I was intrigued by his use of the word *hard*, though. The Nazis conceived of *hardness* as the hallmark of the new Nietzschean superhuman. Members of the band used this word often, I noticed, as do their fans.

"We made this song for Germany," said Lorenz.

I asked Lorenz whether the allusion to the Nuremberg Rally was intentional. Pique played over his odd, pointy features. "There is no reference to the Nuremberg Rally. This is the first time I've ever even *heard* of that. It never would have *dawned* on me. We purposely did a video without people and symbols. I think it's a very nice video. It's almost my favorite video. The ants are so cute."

Look, I said to Lorenz, *come on:* If Rammstein is a left-wing band, why use all this right-wing imagery?

"We wonder about this ourselves," he replied, as if the answer were somehow unknowable. "We never thought that people could see it is as right-wing. We can't see things from the audience's perspective. We just use blood and these symbols because the songs are about violence and aggression." My translator winced.

"We use them to *enthrall* the audience," he added. Lorenz is the runt, the only member of Rammstein who isn't huge and handsome. He's the one who wears the ball gag in his mouth while Lindemann pretends to sodomize him on the stage.

"It's a difficult question, because everyone has the right to listen to the music they want to listen to," he offered in response to a question no one asked.

Kruspe-Bernstein reflected. "We are interested in lyrics that reach and move people and trigger something in people. We try not to refer to things by name, or to name them directly, but to refer to things obliquely, between the lines."

Why, then, does it distress them so that some of us *have* read between the lines?

Returning to my hotel, I saw protesters swarming over Berlin's bridges. They were hanging gigantic peace signs, printed on white bedsheets, above the freeways. Rammstein too opposes the war. "I wonder how anyone can be *for* the war," Lorenz said to me. "Everyone I know is against America. We find it dangerous what the American government is doing. This is a war the Americans started."

When I visited Berlin again recently, I spent some time chatting with the owner of a restaurant near my hotel. He was a thirty-six-year-old Berliner from the former East, and close to the members of the band. He had known them for many years. They often ate at his restaurant.

"Yes," he told me, "if you didn't understand them, you could look at them and be very frightened, because yes, maybe they sound just exactly like Goebbels or something. But they don't mean it. They're playing."

The proof? Rammstein, he said, like most of Germany, had opposed the war in Iraq. "Everyone here, even children too young to understand, opposed the war. We are against war now. That united us like nothing else has done since the Second World War. For the first time we were proud again to be German." The restaurateur was gentle and sweet-natured, with soft, pleading eyes. While we spoke, he insisted the kitchen bring out bratwurst and beer and sweet elderberry chasers. He wouldn't accept payment. I don't think he had any agenda behind his generosity: He was just a very sweet man, eager to set the record straight about his friends.

By his logic, Germans had through their pacifism earned the right to enjoy Rammstein without fretting overmuch about how the band looked. "Rammstein made it possible for artists to play with these themes from our history, to bring them out in the open," he said. He likened the members of the band to the contemporary German painter Neo Rauch, who also grew up behind the Wall, and whose paintings are filled with sardonic tributes to the propaganda of the East German regime.

Rammstein, he added, was helping Germany to rediscover its identity. What he did not explain—and could not explain—is why Germany would *want* to rediscover that identity, even in jest.

## "THESE THINGS START BUBBLING UP"

As for Germany's pacifism, how can we disapprove? Who, after listening to Rammstein, can be anything but grateful that the Germans have renounced war?

But some people think that pacifism requires some scrutiny. For Rammstein, pacifism is linked, as it so often is in Europe, to deep suspicion about America. Rammstein's recent single, *"Amerika,"* "is not a love song" as the lyrics explicitly tell us.

| | |
|---|---|
| *We're all living in Amerika* | We're all living in America |
| *Amerika ist wunderbar* | America is wonderful |
| *We're all living in Amerika* | We're all living in America |
| *Amerika, Amerika* | America, America |
| *Wenn getanzt wird will ich führen* | I'll lead whoever dances |
| *auch wenn ihr euch alleine dreht* | Even when he turns alone |
| *Lasst euch ein wenig kontrollieren* | Let's exercise a little control |
| *Ich zeige euch wie es richtig geht* | I'll show you how to do it right |
| *Wir bilden einen lieben Reigen* | We're building a beautiful region |
| *Die Freiheit spielt auf allen Geigen* | Where freedom plays over every place |
| *Musik kommt aus dem Weißen Haus* | Music is coming out of the White House |
| *und vor Paris steht Micky Maus* | and in front of Paris stands Mickey Mouse. |

The song continues in English, presumably to make sure we get the point:

This is not a love song
This is not a love song
I don't sing my mother tongue
No, This is not a love song
We're all living in Amerika
Coca-Cola, sometimes war
We're all living in Amerika
Amerika, Amerika

When I was last in Berlin, I spoke to Jeffrey Gedmin, an American scholar of European Studies who directs the Aspen Institute's Berlin campus. He is perhaps the most prominent defender in Germany of American foreign policy these days.

We met at a Starbucks in the now entirely reconstructed and Westernized section of east Berlin. It was easy to see from the Starbucks why some Germans might think they were living in America. The place was a perfect replica of any Starbucks in the United States, down to the piped-in Christmas carols, in English. *Pa-rum-pa-pum-pum.* I'd taken a taxi there through a less fashionable east Berlin neighborhood. We drove through street after street of bleak Soviet-era concrete apartment blocks, featureless and colored only by angry smears of graffiti. Little in Berlin looks German, since the original architecture was reduced to smoking rubble by Allied bombing raids. What doesn't now look like America looks like Moscow, and in fact, *"Moskau"* is the title of another Rammstein song:

| | |
|---|---|
| *Diese Stadt ist eine Dirne* | This city is a hooker, |
| *Hat rote Flecken auf der Stirn* | Red spots on her forehead |
| *Ihre Zähne sind aus Gold* | Her teeth are made of gold |
| *Sie ist fett und doch so hold* | She's fat and yet so lovely |
| *Ihr Mund fällt mir zu Tale* | Her mouth falls to my valley |
| *wenn ich sie dafür bezahle* | when I pay her |
| *Sie zieht sich aus doch nur für Geld* | She takes off her clothes but only for money |
| *Die Stadt die mich in Atem hält* | The city that keeps me in suspense |
| *Moskau* | Moscow |
| *Раз, два, три!* | One, two, three! |
| *Moskau* | Moscow |
| *Посмотри!* | Look! |
| *Пионеры там идут,* | Pioneers are walking around there, |
| *песни Ленину поют.* | Singing songs to Lenin. |

Here Rammstein sings in Russian, to make sure *they* get the point. The old antagonism toward the East is still, evidently, very much alive.

I asked Gedmin what he made of German pacifism and anti-Americanism. "I do think," he said, "that we underestimated how hard it was for a country with a grand tradition of history, literature, culture and music—one that committed an act of insanity that lasted for thirteen years—to end up divided, lacking sovereignty, and so heavily, heavily dependent on the United States. A young editor for one of the papers here put it this way to me. He said, 'Imagine this: You're from the grand nation of Germany, and you're responsible for fascism and the Holocaust. You can't liberate yourselves, and you're liberated by gum-chewing Negroes from America.' That sat rather deep with some people. Part of it is understandable. No one wants to be divided, lacking sovereignty, and so heavily dependent. But part of it was that their sense of cultural superiority took a big blow for those forty years. Then comes the fall of the Wall, and these things start bubbling up.

"It's not malign. They're not invading countries. It's a democracy. They have a free press. They have all these things, don't get me wrong: I'm not of the school that says, *Beware, democracy is crumbling in Germany*. But what happened is this: On the East German side, a lot of people figured, I guess, *Bring the wall down, pump in subsidies, give them elections, and they'll be liberal, democratic, and Western*. But they went from one dictatorship to another. They had sixty years of continuous dictatorship, with its institutions and indoctrination. And we know that democracy is institutions. But it's also learned habits and values and behaviors. Much of the country wasn't exposed to those habits and values for over a half a century. You pump in subsidies and give them free elections, but that doesn't mean the virus doesn't keep going around. Not that some East Germans aren't absolutely loyal, brilliant democrats, but some are . . . not. *They're just not*. They're consuming Western goods and they're voting, but . . . Look, this city is an example. Fifteen years after the fall of the Wall, one out of four East Berliners votes for the post-Communist party. Twenty-five percent, fifteen years later? It's a little bit high, and a little bit strange, don't you think?"

Yes, I did think it was strange.

How, I asked, did he understand German anti-Americanism? "It's envy, resentment. Some of it's because of the imbalance of power, some of it's residual because of their dependence on us during the Cold War. But all that bubbles up."

And German pacifism? "Pacifism. They wear that as a badge of honor, but people say funny things, you know. I've asked people, 'Why are you so agitated about certain aspects of American foreign policy?' And they'll say, 'Because *we* would like to assert ourselves that way and we can't.' I've heard a journalist say that. 'Because we would like to assert ourselves that way and we're not allowed to. We have to be quiet. We have to be meek. We have to be reticent. We have to be *pacifists.*'

"This is a country craving independence from the United States. It wants to make its own mark. It's a sensitive country right now. I wrote a column in the *Financial Times* a few weeks ago about Germany's bid to get a UN Security Council seat. And I said a few things that just massively offended people, so much that an official in the government called the chairman of my board and demanded that I be fired. The first thing I had said was that Germany's quest for a UN seat is partly about exerting its national interest. I thought that was pretty clear and inarguable. But they thought, *No! This is for World Peace! This is our contribution to the UN!* So they were very offended by that.

"But there was another thing I said, and *friends* were offended. Friends whom I know and trust. I said, and it's true, 'When Americans say that they really like Germans, what they really mean is that they like West Germans—those Germans they got to know during the Cold War. But this bid to get a UN Security Council seat is in part about the Germans becoming Germans again.' I didn't mean, 'They're marching into a Fourth Reich,' I just meant, *This is no longer West Germany.*"

And Rammstein, I asked? "These taboos have been getting broken for some time. Someone told me it was a fashion, several years ago in Berlin, in certain groups, young people's groups . . . if a disco, or a party, or a concert was really full, young people would say, 'It's packed like a gas chamber in here!' It's pretty bizarre.

"Yeah, something is happening here. During the Iraq War, I did a fair amount of writing and a fair amount of television. I supported the war. I expected to get lots of criticism. I got a very heavy amount of very violent hate mail. Beyond, you know, 'You're an idiot.' Threatening. Mail that we had to give to the police. *I will find you one day and beat the shit out of you and pour napalm on your face.* A lot of it was anti-Semitic. I'm not Jewish, I'm Catholic. Nevertheless, a lot of it used that sort of language. By the way, a lot of it came in e-mail, suggesting that these weren't seventy-year-old Nazis. A lot of it used language like, *You son-of-a-whore.* I got that a hundred times, *son-of-a-whore. Nigger* was used a lot. *Jew-fucker* was used a lot. It wasn't ten or twenty letters. It was a couple of hundred. Of course every society has its racists, and every society has its bigots. This is a country of 82 million people. I didn't get 82 million letters. But I got a lot. And these were letters that were beyond *I disagree vehemently. I think that's reckless and irresponsible.* This was really the kind of stuff where you felt you had to give it to the police. We found red paint one day on the door of the institute, which I guess is supposed to represent blood. Again, that could happen elsewhere, people get out of hand, there are radicals.

"I guess the biggest thing I would say is that Germany is finding itself. There's a reaction against taboos, anything that they feel was imposed from the outside, and there's this reflex to go in the opposite direction."

It certainly does seem so.

## POWER, PATHOLOGY, AND PAYBACK

"Here's another anecdote," Gedmin said. "I had this young student say to me once, 'For the first time in my life, I feel proud to be German.' And I said, 'Great. Why is that?' And she said, 'Because we had the nerve to stand up to the United States.' And she thought that was so obvious. And I said, 'Well, I hope that's not the only basis for your patriotism,' and she didn't get my point. This was spontaneous on her part, she was a very lovely person, and she was feeling very good. She smiled. She could drink a beer: *We're saying no to America.* And that had nothing to do with Iraq, by the way. It was about them and us."

Was there no sense, I asked, that authentic pacifism, or at least an authentic stand against fascism and genocide, would dictate a more vigorous opposition to Saddam Hussein's regime than to ours?

"No."

"Why didn't they connect that logical circuit?"

"Mostly, it wasn't *about* Saddam Hussein—it was about us. *Here's a big power, a hegemon, throwing its weight around without consulting us. This is not the world order we're trying to create.* I think they were afraid of us failing in Iraq, but they were also afraid of us *succeeding* in Iraq. Seriously. Now, you know, we've had problems in Iraq. But if we hadn't had problems, that would have cost us great German resentment, too. Because we would have removed him, the Iraqis would have liked us—and *that* was not what they wanted either. A lot of it is about power, and pathology, and payback.

"By the way, it's the same with Israel. I just saw a new poll—more than 60 percent of Germans believe that Israel's treatment of the Palestinians is worse than the German treatment of the Jews under the Nazis." I had seen the same poll.* I looked around the café and wondered whether more than half of the pleasant, well-mannered people around me, sipping their eggnog lattes and reading their newspapers, really believed that.

"Look, the Germans have a chip on their shoulder. They have a chip on their shoulder because, as this journalist friend of mine said, Americans did them the ultimate injustice. We liberated them. We pro-

---

*The poll was conducted by researchers at the University of Bielefeld. The researchers found that 51 percent of Germans believed Israel's present-day treatment of the Palestinians to be equivalent to the Nazi atrocities against European Jews during the Second World War; 68 percent believed that Israel was waging a "war of extermination" against the Palestinians; 82 percent were angered by Israel's policies toward the Palestinians; 62 percent were sick of "all this harping on" about German crimes against Jews; and 68 percent found it "annoying" that Germans today were still held to blame for Nazi crimes. In a triumph of understatement, the German pollsters remarked that the findings "may be worrying." See Edgar Lefkovits, "Poll: Over 50% of Germans Equate IDF with Nazi Army," *Jerusalem Post,* December 7, 2004.

tected them for forty years. When unification came, and Europe was against them, we stood up and supported them, and . . . they've had enough of that! And with Israel, one could say, they just will *not* forgive the Jews for putting them in the black box of history. Now, you might argue that *they* were guilty of the Holocaust, but somehow, weirdly enough, it gets contorted to, *If Germans have a bad reputation, it's because of those friggin' . . .*" He didn't need to finish his sentence.

"And this other thing—it was on prime-time television, last year, prime-time German television, Friday night, nine o'clock. Public television showed a documentary about conspiracy theories about 9/11. It wasn't *about* the theories, it gave *credence* to the theories . . . how they're absolutely sure it wasn't a commercial aircraft that hit the Pentagon, and all these things. . . . You put this on in prime time, you're actually suggesting that it's a credible piece of journalistic work. And it was *silly.* One other poll: Twenty percent, one out of five Germans, think that the CIA, or Mossad, was behind September 11. That seems kind of high—that's not three percent, two, six. One out of five people in this café think the CIA or the Israelis did it? That's too high, isn't it, for a modern, liberal democratic Germany?"

I looked around again. It *looked* like America.

"I know TV journalists," Gedmin said, "who told me that after September 11, in their editorial rooms, at the television stations, German public television, there was agreement that it was a terrible thing that happened, but there was a big argument, with a good number of their colleagues saying that Americans deserved it. You know, these are educated people, these are international people, these are not neo-Nazis—"

If being for peace means threatening to pour napalm on American faces and arguing that Americans deserved September 11, then perhaps, I thought, I should not be reassured by Rammstein's pacifism. Not, of course, that they've threatened to pour napalm on anyone's face. It's not even napalm they use in their concerts, it's a stunt inflammable called lycopodium. It only looks like napalm.

## SO HARD, SO DARK, SO EVIL

I met the members of Rammstein for the second time, again in Berlin, in December 2004. They were back on tour in Europe for the first time in two and a half years and once again packing stadiums. Hours before they played the Velodrome, thousands of fans crowded the entrance. "We find it funny how Germany talks about the band," a woman from Berlin in her late thirties, staking out her place at the front of the line, explained to me. "In Germany they're in a lot of trouble. But that's because Rammstein is misunderstood. People think they're evil and racist. They don't get the irony."

Their fans were of a wide demographic. Some had arrived in jeans and anoraks; others had come in leather, and one had shown up on a dog leash. There were children in the crowd, and a lone elderly man in a tweed jacket with elbow patches. Many fans were wearing T-shirts with the legend "You are what you eat," a reference to the cannibalism song. Despite the long wait, the crowd only once burst into the traditional skinhead anthem—"Oi! Oi! Oi!"—and this only half-heartedly. They then returned to drinking their beer, eating their bratwurst, and rubbing their hands together against the bitter cold.

"We love Rammstein because they make it so hard, so dark, so evil, and that makes it so interesting for us," said a woman in her late thirties with a hard, lined face. "Rammstein wants to be provocative, they want Germany to open its eyes. Every song has a deeper sense. Germans don't want to open their eyes—they don't want to talk about these things."

"And the men . . . the men are great," said her friend. "If you see Till, tell him I have his face tattooed on my ass, so I can sleep with him every night."

I *would* have told him, but when I ran into him several minutes later, in the corridor backstage, he scowled. "I don't speak. *Nein,*" he said, and stomped off. He looked bloated and unwell. He had deep circles under his eyes, and his dark stage makeup was smeared.

Minutes before I had met a very pretty young woman who was loitering around the backstage entrance. She told me she was one of Lindemann's girlfriends. She proudly showed me his name on her mobile phone and Polaroid pictures of his apartment. He was really stressed, she said, from the pressure of the tour. But he had a loving side, she wanted me to know. At times he would hold her tightly all night. They could be happy if only he would stop sleeping with other women, or at least if he would only stop *lying* to her about it.

I'm not sure if anything she said was true. It had the ring of truth—there are lots of women who live that kind of life and believe those kinds of things. While we were chatting, she suddenly reached for her phone. She exclaimed with delight that Till had just sent her a text message. "What does it say?" I asked.

She looked at the display. Her face saddened. "He told me to piss off."

## A NATION AT WAR WITH ITS FORBIDDEN IMPULSES

Guitarist Landers, who was holding court in a small office backstage, was more forthcoming than Lindemann. I asked him whether it was true, as rumor had it, that the lead singer was so addled by cocaine addiction that he had been forbidden by the band's management to give interviews. "It's not true," he said peevishly. He wasn't yet in his costume or makeup, and he looked less frightening than he does in his videos—in fact, he looked fussy and middle-aged. His assistant had warned me that I had fifteen minutes to speak to him, and *not one minute more*. "We have our politics," Landers said, "and our politics are that Till doesn't do interviews and no exceptions. It's been a very good policy so far. And you have just wasted five minutes."

Well then, Paul, tell me about the song *"Amerika."* What's that all about?

"The song *'Amerika'* is ambivalent, like everything we do. There's no good and bad, there are always two sides to every issue. But it's a fact that America has made itself disliked through its foreign policy over the past few years, and it's very easy living in Europe, being in Europe, to not like America. In general we're not political, as a band, but when America started bombing Iraq we had to say what we thought. For us in Europe, we still don't understand why that happened. The song is about how willingly the world adopts everything that is American, and takes on the American view of life, things, products—buying them and making them their own—and that's why we sing this song. No one is forcing people to consume American things, or to watch Hollywood films. So the song is about how the world willingly adopts American culture and how this occurs. A journalist once asked me if I'm afraid of America, and I said no, not directly of America—I'm more afraid of countries that bow to American power."

And how did he understand Rammstein's role in all of this? "The Germans," he said, "definitely have a problem. Before, it was *Deutschland über alles*—Germany above everything. And now Germany is below everything. Rock bottom. Our problem is that we actually think Germany is pretty good. But almost nobody thinks that. Everybody's very embarrassed to be German, and there's no German identity. Our aim is to help Germany not to be overly patriotic like the Americans, but to be patriotic, and not be ashamed. Every country has its strengths and weaknesses. Some of them have more character, some of them have less character. In my opinion there's a certain type of character that Germans have . . . there's something that Germans have, that no other nationality has. It's hard to describe. It would be a shame if that disappeared." When I asked him what that was, precisely, he told me that Germans made good cars.

"I'm a German too, and like all Germans, we haven't a completely clear conscience. Other people don't do what we do, don't use the images we do, because they're too cowardly. A rock band has to provoke—it's their task, their duty. We love doing it, we love provoking people. It's fun. It's a lot of fun. We love getting attention. We love getting people upset, shocking people—but we think that's good. But it's just fun to do, that's the most important thing. It's the way things have turned out. It's just the way things have happened.

"At first, we thought it was our duty to provoke Germany, to get Germany going in a certain direction. That was at first. But then we realized, it doesn't work that way. It takes time. What we can do is set a certain example. We can show the way. Blaze a trail. But it will take a long time—it will take at least sixty years until things go in that direction. You can't change history, it just doesn't work that way. You see it in Iraq: When you go in, you get into trouble. It just takes time. History takes time. A hundred years."

Or perhaps a thousand.

He wanted to make sure I didn't think his attitude toward America was unbalanced. "There are some good things about America," he stressed. "We're always happy about the naïveté of Americans."

The strict assistant interrupted us. He hustled me off to meet Kruspe-Bernstein, who was waiting in another anteroom. He was already in his makeup, and wearing a costume with a high bat-wing collar. He looked a bit like an escapee from the set of *Dracula*. Kruspe-Bernstein now lives in New York. Unlike Landers, he was warm and friendly—charming, in fact. His English had improved markedly since the last time we met, and we no longer needed a translator.

"You know," he said, "it's funny, I was reading yesterday about fifty reviews of the last shows, in Germany—and not one of them was any good. Not one. And it's so interesting, I just wonder, because we toured through all of Europe, for the last two months, I guess. And everyone really liked us, they thought we were really good, but coming back to Germany not one person, not one writer, not one journalist likes the show? I mean, come on. There's something weird there. I don't know. . . . I think Germany still has a big problem with us. I can't really figure it out. You know, it's almost like a man who would never admit he likes to go to a bordello or something—but he still goes. It's kind of the same with Rammstein, you know? It's a guilty pleasure. It's weird."

So how did he account for this?

"The biggest problem about Germany is that they have either too much respect for themselves or too less respect for themselves. They never have a balance between, you know? They're still carrying . . . They still suffer from the last war. I kind of represent like, myself, just to friends, you know, like being . . . living in New York City, and getting involved in discussion, like, don't be afraid, no, *ja,* kind of afraid to say that you are German, you know, and try to have a balance, you know, and try to use the German as kind of humor, you know? That's what we actually do, with Rammstein. But to go back to humor . . . everyone knows that humor's not the biggest strength Germany has. I asked why, what is it that brings humor out? And I came to the conclusion that you have to be confident about yourself to laugh about yourself. And that, coming back to Germany—I think Germans aren't confident about themselves. And Rammstein is something, we can use humor right now, in a way. In quiet confidence.

"I'm not scared of America. I'm not scared at all. I think the most important thing for everyone—whether a human being or a country— is balance. You have to reach balance. And I think America is stepping out of balance. Obviously, we know that it wasn't about Saddam Hussein. It was never about him."

I didn't have time to debate this point, given that the strict assistant was coming back momentarily. "It must be such a pleasure for you," I said, "after being viewed by the world as the most evil nation in history, for so long, to find that the United States has taken over that role."

He didn't notice my tone. "Oh, yeah," he agreed happily. "Especially the coming-from-the-East part. I mean, that makes it even more special." It's a tough thing, growing up behind that Irony Curtain.

Two things come through very clearly in my conversations with the band: the never-ending guilt of anyone born German, and the growing, peevish disgruntlement that guilt provokes. Rammstein perfectly captures the sentiments of a nation at war with its forbidden impulses, and indeed, when Kruspe-Bernstein surprised himself with his desire to wrestle his own image in the video for *"Mein Teil,"* he happened upon an excellent metaphor for this.

Perhaps the song that best characterizes this attitude is *"Los,"* in which the band taunts its critics:

| | |
|---|---|
| *Wir waren namenlos* | We were nameless |
| *Und ohne Lieder* | and without songs |
| *Recht wortlos* | We were wordless |
| *Waren wir nie wieder* | Still are |

| | |
|---|---|
| *Etwas sanglos* | songless |
| *Sind wir immer noch* | But not |
| *Dafür nicht klanglos* | toneless |
| *Man hört uns doch* | You *can* hear us |
| *Nach einem Windstoß* | After a gust of wind |
| *Ging ein Sturm los* | began a storm |
| *Einfach beispiellos* | matchless |
| *Es wurde Zeit* | time- |
| *Los* | less |
| *Sie waren sprachlos* | They were speechless |
| *So sehr schockiert* | Shocked |
| *Und sehr ratlos* | Powerless |
| *Was war passiert* | What happened |
| *Etwas fassungslos* | Flummoxed |
| *Und garantiert* | and surely |
| *Verständnislos* | Uncomprehending |
| *Das wird zensiert* | Sure to be censored |
| *Sie sagten grundlos* | Groundless |
| *Schade um die Noten* | Too bad about the music |
| *So schamlos* | Shameless |
| *Das gehört verboten* | That should be forbidden |
| *Es ist geistlos* | It's witless |
| *Was sie da probieren* | what they're trying there |
| *So geschmacklos* | Tasteless |
| *Wie sie musizieren* | how they're making music |
| *Ist es hoffnungslos* | Is it hopeless |
| *Sinnlos* | Senseless |
| *Hilflos* | Helpless |
| *Sie sind gottlos* | Godless |
| *Wir waren namenlos* | We were nameless |
| *Wir haben einen Namen* | We have a name |
| *Waren wortlos* | We were wordless |
| *Die Worte kamen* | The words arrived |
| *Etwas sanglos* | Still we are |
| *Sind wir immer noch* | a little songless |

| | |
|---|---|
| *Dafür nicht klanglos* | Yet we're not toneless |
| *Das hört man doch* | You *do* hear it |
| *Wir sind nicht fehlerlos* | Not flawless |
| *Nur etwas haltlos* | Without an anchor |
| *Ihr werdet lautlos* | You will become soundless |
| *Uns nie los* | You'll never get rid of us |

For men who are basically quite stupid, they do come up with some clever puns. The suffix *-los* means "-less" in English but, when used as an adjective, means "off" or "loose." As a command, *Los!* means "go." When Lindemann sings *"Sie sind gottlos,"* he pauses dramatically between *gott* and *los*. For a moment, it sounds as if he is singing, "You are God." The song conveys an eerie combination of self-pity and menace. You *do* hear it—just what you think you hear.

You'll never get rid of us, indeed.

This is an ancient theme in German history, this resentment, this sense that the German nation does not occupy its proper place, that the German people have been unjustly oppressed. Historically, it is nothing new to see these sentiments coupled with outrage that those goofy Americans should by contrast be so powerful. We see this resentment in the Wilhelminian Germany's obsession with its encirclement prior to the First World War. Hitler skillfully exploited the same resentment in his rise to power.

The scariest thing about these men is that plainly they have not learned a thing from history. They're just pissed off that it's oppressing them.

## A LITTLE GAME

Let's play a little game. Read the following and decide: Rammstein or Goebbels? The answers are in the footnotes.

We would not say anything if the U.S.A. were aware of its intellectual and moral defects and was trying to grow up. But it is too much when it behaves in an arrogant manner toward a part of the earth with a few thousands years of glorious history behind it, attempting to teach it moral and intellectual lessons. . . . [T]his degree of arrogance gets on one's nerves.*

We therefore have no appreciation for the Americanism that can be found in certain of our circles. We fail to see why we as the leading musical nation in the world should borrow even a single note from the U.S.A.**

One is never sure which of two characteristics is more prominent in the American national character and therefore of the greater significance: naïveté or a superiority complex.†

It is time to recommend peace and good sense. American public opinion is going the wrong way. It would benefit by returning to the old, tested practices of international courtesy and good manners. . . . We do not expect our appeal to have a great impact on American attitudes. Still, we think it our duty to speak plainly.††

In the past, the Germans have come up with very good ideas, but then they've left Germany and gone, for example, to the States, and actually realized their ideas there—and it's a shame, because it was lost.#

Seeking fortunes in America led to Germany losing people, and the American continent received many people whose contributions are particularly clear.##

---

*Goebbels. See Joseph Goebbels, "Aus Gottes eigenem Land," *Das eherne Herz* (Munich: Zentralverlag der NSDAP, 1943), pp. 421–27.
**Goebbels. See ibid.
†Goebbels. See ibid.
††Goebbels. See Joseph Goebbels, "Was will eigentlich Amerika," *Die Zeit ohne Beispiel* (Munich: Zentralverlag der NSDAP., 1941), pp. 24–30.
#Rammstein. Paul Landers, interview in Berlin, December 20, 2004.
##Neither—it's a trick question. Julius Streicher, "What Is Americanism?" *Der Stürmer,* #23/1944.

In any event, the reader will see that it's not difficult to distinguish between Rammstein and Goebbels. Goebbels was more articulate.

## THAT IS <u>NOT</u> A LOVE SONG

Strict Assistant bustled in to take me to the wings of the auditorium, where stagehands were preparing the explosives. The evening's schedule, taped to the wall, could have doubled as a battle plan: For the song *"Du Hast"*—"You Hate"—there would be "Gas/Lyco/Comets/Grid Rockets/Mortar Hits," and for the encores, "Airbursts," "Flames," and the ominous-sounding "Concussion Boat." The band, their stage manager told me, often had problems getting the legal approval they needed for their pyrotechnics in Germany. By comparison, American authorities were easygoing. "In America, they say, 'Okay, you have a fifteen-foot line from the audience. So whatever you do on stage, you have to keep that distance from the audience. And if you do it behind that line, you'll be fine.' And that's it."

I nodded enthusiastically. "Land of the free, man, I'm telling you."

His face fell. "Well. I have my personal opinion about that."

The warm-up act began precisely on time. The dreadlocked lead singer of Exilia, author of the loudest and ugliest sounds ever produced by human agency, shrieked down the microphone and banged her head spastically up and down for nearly an hour. Earlier, backstage, I had seen her walking down the hall with her dog. The miserable beast had dreadlocks, too.

The audience seemed to want to like Exilia (renamed Ex-Lax by the press contingent); they pumped their fists in the air politely and made the heavy metal sign—a gesture that in southern Italy would mean, "You've been cuckolded"—but in the end couldn't conceal their boredom. The woman on a dog leash, whom I had seen earlier outside, crouched by the speakers and picked lint from her leather corset.

Exilia left the stage and the audience rumbled restlessly. Finally, the lights dimmed. A man beside me pulled out a pack of cigarettes, ripped off the filters, and stuffed them in his ears. Then *"Reise, Reise"* began. A jolt of electricity passed through the crowd. A huge curtain dropped, revealing a row of massive Potemkin amplifiers, flashing with the band's insignia. The guitarists descended like gods from the ceiling by means of some kind of levered contraption. Suddenly, the auditory assault began: It was so fearsome that even the hardest-core fans appeared momentarily stunned. It was not, however, merely loud: It was thrilling. Rammstein is popular for a reason.

Dressed in an imperial German military uniform, Lindemann materialized on stage. The audience was mesmerized by him, and understandably so—he gave off an air of such brute masculinity and barely contained violence that it would have surprised no one had he reached into the crowd, snatched up a fan, and bitten off his head. When he began to sing, the audience, enthralled, began pumping their fists in the air. Dog-Leash Woman began to writhe and snake on the ground.

The band then introduced *"Links." "Links-Zwo-Drei-Vier!" "Links-Zwo-Drei-Vier!"* The keyboardist stomped about in a German military helmet. Mr. Lindemann performed an exaggerated goose step. The crowd shouted *Hi!* in unison. The musicians, wearing flamethrowing gas masks, sprayed fire—seemingly from their eyeballs—over the stage. They burst explosives in the air and shot balls of flames over the audience, generating heat so intense that fans began to pass out. Medics strapped the fallen Germans to gurneys and carted them away. The crowd was vitalized, as if they could easily be persuaded to channel their furious energy toward a target, and when, later, the band sang their hit *"Amerika,"* it seemed quite clear what the target of preference would be. I looked uneasily for the routes to the exits, because that's *definitely* not a love song.

## NOT EUROPEAN—GERMAN

Whether their songs are about love or war, and whether they are on the Left or the Right, one thing is sure: Rammstein's music is German. Not European, *German.* A sensibility has been passed, from generation to generation to generation. The Danes don't make music like this, and neither do the Portuguese. Nor do the Irish, the Macedonians, or the Belgians. This music couldn't have its mesmerizing power in any language but German. Rammstein refuses to sing in English. As keyboardist Lorenz correctly observes, "The German language is very suited to our musical style." To confirm this point, imagine Rammstein's lyrics sung in French. For particular hilarity, imagine them sung by Maurice Chevalier.

It has often been remarked that people reveal their souls in the music they create, and that a nation's music bears a relationship to its social, moral, and political life. Plato devotes considerable attention to this subject in the *Republic*. "Music," he writes, "is the movement of sound to reach the soul for the education of its virtue." Later, he cautions that "the introduction of a new kind of music must be shunned as imperiling the whole state; since styles of music are never disturbed without affecting the most important political institutions." His views are echoed by Aristotle, Rousseau, and Nietzsche, all of whom acknowledge the unique capacity of music to stir human emotions, for good or ill. Napoleon urged legislators to give music the greatest encouragement, for, he noted, it had of all the arts the most influence on the passions.

Has Rammstein had any influence on the German body politic? It's hard to say. Rammstein certainly returned the aesthetic of the Right to the German pop culture mainstream, and Rammstein's vaulting commercial success has inspired scores of imitators. Last September, the strong showing of far-Right and neo-Nazi parties in Germany's regional elections, particularly in the formerly Communist East, sent a chill through Europe. Did the cultural transformation associated with Rammstein's *"Neue deutsche Härte"*—the new German hardness—help these parties return to the mainstream? Who knows? It probably didn't hurt.

Nowhere has the close relationship between music and the soul been more evident than in Germany. The barbarians of Germania, Gibbon noted, were fascinated by music.[17] Nietzsche remarked that the German imagines even God singing songs. The German, Wagner observed, far from looking upon the practice of music as an empty entertainment, religiously approaches it "as the holiest precinct in his life. He accordingly becomes a fanatic, and this devout and fervent *Schwärmerei*, with which he conceives and executes his music, is the chief characteristic of German Music."[18]

Fanaticism: That, too, is a German quality. This is a traditional observation about Germans, one that has been made by Einstein, among others: No matter what the pursuit, Germans will take it to extremes. German music is unique because it is *taken* to extremes, and because it inspires the listener to *go* to extremes. In this regard, too, Rammstein is nothing new. The hero of *A Clockwork Orange* listened to Beethoven. It certainly wasn't Puccini who got him in the mood for a bit of the old ultraviolence. The killers at Columbine loved Rammstein. According to Russian authorities, the murderers at Beslan were listening to Rammstein during the school siege. It is doubtful that they understood the lyrics, but they certainly understood the message. Why is it that they found themselves inspired by *German,* not Chechen, music? What is it about the German musical tradition that has this force?

I am not sure. But at the extreme, it is clear, music becomes a form of exhortation, one that quickly leads to action. And this raises an interesting question: Was Plato right?

## DOESN'T EVERY FAMILY HAVE ONE LIKE THAT?

According to the Laeken Declaration, issued in late 2001 by the European Council, the unification of Europe is near. "At long last," the document reads, "Europe is on its way to becoming one big family." Cheerful news. And this brotherhood is all very touching, considering that it replaces century upon century of unmitigated slaughter and butchery among the European peoples, a tradition of virtually uninterrupted warfare since the sack of Rome. Brotherhood, at last, after the Visigoth Raids, the Saxon Raids, the Vandal Raids, the Hun Raids, Theodoric's War with Odoacer, the Frankish-Alemmanic War, the

Burgundian-Frankish War, the Visogothic-Frankish War, the Gothic War, Aelthelfrit's Wars, the Byzantine-Avarian War, Oswald's War, the Anglian-Picktish War, the Siege of Constantinople, the First Frankish-Moorish War, the First Iconoclastic War, the Battle of Tours, Aelthelbald's Wars, the Second Frankish-Moorish War, the Bulgarian-Byzantine War, Offa's Wars, the Carolingian Wars, the Frankish-Avarian War, the Second Iconoclastic War, the Viking Raids, the Magyar Raids, the Bulgarian-Byzantine War, the Franco-German War, the Spanish Christian-Muslim War, Ardoin's War, the Conquests of Vladimir, the Norman Conquest, William's Invasion of Normandy, the Norman-Byzantine War, the Holy Roman Empire's War with the Papacy, Almorovid's Conquest of Spain, the Second Norman-Byzantine War, the Aragonese-Castilian War, the Anglo-French Wars, the First Portuguese-Castilian War, the Hungarian-Venetian War, the Wars of the Lombard League, the Aragonese-French War, the Anglo-Scottish War, the Danish-Estonian War, the Teutonic Knights' Conquest of Prussia, the Norwegian invasion of Scotland, the Bohemian-Hungarian War, the Hapsburg-Bohemian War, the Aragonese-French War, the next Anglo-French War, the War of the Sicilian Vespers, the Teutonic Knights' War against Poland, the Florentine Wars against Pisa, the Burgundian-Swiss War, the Hundred Years War, the Hungarian-Venetian War, the First and Second Danish Wars against the Hanseatic League, the next Portuguese-Castilian War, the Conquests of Tamerlane, the War of the Eight Saints, the Austro-Swiss War, the Albanian-Turkish War, the Austro-Turkish Wars, the Livonian War, the Eighty Years War, the Defeat of the Spanish Armada, the Hapsburg Brothers' War, the Thirty Years War, the Franco-Spanish War, the Anglo-Spanish War, the Spanish-Portuguese War, the Wars of the First and Second Coalitions, the Wars of the Vendee, the Napoleonic Wars, the Peninsular Wars, the First and Second Turko-Montenegrin Wars, the Danish-Prussian Wars, the Franco-Prussian War, the Serbo-Turkish War, the Serbo-Bulgarian War, the Greco-Turkish War, the Second Balkan War, the First World War, the Second World War, and the most recent Balkan Wars. These are only the first few wars that come to mind; I have probably forgotten rather a number. By way of contrast, the United States has fought *one* war against itself. To give Europe as fair a shake as possible, I have not included in this list such events as the Crusades or the Mongol Invasions, which were not, strictly speaking, domestics, as the cops call family disputes, nor have I listed the equally interminable catalogue of *civil* wars in European states and proto-states, national insurrections, revolutions, and wars of independence or separatism. Nor have I noted the bloody conflicts between the European peoples and their neighbors to the east and south, some of whom are now agitating to be adopted into Europe's newly united, close-knit family. I stress that these were *wars,* not soccer matches.

But for the sake of argument, let's accept the assumption. *E Pluribus Unum!* Thank goodness Europe is a family now: That certainly was a spell of unpleasantness. One feels such the spoilsport in pointing out that certain members of this new European fraternity—the ones who have always been a little wrong in the head, if you get my drift—seem to retain rather a bizarre preoccupation with the smell of burning flesh, the coagulation of blood on the asphalt, and the sound of screaming mothers. How churlish one would have to be to point out that they are still gibbering dementedly about the *horniness* they feel when you scream in fear, red welts oozing from your skin. And surely, this preoccupation with the enlightenment of white flesh, with doomsday, with destruction, with mercilessly breaking you apart like little sticks—it would be unbrotherly to find that odd? He asks where all the dead are coming from, whether you want to perish in skin and hair; he says that love is war and he tells you to run; he warns that there is no escape and no one to save you; you might plead for mercy but none will be given; he kneels in your face and sticks fingers in the ashes; his father, he admits, was exactly like him. But what can you do. He's family. Doesn't every family have one like that?

"I think it's really nice when the countries are also proud of their traditions," said Lorenz.

## THAT'S RIGHT, THE <u>NAZI</u> MANNER

I certainly think it is possible that the members of Rammstein believe their own party line: they do not see themselves as Nazis; they hold themselves to be harmless musical herbivores. No member of the band, from what I can tell, is personally genocidal, an enemy of the Jews, or a particular partisan of the Aryan Nation. There is something all the *more* frightening about the fact that they do not consciously recognize what they're doing: It suggests that this stuff comes out of them by sheer instinct.

But that's not even the point. Whether or not the members of Rammstein properly adhere to the core principles of the Nazi *Weltanschauung* is irrelevant. Recall Hugo Ringler's essay about speaking to the heart: "In a thousand ways it was proved true that often it was *not so much the contents of the speech as it was the manner in which it was delivered* that influenced the listener and won him to us." Rammstein certainly knows how to deliver their message in a manner that influences the listener to open his wallet. As Lorenz puts it, "We can deliver whatever we like, and they'll play it. When no one knows you, they say it's glorifying violence and not suitable for broadcasting, but when you hit the charts, it doesn't count anymore. Then you can make what you want anyhow, and they'll play it."[19] In contemporary Germany, it so happens that the *manner of delivery* that best influences the listener is very much like the Nazi manner.

That's right. *The Nazi manner.* The manner of Old Europe, as Donald Rumsfeld might have it. We can speak frankly among ourselves now. They look like a duck, they quack like a duck. Just go down the checklist. The color: black. The material: leather. The seduction: beauty. The justification: honesty. The aim: ecstasy. The fantasy: death.[20] Check, check, check. And they dominate German popular culture. It is the *Germans* who are fascinated by Rammstein, who are gobbling up this virtually undisguised Third Reich revivalism, devouring it as if they've been starved for years. But that's not Germany, you say? It's just a handful of jackbooted Teutonic nihilists who *happen* to be German? *Then who bought all those albums?* It wasn't the Liverpudlians, that's for sure. They just wanna hold your hand.

That the German people, the bourgeois German establishment, after all that has happened, after all they have learned, could usher Rammstein's every album to the height of the German charts, could feature them nightly on mainstream German television, award them their most enthusiastic accolades while simultaneously, earnestly, denying the patently obvious—that Rammstein is the *living embodiment* of the aesthetic of the Third Reich, the *living embodiment* of the Third Reich's vocabulary, dramaturgy, propaganda, mythology, occultism, death-worship, bloodthirstiness, ferocity, nihilism, power lust, and outrageous sadism—only once again proves Hitler's claim: People are unusually susceptible to the Big Lie.

## THE PERSISTENCE OF NATIONAL PERSONALITY

Now, I am *not* arguing that Rammstein's popularity evidences a full-throated recrudescence of Nazism in Germany, nor that German democratic institutions are under immediate threat. I agree with Jeffrey Gedmin about that. I am arguing that culturally the Germans are unlike any other nation in history; this is equally true of the French, the British, the Spanish, and the Greeks. And I note that *never in history* have mature, fully formed nation-states of such cultural disparity united to form an effective and coherent single actor—not economically, not politically, not in foreign affairs—for more than a few decades. Indeed, the overwhelming tendency of states cobbled together from diverse ethnic groups is to disintegrate, swiftly and violently. The immigrants tend to get killed when this happens. In this regard, one can only read with deep unease such editorials in German newspapers as one written by Hans-Ulrich Wehler, a leading German historian, about "*das Türkenproblem.*"[21]

Perhaps Rammstein is a group of refulgent Nazis in the truest and most sinister sense of the word, or perhaps they're clowns, guilty of nothing more than outrageous blindness to their own appearance. Perhaps they're somewhere in between. That's not the point. The point is that Germany loves them. The point is the persistence of a German national personality so distinctive, so historically continuous, that it is *risible* to imagine these people as the brothers of the French or the sisters of the Belgians or the cousins of the British.

The European Union is a marriage of convenience; the acceptance of massive immigration a matter of economic necessity. A salad of nations and peoples is now tossed together because the arrangement is politically and economically imperative, however grimly distasteful they find one another, however unsuited their temperaments, however grossly they have betrayed one another in the past. Now, I am *certainly* not opposed to the unification of the European people, nor to their cheerful acceptance of a flood of immigrants from faraway lands of which they know nothing. It would be glorious if brotherhood among men were at last to prevail upon this tormented and schismatic continent.

I am simply listening to Rammstein and thinking: Don't bet on it.

# TO HELL WITH EUROPE

S EEN ON A PARIS SIDEWALK in late May 2005, shortly before the French vote *non* to the European constitution: A shady-looking character runs up the street. Suddenly a waiter from one of the cafés comes running up behind him, yelling at him to stop, then charges into him, knocking him to the ground with a dreadful clatter. The waiter straddles him and begins slapping his face, calling him a filthy thief. A police motorcycle roars up. Off hops a cop who cannot be more than twenty-five. He interposes himself between the thief and the waiter, and then, with his finger in the air, begins a lecture. Never raising his voice, he tells the infuriated waiter that no matter what the thief might have stolen—some customer's wallet, it seems—he has no right to settle matters privately. He outlines the procedure for filing a civil or criminal complaint.

Then he says, slowly and quite distinctly, "In France, *we* have the *law*."

As these words rolled over the waiter—they were repeated several times—his face registered first embarrassment, then unease, and then what was unmistakably a deep sense of shame. *In France, we have the law.* Not *There are laws against that, buddy,* as a New York cop would have said, but *We have the law in France,* almost as if, as the representative of the state, he was addressing the untamed and violent aspect of the human heart itself. And then, with the thief in custody, the policeman adjusted his sunglasses, gunned his motorcycle, and was off.

Things to note: The *we* in his declaration—that is, we, the *French*, not we, the Europeans. The appeal to *the law:* This easily mocked people with their passion for abstractions really *does* take some things seriously. The shame registered on the waiter's face as he realized that in some very concrete way, he had violated a social contract to which he himself had given his allegiance.

Contrary to the assurances of its politicians, France's core national values *were* under threat by the prospect of a unified Europe. Anyone in doubt of this should try doing what I did as the vote on the constitution took place: Move from Paris to Istanbul. From this vantage point, one sees immediately that the idea of integrating Turkey into the EU has always been ludicrous. It can be established at a glance: *Turkey is not Europe, and it is certainly not France.* I do not say this merely because the phones, electricity, Internet, refrigerator, stove, hot water, and front door lock failed on me, serially, upon my arrival. I say this because *of course* the working-class Turks to whom I've spoken want to become part of the predicted flood of cheap, unskilled, Islamic labor that would completely destabilize the economies and delicately balanced social orders of the northern European welfare states—if Europe and its periphery were to be glued together and all its borders thrown open, that is.

Istanbul is an extraordinary place. It is utterly alive—an exuberant, thriving, tolerant Islamic city, living proof that it is not just politically correct cant to say that Islam and modernity are compatible. But as for having the *law* in Turkey, no, I don't think so. Why has my electricity been unreliable since I arrived? Because everyone in my neighborhood—the supposedly European neighborhood, I might add—is *stealing* it, causing blackouts.

It is fascinating to see that supposedly thoughtful politicians have seriously been considering the idea that France and Turkey might within our lifetimes be merged into one harmonious national entity. It is an indicator of the level of magical thinking and delusion that has accompanied the EU dream. But deep down, the *ordinary* Frenchman doesn't believe that in Eastern Europe, or Turkey, they have *the law.* They do not much trust that the Germans and the British have their interests at heart. Given European history—and given what I see around me—I can't say I blame them.

The pro-Europe talking heads on French television were busy, in the weeks following the referendum, poking fun at French fears of the so-called proverbial Polish plumber. How they could argue that he was only proverbial is beyond me. If you want to test the theory, try living in an apartment in Paris that needs repainting. Get estimates. The Polish workmen will—literally—ask for ten times less than the French workmen. They will not ask for social security or health insurance either.

If I were a French housepainter or plumber, I, too, would have voted *non.*

Sooner or later, of course, France will have to come to terms with reality: Its extensive social welfare system, its thirty-five-hour workweek, and its highly regulated economy cannot be sustained indefinitely. But many of the concerns that drove French voters to reject the European constitution make perfect sense. French politicians may have delivered enthusiastic encomiums to European unity for the past half-century, but it seems that the French *people* do indeed cherish their sovereignty—particularly their protected national labor markets, as many have observed, but also their distinct cultural identity, their legal and educational traditions, and their social stability.

In all the millions of words written in opinion pieces in France, uttered by television pundits, and spoken by politicians following the referendum, no one said the most plain and obvious ones: To hell with Europe. That's right, *to hell with Europe*—to hell with integration; to hell with the superstate; to hell with playing a role like that of the United States on the international stage; to hell with liking the Germans; to hell with putting up with the English; to hell with the Poles; to hell with the Turks; to hell with them all. No one has said, "It's a nutty idea. It will never work. It would put us in contact with people we've hated for thousands of years." Intellectuals and public figures in France, from left to right, explained their votes by first expressing boundless devotion to the ideal of Europe itself: The vote against the constitution, they said, reflected only a tactical readjustment in the great vision. The fantasy of Europe has adopted so prominent a role in the consciousness of French intellectuals that no one will speak plainly of it. No one is prepared to express what the majority of French voters *really* feel.

But ask a French taxi driver. You'll hear it. *To hell with Europe.*

According to those dismayed by the outcome of the referendum, the no vote represented a mix of incoherent sentiments, chiefly a frustration with structural unemployment, a rejection of market reforms, and a widespread loathing of the Chirac government. All real, these issues. But unemployment in France is a structural problem of very long standing. It would be a problem whether or not the French voted for the constitution. Chirac? Everyone has always disliked him. The one thing the vote *did* surely express, with perfect clarity, was the unwillingness of the French to cede any more of their national identity to the fantasy of a unified Europe.

It is an old fantasy, of course. The great peace of Innocent III was the expression of just such a fantasy: the notion that the Catholic Church was finally in a position to introduce the City of God into the fractious European political arena. That attempt lasted no more than a generation. Why should this one last longer? No effort to unify Europe has ever succeeded. Most have ended in blood.

What no one in the French elite is prepared to say, but what the French electorate has said clearly, is that the European Union is historically nuts. It does not reflect the will of a single nation-state, or the will of an empire, based on the ability of a central political entity to dominate its periphery, or some form of established European national identity with deep historic roots. Even the Austro-Hungarian Empire had in Austrian power—diminished though it was after 1866—a stable and powerful center. All of European history—all of *world* history—argues against a federation with no force to back it up and no way to impose its will on member states. The French voters recognized this, as did the Dutch, who voted *nee* several days later.

The EU is, in effect, an empty empire. The only national identities up for grabs are the old national identities of the chief nation-states of Europe. And no matter how much the EU bureaucrats try to promote a French identity into a European identity, what do you know? The people just aren't buying it.

## THE THIN VENEER OF GAITY

They aren't buying it because the strains are showing. When the mayor of Paris, Bertrand Delanoë, took office, in 2001—the first leftist to take charge of the city since the Paris Commune—the foreign tabloids made predictable jokes about Gay Paree, because Delanoë is, as everyone knows, gay. And Paris *has* been unusually gay under Delanoë. Every summer, he redecorates the banks of the Seine, importing 10,000 tons of sand, potted palm trees, little café tables, and umbrellas so Parisians can enjoy the ambience of the Riviera in the heart of the city. Cool glasses of Ricard by the river during the day! Singers and jugglers at night! Men in Lycra and women in bikinis playing volleyball in the sand! He even decreed a special beach for dogs. He implemented pedestrian days in the city center—and if the merchants didn't like that because they couldn't get their wares to the shops, he shrugged. To hell with them. He organized citywide scavenger hunts. He arranged for Hollywood movies to be broadcast at night onto giant screens outside the city's famous landmarks, and everyone thought the Cathedral of Notre Dame much improved by the ninety-foot-tall likeness of Clint Eastwood, gesturing in the vague direction of the gargoyles and enjoining them to make his day. The mayor has been enormously popular, of course. What's not to like?

The Nuit Blanche celebration—the Sleepless Night—took place on October 5, 2002. This was another one of the mayor's gay ideas: Throw the city's monuments open to the public, all night, and have a giant free party for everyone in Paris. The Louvre, the Eiffel Tower, the Arc de Triomphe all were open. Jazz pianists and cabaret singers played the bistros until sunrise. Giraffe-limbed models in sunglasses put on a fashion show at the Palais Royale. A glass façade of the

National Library became a giant interactive light show: Passersby could operate the display by sending messages with their cell phones. And for those who made it to dawn, free croissants! Outside the Hôtel de Ville, enamored, grateful citizens chanted "Bertrand, Bertrand!"—and this before anyone heard the bad news.

I was on the scene when it happened. In fact, judging from the news accounts, I was about twenty feet away. I missed the entire thing and read about it the next day in the *New York Times*. Frankly, I wasn't all that sober, and neither was anyone else. Delanoë had decked out the foyer and the hall of mirrors like a 1930s nightclub; everyone was preening and flirting and doing the cha-cha, and *zut*, who was paying attention?

I'd been living in Paris for a while, but I'd never been inside the Hôtel de Ville before, and neither had most native Parisians. Under Delanoë's predecessors, the opulent town hall—which looks like a statuesque wedding cake from the outside and a magnificent bordello inside—was closed to the public for security reasons. But Delanoë threw the gates open. There were no metal detectors or pat-downs at the door, because, he insisted, that wouldn't have been festive.

That was why the assailant was able to throw himself on the mayor, who was circulating without bodyguards among the crowd, and stab him in the stomach, missing his aorta by less than an inch. Delanoë was gravely wounded but insisted he be evacuated quietly: "Let the party continue," he said, wanting no one's night to be spoiled. Doctors at Pitié-Salpêtrière Hospital operated on him for more than three hours, and saved his life.

The attacker, Azedine Berkane, was a Muslim immigrant from Algeria. Initially, the media suspected organized terror. But the man, police concluded, was a lone nutball, more John Hinckley than Mohamed Atta. According to *Le Monde*, the police had at least fifteen files on him, half concerning drugs, the others, theft. He had been in and out of psychiatric hospitals and prisons for years. He lived with his parents.

He had stabbed the mayor, he declared, because he hated politicians and he hated homosexuals even more. Berkane came from one of the tough, hopeless Parisian suburbs that recently exploded in rioting and arson. *Le Monde* reported,

> At the foot of his building about twenty young adults described their neighbor's personality. . . . [One neighbor] remembered above all that this childless bachelor "didn't much like homosexuals," and that "he made this clear to everyone he hung out with." On that matter, opinions among the group were unanimous. "He was a bit like us," continued [another neighbor]. "We're all homophobic here, because it's not natural." "It's against Islam," added [yet another neighbor]. "Muslim fags don't exist."[1]

Of course, most Muslim immigrants do not attempt to murder the mayor because he is gay. Nor, for that matter, are all murderers of gay martyrs Muslims: Daniel White, after all, whose last name rather sums up his ethnic situation, killed San Francisco supervisor Harvey Milk. But the story is revealing nonetheless. It is a hint that Europe may have a problem on its hands. It is a hint that the veneer of gaiety may be thin.

This story, and stories like it, are why the French voted *non*.

## REVERSION BY DEFAULT

Throughout the Middle Ages, the life of every single European, from peasant to lord, from knight to tradesman, was ordered and assigned meaning by the Church. The village church was the center of his community. His days and seasons were governed by the rhythms of the liturgical calendar. Sacramental rituals demarcated the milestones of his life. He received the Eucharist on Holy Days. He confessed his sins. He feasted on feast days and fasted on fast days. His cycle plays enacted the drama of creation and judgment. The Church was the source, the only source, of his education, and often his only connection to the world beyond his village. All music, all literature, all art, all philosophy—*all* emanated from the Church. His understanding of his place in the universe came from the stories and examples of the lives of the saints, from devotional treatises, from religious and mystical lyrics, from religious allegories in poetry and prose.

Each man's life was infused with a sense of supernatural meaning. His monarch ruled by divine right. His place in a rigid, hierarchical structure of loyalty was divinely sanctioned. Human history unfolded according to an ineffable divine plan, represented in the paintings and stained glass on the walls of his church. God was directly involved in human affairs: He rewarded the just, and punished the wicked. Plagues and famine were the Devil's work. There was no other explanation for the mysteries of human existence on offer, and none conceivable.

The rise of modern science facilitated the death of Christianity, and thus the nullification of this entire social and political order, by replacing religion as a framework to interpret human experience. The origins of European atheism, however, were political as much as intellectual, rooted in protest against the power and corruption of Europe's Church institutions. (It is not an accident that atheism, like Marxism, captured the imaginations of Europeans, but not Americans.) Nothing about the Scientific Revolution *inherently* entailed the demise of religious belief. Atheism gained strength through its loose association with the triumphs of science, not through its logical emergence from any particular scientific discovery: The existence of God, after all, was never specifically disproved. And no scientific discovery provided anything like a comprehensive and fully satisfying answer to the questions posed by religious inquiry. Nonetheless, medieval piety was extinguished, and with it every ordering principle of medieval life, leaving a vacuum in its wake. This made possible the rise of the nation-state—and made it necessary, as well.[2]

Since the death of Christian Europe, Europe's new social order has been rooted in the nation-state. Nationalism, propagated through the emerging secular channel of print media, restored meaning and ritual to European civic life. National ceremonies replaced those of the

Church. The nation-state in Europe has always been more than an administrative structure; it has been a pseudo-spiritual entity, imparting meaning to the lives of men.

The nation-state was predicated, precisely as the term suggests, on this idea: *one nation, one state.* The nation includes all and only those who share a particular historical, linguistic, and cultural heritage. By definition, it excludes those who do not. Unsurprisingly, nation-states are confounded when they meet large-scale immigration. If Europe is unable to integrate its minorities as the United States does, it is because the United States is, in effect, an empire, and empires successfully integrate minorities. Indeed, the empires of European history—the Roman Empire, the Holy Roman Empire, the French Empire, the Austro-Hungarian Empire—successfully encompassed a multitude of racial and ethnic groups. But the First World War delivered the death blow to the great multinational empires. The Ottoman Empire and the Austro-Hungarian Empire were destroyed. National self-determination emerged as the official doctrine of Europe, enshrined in the Versailles Treaty: From then on, Europe was to be a continent of small nation-states, not empires.*

The European nation-state was predicated as well on the idea of national sovereignty. Following the war, Roosevelt and Stalin were determined to extirpate nationalism forever from Europe, and indeed succeeded in repressing nationalism, in favor of ideological empires, until the collapse of the Soviet Union. Western Europe was rebuilt as a symbol of liberalism, capitalism, and free trade, while Eastern Europe was forced to adopt Soviet Communism. The collapse of the Soviet Union has ended this epoch. No longer under the control of the superpowers, Europe has in many ways reverted by default to the era of Versailles. The treaties that established the European Union work at cross purposes with the essential character of the nation-state. The persistence of the nation-state as the source of social order in Europe,

---

*Enshrined, but poorly applied, leaving the successor states riddled with internal divisions and border disputes, and permitting outraged nationalism to reach its pinnacle in postwar Germany.

despite the stubborn efforts of the superpowers to eradicate it, is key to understanding modern Europe.

## A BLIND BALANCE OF POWER

Directly following the terrorist attack on Madrid, one of al Qaeda's key ideologists, the pseudonymous Lewis Atiyyatullah, published an article in the Global Islamic Media Internet forum. "The international system built-up by the West since the Treaty of Westphalia," he prophesied, "will collapse; and a new international system will rise under the leadership of a mighty Islamic state." Again, al Qaeda's keen sense of history is in evidence: Who in the West is apt to give a moment's thought to the Treaty of Westphalia?

But he is right to think that treaty significant. Modern Europe's political order can be traced directly to the conclusion of the Thirty Years War and the signing of the 1648 Peace of Westphalia, the terms of which afforded the various German principalities both religious autonomy and a measure of political independence. The secular state system that emerged replaced the medieval system of feudal loyalties. Subsequent European wars were fought not for reasons of religion but for reasons of state.

The French Revolution ignited a blaze of nationalism throughout Europe, one that has not yet been extinguished. The French revolutionary armies, followed by Napoleon, his soldiers on fire with faith in France, provoked in their aggression an equal and opposite nationalist vitalization throughout Europe. The 1815 Congress of Vienna represented a compromise with this new nationalism, tempering—but not halting—its advancement.

Europe is still organized along the lines of the Congress of Vienna: It remains a collection of independent nation-states governed by ever-shifting coalitions designed to prevent any one state from repeating the dominance achieved by Napoleonic France. This model has governed Europe for almost two hundred years, with two notable failures—the

First and Second World Wars. The idea of the balance of power has never disappeared. (Indeed, the internal organizations of France and Germany are both governed by balance-of-power calculations. France is essentially a corporate state, with at least half a dozen powerful fiefdoms eternally trying to form coalitions and limit the power of other fiefdoms.)

But a balance-of-power system is inherently blind when confronted with an ideologically driven, internationalist movement. Confronting Communism during the interwar years, Europe found itself in the same position it now finds itself with respect to radical Islam: under assault by an international movement that did not identify itself with a nation-state.* Some—Britain's intellectual elites, for example— underestimated the threat, finding much to admire in the Bolshevik Revolution; elsewhere in Europe, fascist parties rose to power by grossly exaggerating the threat. Then as now, Europe was incapable of marshaling an appropriate, effective, unified response. It reacts to radical Islamism now by default, as a large bureaucracy. Its leaders lack the imaginative power truly to appreciate the nature of their adversary. Europeans expect Islamic radicals to be, at heart, like Europeans: open to negotiation, amenable to reason, susceptible to bribery. They do not appreciate that their posture engenders not reciprocal conciliation but contempt.

This tendency is reinforced by the nature of Europe's governing class. Every modern European country is the legatee of feudalism's system of social stratification. Based originally on birth, it is now based on competitive examinations. The EU countries now constitute a Mandarin system as complete as the Mandarin system of Imperial China. Historically, little has changed but the rules by which the aristocracy is defined. This idea is best traced in France: In large measure, the Revolution destroyed the old hereditary class; Napoleon created a new aristocratic class, however, through the system of the *grandes écoles,* schools designed to produce another kind of self-perpetuating

---

*I am aware that the Comintern was little more than an organ of Soviet foreign policy. Nonetheless, the ideological character of the Soviet Union was such that it felt its revolution universally suitable for export.

class. The French system has now been adopted in all but name by the EU itself, since entry into EU employment is based on an endless series of competitive examinations. As a consequence, Europe's leaders are bred of young Europeans who want *nothing more than to pass those examinations.* The kind of mind produced by elite schools and competitive examinations: bureaucratic, anti-entrepreneurial, and risk-averse.

Of course, the conflict with the Islamic world is nothing new for Europe. Europe's conflict with the Islamic world dates from the era of the first caliphs. Clearly it remains unresolved—at least, much of the Islamic world thinks so. But with the collapse of faith in Europe, the nature of this conflict has changed. In the era of the Crusades, Islam and the Christian West were equals in piety and passion. The eschatology of the Crusaders was uncannily similar, in tone and vocabulary, to that voiced in the ancient and contemporary mosques of the Middle East and broadcast daily now, via satellite dish, into the homes of Muslims in Europe. European eschatology has since changed completely. Islamic eschatology has not.

The Crusaders had two chief goals: to rescue their coreligionists and to liberate Jerusalem. So do the jihadis who murdered 200 Spaniards in Madrid. But the fervor now runs only one way. No European is now prepared to die for Jerusalem or his fellow Christians. Few Europeans are even prepared to admit that there is, indeed, an unresolved conflict. But there is, and most Europeans cannot, or will not, confront it.

## THE LONG WITHDRAWING WHIMPER

All these ancient conflicts and patterns are now shambling out of the mists of European history. This is why Europe has lately appeared so bewildering—and often so thoroughly obnoxious—to Americans. At the beginning of this book, I proposed that we must understand this to understand Europe, and must understand Europe to construct an intelligible relationship to it. Upon what principles, then, should this relationship be based?

The first principle must be this: European anti-Americanism is a cultist system of faith, rather than a set of rational beliefs, and as such is impervious to revision upon confrontation with facts, logic, evidence, gestures of good will, public relations campaigns, or attempts on the part of the American secretary of state to be a better, more sensitive listener. I do not believe the United States to be beyond reproach. Like all societies, America has defects, often grave, and in some instances Europeans are correct to note them. But the vast bulk of this criticism is exuberantly irrational. Americans need not attempt to correct Europe's antipathy toward the United States by means of pained introspection and efforts to improve themselves: it will not work. Nothing Americans might do, short of dying politely en masse, will change this. The American Left's contention that it is the current administration's foreign policy that has made the United States an object of hatred is a naïve delusion.

Americans need not be much impressed by, or attempt to emulate, Europe's controlled economies and social welfare policies. French newspapers chortled gleefully during the 2001 economic slowdown, when unemployment in the United States reached 5.5 percent. This occurred precisely as the French government was admiring itself for *reducing* levels of unemployment to 8.7 percent. Americans who are tempted to consider high levels of structural unemployment a reasonable price to pay for cradle-to-grave social welfare should consider more closely the social costs of that unemployment, particularly the barrier it constitutes to the economic integration and advancement of immigrants, and thus to the entire polity's harmony and welfare.

Precisely as the United States has succeeded dramatically in slashing its rates of violent crime over the past decade, European crime rates have soared. If former French minister of justice Marylise Lebranchu was quick to reassure her countrymen that in matters of police technique, "The government has no desire to copy the American model," this is not because the French model has proved superior, as any quick trip to the suburbs of Paris will prove, if you survive it. Where police tactics have worked in Europe—as in Marseille—they have worked by emulating Americans ones. Where they have not emulated the Americans, they have failed.

There is a popular myth, accepted by most Europeans and a surprising number of Americans, that Europeans enjoy a superior quality of life, that their societies are less plagued by inequality, that European societies are less violent, more civilized, more rational, even that Europe's popular culture is more tasteful. This simply is not so. When films by Michael Moore receive rapturous ovations at Cannes, the audience stopping just short of ululating and firing AK-47s into the air, it is not because Michael Moore makes a great many excellent points. It is because Michael Moore, like Europe, is lost in what is evidently a pleasurable miasma of perverse fantasy, internal contradiction, and hysteria.

Our policy and posture toward Europe must be informed by the belief that this popular myth is just that, a myth, and by a deeper appreciation of European history. Politicians with no appreciation of that history should not determine our policies toward Europe. Ted Kennedy, lamenting the failures of the Bush administration, proposed that "we should have strengthened, not scorned, the alliances that won two World Wars and the Cold War." But it is logically impossible to strengthen the alliances that won the two World Wars and the Cold War. The two World Wars were fought *against* Germany, but the Cold War was fought *in alliance* with West Germany; Russia was our *ally* in the First World War and the Soviet Union was our *ally* in the Second World War, but the Soviet Union was our *enemy* in the Cold War; Japan was our ally in the First World War and our enemy in the Second World War and our ally again in the Cold War, as was Italy; Turkey was our enemy in the First World War, neutral in the second, and our ally in the Cold War; Vichy France was our enemy for a time, too. So really, Britain is the only major power to which this statement might logically apply, and no one could fairly argue that this is an alliance we scorned. Am I quibbling here? No, not really. Anyone who has spent time thinking about Europe and its history would be incapable of making such a comment in a well-rehearsed and widely broadcast speech. And no one so unfamiliar with the history of our European alliances should be giving us advice about those alliances now.

As someone who *has* spent time thinking about Europe and its history, I do not prophesy the imminent demise of European democratic institutions, nor do I predict imminent catastrophe on European soil. But I don't rule out these possibilities either. Europe's entitlement economy *will* collapse. Its demography *will* change. The European Union may unravel. Islamic terrorists may succeed in taking out a European city. We have no idea what these events would herald, but it is possible and reasonable to imagine a very ugly outcome.

And once again, the only people to whom this will come as a surprise are those who have not been paying attention.

# AFTERWORD FOR THE PAPERBACK EDITION

## I TOLD YOU SO

THIS BOOK BEGAN with a prediction that the next major terrorist attack on America would come from Europe. So when recently it emerged that British counterterrorism officials had foiled a plot to blow up as many as a dozen transatlantic airliners with liquid explosives, the news did not come as a surprise to me. In fact, shortly after September 11, 2001, I spoke to American counterterror officials who told me they were concerned about precisely this scenario. Nor was I surprised to learn that the arrested men and women were British citizens, some of a "wholly ethnic British" background, as the newspapers delicately put it. (In plain speech: They were white).* Authorities suspected that a British charity ostensibly dedicated to earthquake relief in Pakistan had helped to fund the plot. Again, no surprise there.

From the moment the word *terrorist* passed over the news feed, it was assumed by the public that the suspects were Islamic radicals, as indeed they were. But no mention of this was made for an entire news cycle—as if quite possibly they were extremist members of the Order of the Elks or radical Rotarians, and only time would tell. *Bloody Elks, it's always them, innit, mate?* The media's delicacy was also un-

---

*Note this interesting euphemism. Would American newspapers describe white men as being from an "ethnic American background"? Of course not. There is no such thing. This phrase suggests why immigrants have an easier time in America than they do in Britain. Johnny Walker Lindh was never described as the "ethnic American" Taliban.

surpising, for mentioning Islam in the same breath as terrorism is now considered in Europe to be a breech not only of good manners but the law. According to European Union guidelines drafted in April 2006, officials are to avoid the phrase "Islamic terrorism" to avoid causing "frustration among Muslims."[1] The words *fundamentalist* and *jihad* are also to be eschewed. Quite right, too; we wouldn't want some frustrated Islamic fundamentalist going on a jihad now, would we?

The suspects were who I said they would be in this book's introduction: deranged homegrown ideologues who sought to take advantage of the freedom of movement afforded them by their European passports to attack the United States. It was this prediction, among others, that caused certain critics to argue that my view of Europe was unduly pessimistic. In light of the events of the past six months, I would suggest that the views offered in this book were, on the contrary, unduly bright.

I wrote in this book, for example, that the Somali-born Dutch parliamentarian Ayaan Hirsi Ali represented an important light of moral courage in the Netherlands. That light has now been extinguished. In April, Hirsi Ali was evicted from her apartment in The Hague. Her neighbors had filed a lawsuit charging that Hirsi Ali was likely to be murdered by terrorists; her neighbors could be caught in the cross fire, and therefore Hirsi Ali's very presence violated their right, enshrined in the European Convention on Human Rights, to feel safe in their homes. The court, agreeing—and inadvertently illustrating the consequences of relinquishing sovereignty to the Council of Europe—effectively ruled that Hirsi Ali had no right to live near anyone. *No Hirsi Ali, no problem.* Perhaps Hirsi Ali's neighbors' right to security had been infringed, but the court's decision to penalize Hirsi Ali for this, rather than those who wished to *kill* Hirsi Ali, reflects a species of moral reasoning so dismal that one might think it parody.

As if this were not sufficiently craven, in May 2006 Dutch immigration minister Rita Verdonk revoked Hirsi Ali's citizenship outright on the grounds that she had lied on her citizenship application, in 1992. This had been public knowledge for years, and the lies were trivial. She had used her grandfather's last name on her application rather than her father's, and she had neglected to mention that she had arrived after transiting through Kenya and Germany. According to Hirsi Ali, she lied to avoid retribution from her family. If that is the case, she in no way violated the spirit of the asylum laws, if indeed those laws had anything to do with providing real asylum. She admitted the falsehoods in 2002; her party at the time accepted her explanation, and, until recently, so did Dutch immigration authorities. Yet suddenly—at precisely the moment the courts were concluding that Hirsi Ali's very existence was a violation of her neighbors' human rights—Verdonk decided that Hirsi Ali must lose her citizenship. It is impossible to imagine that this was a coincidence or that the reasoning behind the decision was not the same: *No Hirsi Ali, no problem.*

In response to widespread criticism, the Dutch government reinstated Hirsi Ali's citizenship in June 2006, but she had by then resigned from parliament. She plans to leave the Netherlands and come to the United States to work with the American Enterprise Institute. Who can blame her?

One year after the London Tube bombings, and one month before the exposure of the plot to blow up U.S.-bound aircraft, the *Times of London* conducted a poll among British Muslims. It found that 13 percent of them considered the Tube bombers "martyrs." That is, slightly more than 200,000 British Muslims thought the murderers not only admirable, but sanctified. This constitutes a minority of Muslims, true, but obviously not a trivial minority. In the same month, a previously unknown group of Islamic terrorists narrowly failed to blow up German passenger trains in Dortmund and Koblenz. Only a design flaw prevented the bombs, concealed in suitcases, from exploding and killing civilians in numbers similar to those in the attacks in Madrid and London. "But why is Germany in the crosshairs of international jihadism?" asked a bewildered columnist in Germany's *Spiegel*. "After all, al Qaeda's two major attacks in Europe to date were attributed to the fact that the governments of Spain and Britain were involved in the Iraq war, which Germany is not. And Germany itself was not the direct target of the previously thwarted attacks. In one case it was an Iraqi politician and in the second it was German Jews, whom Islamists planned to attack because of their religious affiliation, not their citizenship."[2] Imagine that! Despite all that earnest German pacifism and all that stern denunciation of Israel, the terrorists are refusing to confine their attacks to Jews. How inexplicable and unsporting! (Note the columnist's assumption that an attack on German Jews is *not* an attack on Germany.)

But no matter how often the bombs go off or narrowly fail to go off, it seems impossible to persuade a large segment of the European public—and the American one—that the threat is real. Within minutes of the announcement that a plot to blow up aircraft had been foiled, rumors began circulating on the Internet suggesting that there had been no plot, only a hoax perpetrated by the Bush and Blair administrations to shore up support for their foreign policy and strip their subjects of their remaining civil liberties. "More propaganda than plot," sneered British broadcaster and former ambassador Craig Murray. "Be skeptical. Be very, very skeptical."

I'm all for skepticism, as a rule. But it would take the very opposite quality—extraordinary credulity—to endorse Murray's view. You would have to believe that an enormous number of people with no obvious interest in perpetrating such a hoax had been convinced to go along with it—including hundreds of members of MI5, Scotland Yard, and the SAS; local British and American law enforcement authorities of mixed party affiliation; the government of Pakistan; and significant numbers of the Pakistani intelligence service (which is said to have provided key information leading to the arrests). You would have to imagine that Bush and Blair seriously expected everyone in the loop to keep their mouths shut about the hoax forever. All the evidence to be presented at the trial would have to be manufactured—the detonators and the bombmaking chemicals and the thousands of hours of surveillance tapes, photographs, and videos—and the silence of the technicians who manufactured the evidence would have to be guaranteed forever. (I can think of only one way of ensuring that.) British authorities claim to have several of the suicide bombers' farewell videos in their possession. Did they convince actors to play the terrorists? What actor would play that role, knowing it would be used as evidence to send him to prison? It could all theoretically be done, I suppose— though, for my money, I'd hazard that if our leaders had the organizational talent, cunning, discipline, and diplomatic skill to pull the whole scam off without a hitch, we wouldn't be losing in Iraq.

Some of the skeptics speculated that this Potemkin plot was concocted by the Bush administration as a panicked response to Joe Lieberman's Senate primary defeat by Ned Lamont. This requires imagining that foreign conspirators in the hoax knew who Joe Lieberman was, first, and gave a rat's patoot about his political fortunes, second. And it requires believing that at some point, George Bush placed a phone call to Pakistani president Pervez Musharraf and asked him to arrest a few dozen innocent citizens, torture them for verisimilitude, and then subject them to a show trial—just to distract Americans from the fortunes of the Democratic Party's Lieberman wing. How can anyone in full possession of his faculties seriously entertain this idea? *What's that, Pervez? You say you don't have the first clue who this Lieberman guy is and he's sure as hell not your problem? . . . Oh, no, you've got it all wrong; Lieberman's not a Jewish name, Pervie, we wouldn't ask you to do that for a . . . Perve? You still there, Perve?"*

It is psychologically fascinating to recognize that so many people are willing to dream up these extraordinarily unlikely scenario, and blindly put their confidence in them, in preference to confronting an unpleasant but perfectly obvious truth: Europe is home to a significant number of homicidal maniacs who want to kill as many of their countrymen, and as many Americans, as they possibly can. In Freudian analysis, the term "displacement" refers to an unconscious defense mechanism whereby the mind redirects emotion from a dangerous object to a safe one. This concept, in conjunction with the equally useful Freudian concept of denial, goes quite some ways toward explaining what we are now seeing in Europe.

Two days after the plot was revealed, an unknown number of suspects remained at large. I was in Paris and scheduled to fly out of Orly Airport. I personally had no doubt that the plot was real. Trying to convince myself that this must, in fact, be the *best* time to fly, since security would now be so rigorous, I looked on Google to see what new, reassuringly tough screening measures the French airports had put in place. To my astonishment, I discovered that Orly's security screeners had gone on strike. France-2 television showed them marching gaily through the terminal at Charles de Gaulle International Airport, carrying huge banners demanding more job security.

Now, no one, no one on this *planet,* has more job security than a French government employee. Short of having the next hundred years' worth of paychecks stapled directly to their pampered posteriors in dollar-denominated T-bills, there is *no way* French government employees could be more secure in their financial futures than they already are. Yet the strike couldn't be postponed by even a day—even if it put at risk the lives of every man, woman, and child traveling through French airports.

Interior Minister Nicolas Sarkozy, having convened an emergency meeting in Paris to discuss the terrorist threat, called for 100 percent searches of all hand luggage on flights heading for the United States. *Not possible,* responded the head of the security screeners' union. *You see,* he said, *we need higher wages and better working conditions.*

I, for one, thought what they really needed was to be taken out and shot.

I stressed in this book that Europeans have taken the idea of a right to job security to its pathological outer limits, and this point was beautifully demonstrated not only by the security screeners' strike, but also by the recent protests in France against the *contrat première embauche.* Last March, French students took to the streets to protest the new law, which was proposed to combat unemployment by giving employers more flexibility to fire—and thus hire—young employees. This was the second time in four months that France had been seized with violent protests. But the goals of the golden flock of imbeciles on the streets in March were in fact in perfect conflict with those of unemployed immigrants who took to the street in the previous round of protests. If the suburban rioters wanted a change in their circumstances, the students wanted things to stay exactly the same. And because the students' anxieties closely mirrored the concerns of the majority of the French public, the CPE was swiftly defeated. No surprise—in France, job security will win every time.

No one in France is willing to admit that French labor laws are absurd; no one will say that barring their reform, France faces economic eclipse, if not collapse. So powerful is the sense of entitlement in France that even during a crisis involving a genuine threat to *bodily* security, French luggage screeners felt confident that they could blackmail the government in the name of *job* security and get away with it. I very much doubt that the economic and social reforms needed to ameliorate the desperate conditions in French slums will ever be put in place. Thus, for those at the bottom of the French socioeconomic heap, all that stretches out before them is hopelessness, indolence, and the dole.

I'm under no illusion that reforming Europe's labor laws and welfare economies would be the miracle cure for Islamic radicalism. If that were the case, Britain, with one of the most liberalized economies in Europe, would be the European country with the least significant problem on its hands, whereas the reality is just the opposite. The men and women, including one pregnant woman, who planned to detonate themselves over the Atlantic in August appeared to be, like the London Tube bombers before them, comfortably middle class. They were full beneficiaries of Britain's liberalized economy. Some were university educated. They were not planning to commit murder because they were poor and oppressed, no more than Theo van Gogh's murderer, Mohammed Bouyeri, acted from desperate poverty. They were acting, as Bouyeri said at his trial—and as these miserable wretches surely will at theirs—out of conviction. An *ideology* is again the source of the violent impulse spreading across Europe. This seems a particularly difficult point for many to grasp. Despite the fall of the Berlin Wall, the Marxist assumption that ideology must be the consequence, not the cause, of economic circumstance remains almost impossible for many Europeans to shake.

After this book was published, some suggested that I believed the solution lay in a Christian revival throughout Europe. Let me make myself even clearer: I don't, and I have called for no such thing. My observations about the sociological consequences of the decline of religious faith in Europe are descriptive, not prescriptive; I doubt that it would even be possible for the forms of Christianity that once prevailed on the Continent to return, not least because the political structures to which they were attached have been erased. The key point of my book is to recognize that certain forms of essential human longing remain, and equally to recognize that they are now being expressed in *other* forms. Once this is acknowledged consciously—as in psychoanalysis—there is a freedom to choose more appropriate behavior, whether religious or secular.

I am, however, an advocate of Enlightenment values, including the strict separation of church and state. Europe is certainly far from those values now, as the cartoon riots, which erupted shortly after this book's publication, made it all too clear. On September 30, 2005, Denmark's *Jyllands-Posten* newspaper published an article entitled "The Face of Muhammad," consisting of twelve cartoons—only some of which depicted Muhammad—and a text by Flemming Rose, the newspaper's culture editor, explaining that the cartoons had been commissioned to test the new boundaries of freedom of speech in Europe. The ensuing protests and violence were fomented by opportunistic Danish imams who made political capital of the cartoons by touring the Middle East and pointing out to certain fascinated heads of state the intriguing opportunities for mischief-making inherent in the situation. Expressing infinite contempt for every value of the Enlightenment, protesters outside Danish embassies in Europe loudly cried for Osama bin Laden to "bomb Denmark," to "nuke Germany, nuke France, nuke the USA," to "behead those who insult Islam" and "spread blood in the streets of England." Interestingly, some protesters were seen burning the flag of the European Union. One must be grateful for the EU's decision to ban such terms as "Islamic fascism," for surely it would be fearsome to see such men when they were *really* "frustrated."

I was initially heartened to see Danish prime minister Anders Fogh Rasmussen setting a fine example of defiance in the face of intimidation, refusing even to discuss the idea that the Danish government should be in the business of censoring political speech. "This is a matter of principle," he said. "I won't meet with [Muslim ambassadors] because it is so crystal clear what principles Danish democracy is built upon that there is no reason to do so . . . I will never accept that respect for a religious stance leads to the curtailment of criticism, humor, and satire in the press." His splendid words inspired in me a shy flicker of hope until, soon afterward, I received an utterly dispiriting e-mail from Denmark. Several months prior, I had posted an ad on craigslist seeking someone to care for my pets in Istanbul while I went to the United States on my book tour. Two elderly Danish women had replied, and recently I had written back, asking if they were still free to come. Their message offered their regrets. It seemed, they wrote, that it was unsafe and inadvisable for Danes to visit any Muslim country. There had been demonstrations against their embassy in Istanbul, they noted, and all travel from Denmark to Egypt had been halted. The violence was spreading quickly. Then the punch line: They *apologized* for the situation. They understood full well, they wrote, why Muslims were offended by their newspaper's treatment of the Prophet. Would I please extend their apologies to all of my Turkish friends?

Could anything more poignantly sum up the thesis of this book? By all accounts, the attitude evidenced by these two bewildered and kindhearted old ladies was widespread among the Danish public. Indeed, throughout Europe, tentative displays of backbone were followed immediately by whimpering, tail-wagging supplication, as if the muscles supporting the European spine had atrophied through disuse.

Some in the press did make an attempt to stand up for the principle of freedom of speech. Directly after the riots began, *France Soir* carried a fine editorial stating that the cartoons were indeed blasphemous, and if Muslims didn't like it, tough. The Catholic Church, noted the editorialists, had once claimed the right that Muslims were now demanding. France had taken care of that problem with the Revolution. Good stuff, that editorial, and long overdue. One day later, the editor was sacked.

The Council of Europe's Committee of Ministers condemned the Danish media's "intolerance." The Swedish government closed down a political party's website for displaying the cartoons. A Norwegian editor who ran the cartoons apologized abjectly. European companies with interests in the Muslim world competed to see who could distance themselves fastest from the cartoons and from their own principles.

Shortly after the controversy arose, Norwegian political cartoonist Finn Graff explained in an interview that he wouldn't dream of drawing cartoons that offend Muslims—"out of respect." This is the same man who recently depicted the prime minister of Israel dressed in the regalia of a concentration camp commander at Auschwitz.

European enthusiasm for cartoons that depict Jews dressed as Nazis has been much in evidence during the recent Israeli war against Hezbollah in Lebanon. For the sake of argument, let's assume that Israel's actions in Lebanon were unjustified, stupid, cruel, disproportionate, outrageous, and a violation of international law. This is the view held by a majority of European statesmen and is the official editorial stance of a vast majority of European news outlets. Even assuming that this is so, why are Europeans so exercised about it?

This is a serious question. The reader might think, given our assumptions, that the answer is self-evident: Israeli actions were unjustified, stupid, cruel, disproportionate, outrageous, and a violation of international law. And this, of course, is why we have also seen an outpouring of rage throughout Europe toward Pakistan—Pakistani mosques daubed with loathsome and hateful graffiti, politicians denouncing Pakistani brutality, anguished editorials in every major European press organ about the civilian deaths for which Pakistan is responsible. It is only natural, since Pakistani nationalists appear to have been behind the July 11, 2006, bombing of Bombay commuter trains and stations that deliberately killed more than 200 civilians. Any thinking person would be outraged by such as atrocity, would he not?

Apparently not. The event made headlines in Europe for all of

about six hours, then disappeared completely from public consciousness. Of course, there was a particularly embarrassing aspect to that
crime—the bombers seem to have been funded by British businessmen.[3] Even so, civilians were killed deliberately, and one might expect
Europeans, with their exquisite sensitivity to civilian deaths, to take
notice.

But they didn't. One might wonder if the difference is that Israel is
a recipient of American military aid. That, perhaps, is why Europeans find Israeli human rights abuses so much more difficult to stomach—because America could stop them if it so chose. That is what I
am often told when I press critics to explain what's so *different* about
Israel. But Pakistan, too, receives massive military assistance from the
United States. As does Turkey, for that matter, and Turkey has had
more than a few mishaps involving civilians in its war with Kurdish
separatists—so many, in fact, that one begins uncharitably to suspect
a pattern. This is why we have seen so many anti-Turkish demonstrations on the streets of London and calls to send the Turks to the gas
chambers; it's why we've seen the Spanish prime minister dressed in
colorful Kurdish pantaloons as a mark of solidarity, why European
jounalists are streaming into razed Kurdish villages to snap photos of
dead children and wailing families. Except that none of this has taken
place, not least because the Turkish government won't let journalists
anywhere *near* those villages. I live in Istanbul and have heard quite a
few firsthand stories about what happens to journalists who ask what
happened to those civilians. Let's just say, since I cherish my life here,
that enchanting Turkey has everything to offer the discerning tourist.

The truth is that it takes a special hatred of *Jews* to prioritize Israeli atrocities so far above others in a world awash with cruelty, violence, and violations of international law. Shiites killing Sunnis? Eyes
go glassy with boredom. Muslims killing Hindus? Footnote! Africans
killing other Africans? Hell, it would be news if they weren't. No one
in Europe notices, protests, cares, or bestirs himself. As I wrote earlier
in this book: Yes, you can criticize Israel without being an anti-
Semite—in fact, I am about to. But generally, you won't bother.

Now look at the assumptions we have adopted—have Israeli mili-

tary actions in Lebanon been unjustified, stupid, cruel, disproportionate, outrageous, and a violation of international law? Cruel, certainly.
Stupid? Given that Israel seems to have lost the war, yes, by definition
their actions were stupid. Unjustified? Only in some pacifist universe
where nations are expected to allow their neighbors to lob missiles
over their borders without doing a thing about it. A violation of international law? Well, for all the talk of about Israel's "disproportionate"
use of force, I have seen no European politician or newspaper editorial
attempting to explain what a "proportionate" level of force might
look like—should Israel respond by lobbing an equal number of
Katyushas back over the border, at Lebanese civilians, perhaps?—and
these howls of outrage are almost always issued with *no* acknowledg-
ment of the context: Hezbollah's expressed profession of its intention
to eradicate a United Nations member state.

France took a particularly vocal lead in criticizing Israeli actions,
pushing aggressively for an immediate cease-fire—one that would be
monitored by a United Nations peacekeeping force. The French volunteered splendidly to lead it. As soon as Israel accepted the cease-fire,
however, *Le Monde* reported that the French contribution to this
peacekeeping force would, in fact, be "small and symbolic." Perhaps
ten officers. French defense minister Michèle Alliot-Marie defended
this decision by saying, "You can't send in men telling them, 'Look
what's going on but you don't have the right to defend yourself or to
shoot.'" Quite. But that, of course, is exactly the posture they are insisting the Israelis must adopt. Shortly after this, the Italians announced that they would put up 3,000 troops and take command of
the force in France's place. French president Jacques Chirac, presumably itching to head-butt his Italian counterpart, replied by grudgingly
offering to send 2,000 troops. Better late than never, I suppose.

Since the war in Lebanon began, the criticism of Israel in Europe
has been obsessive, incessant, unrelenting. Anti-Semitic crime has
surged again. Jews in Norway, following an assault on a man wearing
a yarmulke on the street in Oslo, have been advised not to speak Hebrew in public or wear clothing that might identify them as Jews. In
Rome, some twenty shops owned by Jews were vandalized with

swastikas. Flyers with Hezbollah slogans were left at the shops and signed by group calling itself Armed Revolutionary Fascists. In Belgium, an urn that contained ashes from Auschwitz was smashed and the shards smeared in excrement. Rallies were held on the streets of Berlin, not far from the Brandenburg Gate, where protesters chanted, "Death to the Jews." In Madrid, protesters took to the streets chanting, "Nazis, Yankees, Jews: No more chosen people!" A mass rally in solidarity with Hezbollah took place in London in July. Note: not a protest, per se, against Israeli military tactics, but a rally in solidarity *with Hezbollah*—the group that killed 241 U.S. Marines, sailors, and soldiers in Lebanon, in 1983, and is basically a Special Forces brigade of the Iranian army. Any place where they are victorious would look just like Iran.

Dutch Socialist Party leader Jan Marijnissen gave that idea some deep thought and concluded that Hezbollah's genocidal campaign against the Jews reminded him of the Nazi epoch, although not quite in the way one might imagine. He proposed that Hezbollah might reasonably be equated with the Resistance. "During World War II, Dutch people thwarted Nazi Germany's destruction machine by blowing up town halls, because this was where the Jews were registered. Things are not all that different in the Middle East. Islamic fundamentalism, including the terrorist wing, is a reaction to Israel's occupation of Palestine, to America's presence in the Middle East and to the West's support of undemocratic regimes in the Middle East," he said. Let's leave aside his fantasies about the record of the Dutch Resistance. The key points are these: Lebanon, first of all, is not in Palestine. Israel does not occupy Lebanon and hasn't for years. Israel unilaterally withdrew from Gaza, and more than 2,000 U.S. troops have died in Iraq because American policy in the Middle East, for the past five years, has been to replace undemocratic regimes with democratic ones. He must have missed those items in the newspaper, but that's understandable, since they were probably buried on page 32, after thirty-one pages of cartoons equating Jews and Nazis.

In Norway, the well-known writer Jostein Gaarder published a gorgeously histrionic editorial, to much general applause, announcing that "Israel is history. We no longer recognize the State of Israel. There is no way back. The State of Israel has raped the world's recognition and will not receive peace before it lays down its weapons. . . . We laugh at this people's fancies and weep over their misdeeds. To present themselves as God's chosen people is not just stupid and arrogant, but a crime against humanity. . . . There are limits to our patience, and there are limits to our tolerance. . . ."[4] Echoing this sentiment, Spanish newspapers were suddenly awash with those original, hilarious Jews-dressed-like-Nazis cartoons. Prime Minister "White Flag" Zapatero, who blazed the trail in condemning the publication of the Muhammad cartoons—he wrote in the *International Herald Tribune* that "the publication of these caricatures may be perfectly legal, but it is not indifferent and thus ought to be rejected from a moral and political standpoint"—had not a word to say about cartoons equating Jews and Nazis, which, I suppose, suggests that he thought they ought *not* to be rejected from a moral and political standpoint. Zapatero then pitched up in public wearing a Palestinian *kaffiyeh*. No significance to that, he assured worried Spanish Jews: someone just handed it to him at a public appearance and he put it on to be polite. Forgive me the cynicism of suspecting that had he been handed a T-shirt embossed with a Star of David, he might not have slung it on with such mannerly alacrity.

*But Israeli air strikes in Lebanon killed children.* Indeed they did, and let me be the first, or rather the millionth, to say that those deaths were a disaster, monstrous, all the more so since the children seem to have died for nothing—and certainly not for Israel's greater security or Lebanon's. But I note that at roughly the same time, the government of Sri Lanka bombed an encampment filled with what they claimed were terrorists, but what UNICEF claimed were orphans. Reportedly, fifty-one schoolchildren were killed on the spot. The Sri Lankan military swiftly agreed that yes, the intended targets were children. "If the children are terrorists, what can we do?" shrugged a Sri Lankan military spokesman.

Do the experiment yourself: go to Google and see what the European press had to say about this on the *day following* this gory slaughter in Sri Lanka. Try entering the search term *Sri Lanka*. You will not, I assure you, find a single editorial declaring that "Sri Lanka is history." The story of the massacre is not even the highest-ranked news item. That honor belongs to the revelation that the opening match of the Unitech Cup triangular cricket tournament had been called off due to soggy ground conditions.

While singularly preoccupied with Israeli excesses, Europeans have been oddly quiescent about Iranian ones. The French foreign minister, Philippe Douste-Blazy, at the height of the Lebanon crisis—which was, of course, started by Iran—remarked with a straight face that Iran was "a great country, a great people, and a great civilization which is respected and which plays a stabilizing force in the region." *Beg pardon?* Iran's merry nutball of a leader, Mahmoud Ahmadinejad, breathlessly anticipates the return of the Twelfth Imam, who will be coaxed from his Occultation, the president has hinted, by means of a regional nuclear exchange. His nation is on the verge of acquiring nuclear weapons. He has repeatedly threatened his neighbor with annihilation. Iran is the world's chief sponsor of Islamic terrorism. It harbors al Qaeda terrorists, causes havoc in Iraq, controls Hezbollah in Lebanon, has turned Syria into a client state, pulls Hamas's puppet strings in the Palestinian Authority, meddles to profoundly evil effect in Afghanistan and Pakistan, denies the Holocaust, and would see the world's women reduced to the status of cattle. Ahmadinejad contemplates with a visible sensual excitement the prospect of annihilating every last Jew on the planet. Yet Iran, according to official France, is a great stabilizing force in the Middle East. I invite the critics who have called me an alarmist about Europe to consider Douste-Blazy's comments and their implications and then share with me the secrets of their enviable composure.

The foreign minister's remarks, and the mentality they reflect, indicate that there is no political will in Europe to take effective action in the face of the Iranian threat. I don't expect that the prospect of being hauled before the Security Council much disturbs Ahmadinejad's rest; after all, Britain, France, and Germany have been threatening Iran with the Security Council since 2003, and what of it? I can't say I know what to do about Iran any more than anyone else does. But at least I can see that whatever that country is, it is *not* a stabilizing force in the region. I reckon that puts me well ahead of the game.

Since the publication of this book, many readers have written to ask me where the solution to Europe's problem lies. I propose the following. As matters of policy, radical clerics funded by Wahhabi Saudi or subcontinental Deobandi money—any cleric in Europe who incites violence and lawbreaking and who advocates the destruction of Western civilization—must be deported or imprisoned. Start with the Danish imams who began the cartoon wars. Cut off their funding; arrest them. Enforce all European laws pertaining to domestic abuse and violence against women with especial vigor. End all state support for extremist Islamic clubs—or any Islamic club where men and women do anything but pray for peace or play backgammon. At the same time, reward moderate Muslims by respecting and encouraging *legitimate* religious aspirations and practices. Provide funding and support for groups that promote the reform and liberalization of Islam, and welcome law-abiding, Westernized Muslims with open arms and real economic opportunities.

Demand that all immigrants learn the language and history of their adoptive countries. Do not cower or capitulate to the threat of violence. Make it perfectly clear that the price of admission to European society is accepting such European practices as the lampooning of religious figures. End the practice of firehosing cash into hermetic immigrant ghettos. Finally, bring back some form of military conscription: A structured military organization is an excellent place for unemployed young men who are prone to radicalism and violence. If the state does not impose this structure on them, they tend to form their own kind of military organization. The Dutch abolished compulsory military service in 1996, shortly before violent extremism in the Netherlands began making headlines. That was obviously a mistake.

The point of this book, however, is not to propose solutions—all of the measures I've stated here are obvious and have been proposed by many others. It is to explain why Europe is incapable of seeing and solving its own problems. The inability to recognize and confront growing Islamic radicalism is only one symptom of a deeper European crisis, and that crisis is the source of the phenomena I have described in this book. Some readers have asked why I devoted so much space to figures such as José Bové and the members of Rammstein. I did so because they are windows through which we see a broader European mood—a widespread cultural and moral void, the existence of which encourages every species of historically dangerous European lunatic to rise from the dead. In all matters, not just ones pertaining to Islam, Europeans seem increasingly to be acting as slaves to historic forces they do not even recognize.

If it is pessimistic to observe this, then so be it.

*Istanbul, August 23, 2006*

# N O T E S

C H A P T E R 1 :  **EUROPE ON FIVE DOLLARS A DAY AND A FLAMETHROWER**

1. Doug Saunders, "British Bombers Likely Recruited at Government-Funded Centre," *Globe and Mail,* July 14, 2005.
2. The complete poll data, including the methodology and precise wording of the questions, can be consulted at http://www.yougov.com/archives/pdf/TEL050101030_1.pdf
3. http://edition.cnn.com/2005/WORLD/europe/05/20/britain. protest/index.html
4. "London Bombers Have Ties to United States," ABC World News Tonight online, July 15, 2005.
5. Ipsos News Center Poll, *Measuring Hope for the Future and Quality of Life: A 12-Country Survey,* September 4, 2002.
6. Michael Ledeen, *The War Against the Terror Masters,* updated edition (New York: St. Martin's, 2003), pp. 242–44.
7. Michael Gonzales, "Vive le Checkbook: How France Bankrolls America's Enemies," *Wall Street Journal,* November 29, 2003.
8. Report on the Manipulation of the Oil-for-Food Programme, issued by the Independent Inquiry Committee into the United Nations Oil-for-Food Programme, October 27, 2005.
9. Paul Krugman, "French Family Values," *New York Times,* July 29, 2005.

C H A P T E R 2 :  **SELF-EXTINGUISHING TOLERANCE**

1. Khaled Shawkat, "European Cinema Exposes Anti-Muslim Practices," *Islam Online,* February 7, 2005.

2.  Marlise Simons, "Militant Muslims Act to Suppress Dutch Film and Art Show," *New York Times,* January 31, 2005.

3.  http://hammorabi.blogspot.com/2005/01/special-sincere-thanks-to-our-friends.html

4.  http://iraqilibe.blogspot.com/2005/01/best-eid-i-ever-had.html

5.  This theory was offered by Juan Cole, a professor of history at the University of Michigan and one of academia's great comic geniuses. See his blog, "Informed Consent," http://www.juancole.com/2004/12/manipulation-of-blogging-world-on-iraq.html

6.  For a full discussion of this point and the new historiography of this period in Dutch history, see Jan Herman Brinks, "The Dutch, the Germans and the Jews," *History Today,* 49:6 (June 1999). This chapter draws heavily upon his scholarship.

7.  *Report of the Netherlands Minister Relating to Conditions in Petrograd,* Publications of the Department of State, Papers relating to the Foreign Relations of the United States. Russia, 1918 (in 3 vols.); here vol. 1, United States Government Printing Office, Washington, DC, 1931, pp. 675–79; here pp. 678 and 679. Cited in "The Dutch, the Germans and the Jews."

8.  "The Dutch, the Germans and the Jews."

9.  Ibid.

10. Wolfgang zu Putlitz, *In Evening Dress Among the Brownshirts: Memories of a German Diplomat,* The Hague, 1964, p. 210, cited in "The Dutch, the Germans and the Jews."

11. Cited in "The Dutch, the Germans and the Jews."

12. See, particularly, Jacob Presser, *The Destruction of the Dutch Jews,* translated by Arnold Pomerantz (New York: E. P. Dutton, 1969). Historian David G. Dalin considers the record of the Catholic Church in the Netherlands notably honorable, however: Dutch bishops distributed a pastoral letter read in every Catholic church in the Netherlands denouncing "the unmerciful and unjust treatment meted out to Jews by those in power in our country." *The Myth of Hitler's Pope* (Washington, D.C.: Regnery, 2005), p. 79.

13. "The Dutch, the Germans and the Jews."

14. Ibid.

15. Anne Frank. *Anne Frank, The Diary of a Young Girl: The Definitive Edition,* edited by Otto H. Frank and Mirjam Prossler. (New York: Doubleday, 1995), p. 54.

16. See http://www.cidi.nl/dossiers/ae/ae.html, "The Background of Abou Jahjah" *(Achtergronden Abou Jahjah),* citing diverse Belgian documents and particularly an article in the French-language Belgian newspaper *Le Soir* of December 6, 2002.

17. Abigail R. Esman, "The Arabian Panther," *Salon,* June 14, 2004.

18. According to the *NRC Handelsblad,* March 1, 2003, she said: *"Dat zijn geen effectieven uitspraken, maar ik keur die ook niet af,"* meaning, "Those are not tactically wise expressions, but I don't reject them either."

19. "The Arabian Panther." *Op. cit.,* citing the Dutch newspaper *Algemeene Dagblad.*

20. Ibid.

21. "Somali Refugee Follows in Fortuyn's Footsteps with Attack on Imams," *Telegraph,* November 1, 2003.

22. Address by Mayor Job Cohen to Amsterdam City Council on November 3, 2004, http://www.amsterdam.nl/contents/pages/00005460/addressbymayorjobcohentoamsterdamcitycouncil.pdf

23. "Feestvieren in de bajes," *De Telegraaf,* September 13, 2005.

24. Chantal Delsol, *Icarus Fallen: The Search for Meaning in an Uncertain World.* Translated by Robin Dick (Wilmington, DE: ISI Books, 2003).

25. Ibid.

26. Emma Goldman, *Living My Life* (New York: Alfred A. Knopf, 1931), vol. 1, chap. 23.

27. Twain, Mark. *What Is Man and Other Essays.* (Fairfield, Iowa: 1st Word Library-Literary Society, 2004), p. 177.

28. Steve Sailer, "Did Fortuyn Have It Coming?" United Press International, May 8, 2002.

29. Ibid.

CHAPTER 3: **WHITE TEETH**

1. ICM Polls, Muslims Poll, December 2002. http://www.icmresearch.co.uk/reviews/2002/bbc-today-muslims-dec-

02.htm. Note the extraordinarily different responses to questions 7 and 10, which are logically the same question but phrased differently.

2.  "London-Based Radical Salutes Bombs 'Victory,'" *Times* (London), July 17, 2005.

3.  "The Men Who Blame Britain," *Telegraph,* July 20, 2005.

4.  Dilpazier Aslam, "We Rock the Boat: Today's Muslims Aren't Prepared to Ignore Injustice," *Guardian,* July 13, 2005. Shortly afterward, in response to widespread outrage that Aslam's political affiliations were not revealed in this article or his byline, his editors asked him to renounce his associations with Hizb ut-Tahrir. He refused and resigned instead.

5.  The film can be viewed at http://johnathangaltfilms.com/.

6.  "Poison Warfare Suits Found in Mosque Raid," *Herald Sun,* January 27, 2003.

7.  *The Muslim News Online,* http://www.muslimnews.co.uk/yoursay/ index.php?ysc_id=3.

8.  Mohammed Abdul Aziz, "Understanding British Muslim Alienation and Exclusion: Exploring the Challenges and Developing Working Solutions" (2004, unpublished draft document), and Humayun Ansari, *Muslims in Britain* (Minority Rights Group International, August 2002), http://www.ingentaconnect.com/content/mnp/ijgr/2003/ 00000010/00000004/art00006

9.  Zadie Smith, *White Teeth* (London: Penguin, 2001).

10. Personal correspondence, October 15, 2005.

11. Tariq Modood, Sharon Beishon, and Satnam Virdee, *Changing Ethnic Identities,* London, Policy Studies Institute Report 794. Statistics on Muslim intermarriage in the United States vary so greatly that I am reluctant to assert a concrete figure. By law, the official U.S. census does not gather information about religious practice, so that's no help. Two-thirds is my best guess, averaging several different sources. See, for example, Yvonne H. Haddad, "The Muslim Experience in the United States," *The Link,* 12:4. One simple reason for higher rates of intermarriage among Muslim immigrants in America may be that they are so much more geographically dispersed. If you don't meet as many

other recent immigrants, you are less likely to marry them. (http://
www.psi.org.uk/publications/publication.asp?publication_id=19)

12. Hanif Kureishi, *The Buddha of Suburbia* (London: Faber and Faber,
    1990), p. 40.
13. Marina Gask, "Editor's Introduction," *Top Santé,* November 2004.
14. I am indebted to my good friend Damian Counsell—another
    immigrant in Britain—for this thought.
15. Bernard Lewis, "Islam and Liberal Democracy," *Atlantic Monthly,*
    February 1993.
16. The insightful Brazilian poet Nelson Ascher offered these reflections
    on Lewis and Said to me in personal correspondence, for which I
    thank him.
17. *Report of the High Level Committee on the Indian Diaspora,* Ministry
    of External Affairs, New Delhi, 2002.
18. *The Education and Child Poverty Report,* End Child Poverty group,
    March 25, 2003, http://www.ecpc.org.uk/downloads/
    Education%20and%20Child%20Poverty.pdf
19. I thank Damian Counsell for this observation.
20. A full and excellent description of queuing theory and its applicability
    to immigrants in the United States and Britain can be found in Susan
    Model, "Non-White Origins, Anglo Destinations: Immigrants in the
    US and Britain," in G. Loury, T. Modood, and S. M. Teles, eds.,
    *Ethnicity, Social Policy and Social Mobility in the United States and
    the United Kingdom* (Cambridge, England: Cambridge University
    Press, 2002). This theory provides an intriguing explanation of the
    comparative success of Muslim Asian immigrants in America.

    Let us imagine a queue such that the ethnic group viewed most
    favorably by employers (yellows) is at the head, and the group
    members viewed least favorably (greens) are at the tail. Purples are
    somewhere in the middle. Suppose we have two labor markets, market
    A and market B. Assume that market A contains only yellows and
    purples. Market B contains all three groups. According to the theory,
    purples will do better, *ceteris paribus,* in market B than market A,
    because the presence of greens benefits purples. Purples will accrue

advantage if the yellow group shrinks or the green group grows. About 27 percent of the U.S. labor force consists of immigrants and ethnic minorities, compared with 10 percent of the British labor force. Assuming most employers in both countries prefer whites to other ethnicities, the theory predicts that Asian minorities in the United States will fare better than their compatriots in Britain, because the United States contains two large, low-ranking groups—blacks and Hispanics—who are less well represented in Britain. This increases the chances that Asian minorities will be at the top of the U.S. labor queue. As long as these large groups hold a lower position on the American ladder of discrimination, Asian immigrants will be more successful in the United States than in Britain.

This appears to be what has happened. When American employers are asked to rank groups in terms of their desirability as employees, whites score highest. Immigrants from the Indian Subcontinent are seen as mid-rank, followed by blacks, Arabs, Mexicans, and Puerto Ricans. If Zia, then, found himself to be an "honorary white man" in the United States, it is perhaps because of the prevalence there of *real* black men. (I am observing, not celebrating, these circumstances.)

21. "We Can Take It," *Mirror,* July 8, 2005.
22. "A Letter to the Terrorists, from London," *London News Review,* July 7, 2005.
23. Harold Pinter, "The American Administration Is a Bloodthirsty Wild Animal," *Telegraph,* December 11, 2002.
24. Margaret Drabble, "I Loathe America," *Telegraph,* May 8, 2003.
25. Brian Reade, "God Help America," *Mirror,* November 4, 2004. Of course, many on the American Left hold identical sentiments.
26. Salman Rushdie, "Anti-Americanism Has Taken the World by Storm," *Guardian,* February 6, 2002.
27. http://www.memritv.org/Transcript.asp?P1=788
28. Fifth Volcker Report, p. 86. Galloway denies this, of course. (http://www.iic-offp.org/story27oct05.htm)
29. K. Sinclair, *A History of New Zealand* (London, 1988), p. 59.

C H A P T E R   4 :   **THE HOPE OF MARSEILLE**

1. The French philosopher and essayist Ernest Renan provided the definitive expression of this doctrine in his famous speech to the Sorbonne, *"Qu'est-ce que la Nation?,"* in 1882.

2. Cited in Patrick Parodi, "Citizenship and Integration: Marseille, a Model of Integration?" in *History-Geography* (Marseille, Académie Aix-Marseille, 2002). My translation.

C H A P T E R   5 :   **WE SURRENDER!**

1. Chantal Delsol, *Icarus Fallen: The Search for Meaning in an Uncertain World.* Translated by Robin Dick (Wilmington, Del.: ISI Books, 2003).

C H A P T E R   6 :   **NO PAST, NO FUTURE, NO WORRIES**

1. Antonio Golini, *Possible Policy Responses to Population Aging and Population Decline: The Case of Italy* (Expert Group Meeting on Policy Responses to Population Aging and Population Decline, Population Division, Department of Economic and Social Affairs, United Nations Secretariat: UN/POP/PRA/2000/7, September 26, 2000).

2. "No Easy Answers Around the World to Population Decline," *The Scotsman,* October 15, 2004.

3. Oriana Fallaci, *The Rage and the Pride* (New York: Rizzoli, 2001).

4. For an interesting depiction of the immaturity and fecklessness of the Italian male, see *L'Ultimo Bacio* ("The Last Kiss"), directed in 2002 by Gabriele Muccino, one of the most successful movies ever produced in Italy. At the center of the film are five young men, each striving to exceed the others' irresponsibility toward their girlfriends and the children they have fathered.

5. Stendhal, *Rome, Naples et Florence* (Folio Ser.: No 1845). (Paris: Gallimard, 1981).

6. Personal correspondence, December 7, 2004.

7. David Horn, *Social Bodies: Science, Reproduction, and Italian Modernity* (Princeton, N.J.: Princeton University Press, 1994), p. 59.

8. "Germany's Declining Population—Kinder, Gentler," *The Economist,* June 12, 2003.

9. *Icarus Fallen.*

CHAPTER 7 :    **BLACK-MARKET RELIGION: THE NINE LIVES OF JOSÉ BOVÉ**

1. I owe my description of the early Bovés, and my knowledge of medieval millenarianism—as does every contemporary scholar—to the great and eloquent historian of medieval heresy Norman Cohn. *The Pursuit of the Millennium* (New York: Oxford University Press, 1970), pp. 41–42.

2. "A World Struggle Is Underway," interview with José Bové by Lynn Jeffress, with Jean-Paul Mayanobe, www.zmag.org.

3. "Anti-Globalization Activist José Bové Is at It Again," Agence France-Presse, January 30, 2001.

4. José Bové and François Dufour, *The World Is Not for Sale: Farmers Against Junk Food* (London: Verso, 2001), p. 18.

5. Phil Reeves, "José Bové Takes His Magic Potion to the West Bank," *The Independent,* June 21, 2001.

6. "José Bové: A Farmer's International?" *New Left Review* 12, November–December 2001.

7. *The Pursuit of the Millennium,* p. 48.

8. *The World Is Not for Sale,* p. 146.

9. *The Pursuit of the Millennium,* pp. 59–60.

10. "A World Struggle Is Underway."

11. *The World Is Not for Sale,* p. 34.

12. Eric Hoffer, *The True Believer* (New York: Perennial Classics, 2002), p. 41.

13. "Anti-Globalization Activist José Bové Is at It Again."

14. *The Pursuit of the Millennium,* pp. 99–100.

15. "José Bové: A Farmer's International?"

16. "Report from French Farmers," José Bové, *Synthesis/Regeneration* 16, Summer 1998.

17. *The World Is Not for Sale,* p. 208.

18. "Report from French Farmers."

19. "A World Struggle Is Underway."

20. *The World Is Not for Sale,* p. 168.

21. Ibid., p. 198.

22. Ibid., p. 185.

23. Ibid., p. 186.

24. Ibid., p. 186–87.

25. Ibid., p. vii.

26. Ibid., p. xii.

27. Ibid., p. 57.

28. Ibid., p. 138.

29. Michael Driessen, http://www.wisemonkeynews.com/article/politics/40/Jose+Bove+fights+the+Mc-Domination+of+the+world/

30. Hal Hamilton, "Reflections from France." http://www.sare.org/sanet-mg/archives/html-home/46-html/0025.html

31. *The Pursuit of the Millennium*, p. 121.

32. *The World Is Not for Sale*, p. 185.

33. *The Pursuit of the Millennium*, p. 83.

34. http://www.foodfirst.org/action/2003/josebove.html

35. *The World Is Not for Sale.*

36. Donella Meadows, *The Global Citizen*, July 13, 2000, http://www.pcdf.org/meadows/Jose_Bove.html

37. James W. Ceaser, "A Genealogy of Anti-Americanism," *Public Interest*, Summer 2003.

38. *The World Is Not for Sale*, pp. 60–61, 78.

39. Ibid., p. 71.

40. *The True Believer*, p. 81.

41. I am indebted to the Brazilian poet Nelson Ascher for corresponding with me at length about these connections. I no longer recall which thoughts were originally his and which were mine, so to be on the safe side, let's say that all the good ideas are his.

42. *The World Is Not for Sale*, p. 27.

43. *"Le Peuple Palestinien est debout,"* interview with José Bové by Fatiha Kaoues, April 24, 2002. My translation. http://oumma.com/article.php3?id_article=378

44. *The World Is Not for Sale*, 11.

45. *The True Believer*, p. 11.

46. H. L. Mencken, *Memorial Service,* first printed in the *Smart Set,* March 1922. Cited in H. L. Mencken on Religion, S. T. Joshi (New York: Prometheus, 2002), p. 297.

CHAPTER 8 :   **BLACK-MARKET NATIONALISM: I HATE**

1. John Felstiner, *Paul Celan : Poet, Survivor, Jew* (New Haven: Yale University Press), p. 39. The translation is Felstiner's.

2. Translated by Evan Goodwin, "Little Blue Light—Georg Trakl," Littlebluelight (May 29, 2003). http://www.littlebluelight.com/ lblphp/quotes.php?ikey=27.

3. Gottfried Benn, *Morgue and Other Expressionist Verse* (1912–1913). Translated by Supervert32C Inc., 2002. http://supervert.com/elibrary/ gottfried_benn.

4. *Der Kongress zur Nürnberg 1934* (Munich: Zentralverlag der NSDAP., Frz. Eher Nachf., 1934), pp. 130–41.

5. Wolfgang Spahr, *Billboard,* August 7, 1999.

6. Winston Cummings, "Teutonic Values," *Hit Parader,* December 1998.

7. Colin Devinish, "Rammstein Raise Furor over Video with Nazi-Era Footage," Sonicnet, August 1998, at www.vh1.com/artists/news/ 500908/08311998/rammstein.jhtml

8. Gabriella, *New York Rock,* November 1998, at www.nyrock.com/ interviews/rammstein_int.htm

9. Chris Gill, "Rammstein: Battering Ramm," *Guitar World,* 6:9 at www.rammsteinsite.com/articles6.html

10. http://www.newsfilter.org/antimtv/bands/rammstein.htm

11. Wojtek Goral, "Nazis? Heil No!," *London Records,* 2001.

12. Examples of posters in this genre may be found at http://motlc. wiesenthal.com/gallery/pg01/pg9/pg01931.html and http://www. calvin.edu/academic/cas/gpa/posters/rad.jpg

13. "Teutonic Values."

14. Hugo Ringler, "Heart or Reason?: What We Don't Want from Our Speakers," *Unser Wille und Weg,* 7 (1937), pp. 245–49. Translated by Robert D. Books, May 1972.

15. Interview with Flake Lorenz, *Deutscher Video Ring Magazin,* May 2001.

16. Dante Bonutto, online interview with Rammstein in *Blistering,* http://www.blistering.com/fastpage/fpengine.php/templateid/7967/ menuid/3/tempidx/5/catid/4/editstatus//restemp/N%3B/fPpagesel/2

17. I thank my editor at *Azure,* Daniel Doneson, for pointing this out to

me and for directing me to a number of interesting sources for the study of the relationship between music and politics.

18. *Schwärmerei* means excessive or unwholesome sentimentality. Richard Wagner, *Über deutsches Musikwesen,* Sämtliche Schriften und Dichtungen: vol. I, translated by William Ashton Ellis, The Wagner Library, Edition 1.0, http://users.belgacom.net/wagnerlibrary/ prose/wagongm.htm

19. Andrea Nieradzik, "Beautiful Sons," *Musik Express,* March 2001.

20. See the final lines of Susan Sontag's "Fascinating Fascism," *Under the Sign of Saturn* (New York: Farrar, Straus & Giroux, 1975).

21. Hans-Ulrich Wehler, "Das Türkenproblem," *Die Zeit,* September 12, 2002.

CHAPTER 9 : **TO HELL WITH EUROPE**

1. Pascal Ceaux, Franck Colombani, and Alexandre Garcia, "L'agresseur de M. Delanoë n'aimait ni les élus ni les homosexuels," *Le Monde,* October 8, 2002. My translation.

2. No one can discuss the rise of modern nationalism without revealing the influence of the seminal theorist of nationalism, Benedict Anderson. See, for example, Benedict Anderson, *Imagined Communities: Reflections on the Origin and Spread of Nationalism* (London and New York: Verso, 1991).

AFTERWORD FOR THE PAPERBACK EDITION:
**I TOLD YOU SO**

1. "Islamic Terrorism Is Too Emotive a Phrase, Says EU," *Telegraph,* April 12, 2006.

2. "Germany in the Crosshairs," *Spiegel Online,* August 22, 2006.

3. "Train Bombers Funded by British Businessmen," *Times of London,* July 17, 2006.

4. *Aftenposten,* August 5, 2006.

# ACKNOWLEDGMENTS

My agent, Daniel Greenberg, is what every writer dreams of in an agent. He's aggressive on my behalf, ever-tactful and encouraging with me, and his advice, generously offered, is always *good* advice. Best of all, he always answers my phone calls and e-mails right away. (Other writers will appreciate how rare and wonderful this is in an agent.) Thank you, Daniel, for seeing the potential in this book and for finding it a good home.

That good home was with Crown Forum, and specifically with my editor, Jed Donahue. An editor who publishes books about politics needs to be able to see not what is in the headlines that day, but what will be in the headlines in two years' time. When Jed first saw the proposal for this book, Theo van Gogh was alive, London had not been attacked, and no one was giving a moment's thought to the suburbs of France. Jed had the foresight to anticipate Europe's crisis at a time when many people did not. He has also forced me to return again and again to this question: Why should anyone *care* what happens to Europe? If more writers were asked by more editors why anyone should give a damn about their books, I suspect a lot of books would be a lot better.

My thanks to Crown Forum's art director, Whitney Cookman, for this book's eerily menacing cover; to production editor Susan Westendorf; to indexer Leoni McVey; and to copy editor Toni Rachiele, who scrubbed this manuscript with a Kärcher. If Toni sees a reference to the world's forty-nine least developed countries, she is the kind of copy editor who goes to the footnote, counts each country by hand, then reports that there are in fact *fifty* on the list I cite. She applied the same meticulous care to every word in the book. It is customary at this point for authors to avow complete responsibility for any errors remaining in the text, but frankly, I don't think it's necessary; I can't imagine anything escaped her. (If something did, it's still my fault.)

I am also particularly thankful for the excellent editorial advice I received from David Hazony and Daniel Doneson, editors of the journal *Azure. Azure* published two chapters of this book in abridged form. I thank them, as well, for inviting me to the Shalem Center and permitting me to air my ideas among their colleagues. I also thank *Policy Review* and the *Washington Post* for publishing some of the material in this book and giving me the chance to think out loud, in print, about the significance of the decline of faith in Europe and the limits to Europe's integration project.

Many people were kind enough to read this manuscript, in part or in whole. I thank in particular Damian Counsell, William Hill, Steven Lenzner, and Ulrich Schollwöck. Norah Vincent offered not just intellectual but emotional support on those days when the phrase "To hell with Europe" seemed like more than just a good title for a chapter. To Bill Walsh, who again saved me from committing to print errors too embarrassing to contemplate, I extend my limitless gratitude. I also thank Mustafa Akyol, Nelson Ascher, Cristina Iampieri, Bruce Gatenby, Jeffrey Gedmin, Judith Wrubel Levy, Phiroze Neemuchwala, Rubel Quadar, and of course Zia Rahman, who were all notably generous with their time and thoughts about Europe, both in correspondence and conversation.

As always, I thank my father and brother. Every chapter in this book began as a conversation with one or the other of them. I also thank my father and grandmother for their translations of Rammstein's lyrics—the reader may imagine what my grandmother thought of that task—and my mother for her thoughts about the German musical tradition.

David Gross traveled with me through Europe while I looked for answers to my questions. He took many photographs of what we saw together. Some of these can be seen at www.mimetic.com. I could not ask for a more patient and curious companion on the long journey— or a better friend.

And one final word in memory of my grandfather. No one knew this continent better than he, and no one taught me more about it. I'm sure he knows how grateful I am.

# INDEX

Genocide, in former Yugoslavia,
12
Germany
birthrate decline in, 141
feelings of guilt in, 219–221
foreign policy of, 13–14
nationalism in, 180–231
Global capitalism, Bové and,
167–169
Globalization, Bové on, 161,
166–168
GMOs. *See* Genetically modified
organisms (GMOs)
Goebbels, Joseph, Rammstein
quotes and, 221–222
Government. *See* Local
government; specific countries
*Grandes écoles,* 242–243
Great Britain. *See* Britain
Great Peasant Revolt (1999),
146–147
Great Satan, America as, 71
Green Revolution, GMOs and,
153
*Guardian, The* (newspaper), 87
Guilt, German feelings of,
219–221

Heresy. *See also* Bové, José;
Christianity
Cathar, 169–171
Hinduism, in India, 73, 74–75
History
cultural transmission and,
139–140
European, 6–7
Hitler, Adolf. *See* Nazis and
Nazism
Hizb ut-Tahrir organization, 42
Hoffer, Eric, 152–153, 173,
178–179
Housing, Italian population and,
135–136
Hunger, reduction of, 155–156

Idealism, death of, 8
Identity, German, 203
Ideology, 9–10
Immigrants and immigration
American and Anglo-Saxon
models of, 93–94
in Britain, 57–62, 72–77
European adjustment to,
11–12, 134
Fortuyn on, 35–36
French assimilation of, 91–92
French model of, 93
in Marseille, 96–97, 105–108,
109–115
Muslims as majority of,
132–133
U.S. compared with Britain,
80–84
van der Graaf and, 36–37
India, Muslims and Hindus from,
71–77
Industrial democracies, population
declines in, 135
Industrialization, meaning in life
and, 172–173
Intellectuals, anti-Americanism of
British, 86–90
Intifada, France and, 92, 95
Iraq
elections in, 19–20
oil-for-food program and, 14
Spanish terrorism and,
123–124, 125–128
Iraq War, Germans and, 206–
207
Islam. *See also* Islamic radicalism;
Muslims
Fortuyn on, 35–36
Islamic radicalism *(cont.)*
van Gogh, Theo, murder and,
27–29, 253
women in, 26–27
Islamic radicalism, 11–12, 262
assimilation and, 59–62

# ABOUT THE AUTHOR

**Claire Berlinski,** born and raised in the United States, has lived and worked in Britain, France, Switzerland, Thailand, Laos, and Turkey as a journalist, academic, and consultant. Her articles have appeared in the *New York Times*, the *Washington Post, National Review*, the *Weekly Standard*, and *Policy Review,* among other publications. She holds a first-class degree in modern history and a doctorate in international relations from Oxford University, as well as a diploma in French literature from the Sorbonne and a degree in philosophy from the University of Washington. Berlinski is also the author of *Loose Lips,* a novel. *Menace in Europe* is her first nonfiction work. She now divides her time between Paris and Istanbul.